Southern Voices from the Past

Women's Letters, Diaries, and Writings

CAROL BLESER, GENERAL EDITOR

This series makes available to scholars, students, and general readers collections of letters, diaries, and other writings by women in the southern United States from the colonial era into the twentieth century. Documenting the experiences of women from across the region's economic, cultural, and ethnic spectrums, the writings enrich our understanding of such aspects of daily life as courtship and marriage, domestic life and motherhood, social events and travels, and religion and education.

The Diary of Dolly Lunt Burge, 1848–1879

The Diary of *Dolly*

The University of Georgia Press

ATHENS AND LONDON

Lunt Burge

1848–1879

EDITED BY

Christine Jacobson Carter

© 1997 by the University of Georgia Press
Athens, Georgia 30602
All rights reserved
Designed by Sandra Strother Hudson
Set in Janson by G & S Typesetters
Printed and bound by Braun-Brumfield

The paper in this book meets the guidelines for
permanence and durability of the Committee on
Production Guidelines for Book Longevity of the
Council on Library Resources.

Printed in the United States of America
01 00 99 98 97 c 5 4 3 2 1

Library of Congress Cataloging in Publication Data

Burge, Dolly Lunt.
The diary of Dolly Lunt Burge, 1848–1879 / edited by
Christine Jacobson Carter.
p. cm.
ISBN 0-8203-1863-9 (alk. paper)
1. Burge, Dolly Lunt—Diaries. 2. Madison (Ga.)—
Biography. 3. Women plantation owners—Georgia—
Diaries. 4. Plantation owners—Georgia—Biography.
5. Women teachers—Georgia—Diaries. 6. Georgia—
History—Civil War, 1861–1865—Personal narratives.
7. United States—History—Civil War, 1861–1865—
Personal narratives, Confederate. I. Carter, Christine
Jacobson. II. Title.
F294.M25B87 1997
975.8'152—dc20
[B]
96-19304

British Library Cataloging in Publication Data available

To Rob, Mom, Dad, and Sandy

CONTENTS

When she began her diary in February 1848, thirty-year-old Dolly Lunt Lewis had already married, left her family and native state of Maine, moved to Georgia with her struggling physician husband, lost him and their only child to illness, and established herself in Madison, Georgia, as a schoolteacher and devout Methodist. Over the next thirty-one years, Dolly remained a faithful Christian, married twice and was widowed twice more, and raised four children. For a time, she also managed a large plantation and sizable estate single-handedly. She witnessed the Civil War and Sherman's march to the sea, adapted to a free labor system, and helped raise her grandchildren. Dolly's full life was extraordinary for the range of roles she filled and the myriad experiences she had. That her life span coincided with critical transformations in America and that she recorded her life experiences in this historical context make her diary all the more spectacular.

Yet Dolly's diary also depicts a life that is wonderfully ordinary—for her race and class. She was not a famous woman. The only celebrities she knew and described were early founders of Emory College in Oxford and Wesleyan Female College in Macon. Indeed, many of Dolly's experiences were replicated by countless other women and men who did not leave such epic narratives. Through her eyes and pen, we gain an appreciation of the everyday dramas and decisions that many others experienced living in the nineteenth-century South. She offers us a rare glimpse of the commonplace: the faithful Christian woman; the conscientious schoolteacher; the widow who marries a widower; the mother who nurses her ill children; the planter who nervously eyes the cost of cotton each season; and the former slave owner whose plantation becomes a tenant farm after the Civil War. Dolly recorded not only the day-to-day tasks, but also her hopes and fears about her life and her family. She used the diary's pages to monitor her relationship with God, analyze her misgivings about remarriage, and offer thanks for familial calm, as well as to consider her part in broader social issues such as the justness of slavery and the male-dominated legal system. Likewise, she spoke for countless other women on the Civil War home front, who watched in horror as soldiers pillaged, burned, and stole their property.

Dolly began her diary in 1848 as a record of her daily activities and thoughts. As an evangelical Christian, she understood that she would be held accountable for her actions and her spiritual growth. During its first few years, the diary served as a notebook wherein Dolly considered sermons and religious ideas and worried constantly about her lack of proper submission to God. Occasionally, she reflected on her schoolroom duties. Later, when Thomas Burge proposed to her in 1849, she used the diary to wrestle with her conflicting emotions and accept the possible implications of marriage to a Georgia planter she barely knew. After she accepted his proposal, the diary became a place for records of daily tasks accomplished, crops planted and harvested and sewing completed, as well as lengthy descriptions of her newfound peace and joy as a mother and wife. When Thomas died nine years later in 1858, she turned to the diary for solace amid her grief and to express her frustrations with managing his estate. During the war, Dolly seemed to recognize that she was documenting a revolutionary event, and she described in detail the armies that swarmed through the countryside.

Later in her life, Dolly wrote less frequently, usually to record significant life changes: a new marriage in 1865 to a Methodist minister, her daughter

Sadai's departure for school and eventual marriage, her third experience of widowhood in 1873, and her final return to her plantation home. Dolly's diary served mostly personal record-keeping and soul-searching purposes. She occasionally made explicit reference to her diary as a personal, historical record or family document, and she omitted from its pages the details of her family's legal battles (which are found in court records). Most likely she expected that others would someday read and use her diary to remember loved ones, understand a way of life, and appreciate the enormous impact of civil war on a region's women and children.

Over the last thirty years, scholarship on the nineteenth-century South and scholarship on American women's lives have grown in parallel, often interconnected ways. Historians have explored a breadth of topics that contribute to our understanding of Dolly's life in the Georgia piedmont. For example, scholars have debated the nature of plantation households, relationships between slaves and masters, and the bonds between parents and children. They have examined courtship rituals, religious developments, educational opportunities for women, and the effects of war and Reconstruction on southern gender, race, and class dynamics. This publication benefits from these great strides made in southern, women's, and family history, and interested readers should look to the notes to the introduction for the key works that inform my interpretation. Similarly, this work is part of a welcome tide of relatively new interest in women's diaries and letters, which contribute crucially to our understanding of the American past. This republication of *The Diary of Dolly Lunt Burge* comes at a most auspicious time, offering a valuable perspective on nineteenth-century life in Georgia and women's experiences of religion, family, and work.

Scholars have long recognized the significance of Dolly's diary and the importance of making it available to a wide audience. In 1918, Julian Street published *A Woman's Wartime Journal: An Account of Sherman's Devastation of a Southern Plantation*, which is a liberal transcription of certain 1864 and 1865 passages from her diary. At that time Dolly's family retained ownership of the diary. In 1952, Dorothy Gray Bolton (Sadai's daughter), Joseph Howard Gray (Sadai's son), and Merritt Dutton Morehouse (Sadai's grandson) gave Dolly's diary, along with other papers from the Burge, Gray, Parks, and Bolton families, to Emory University. Eight years later, in 1960,

James Robertson, a southern historian who taught at Emory University, transcribed and edited the entire diary for serial publication in the *Georgia Historical Quarterly*. His work was reprinted in book form by the University of Georgia Press in 1962 as *The Diary of Dolly Lunt Burge*, which has long been out of print. Robertson's painstaking transcription of nearly illegible passages and extensive identification of certain people and events made my transcription, editing, and annotation much easier. I benefitted also from his biographical introduction to the diary, which brought together much of the narrative of Dolly's life and offered me clues to answering some of my own questions about her story. Most recently, in 1983 the American Women's Diaries microfilm series reproduced Dolly's entire diary in its original form.[1]

This publication builds on the work of these earlier efforts, especially Robertson's, to offer a more complete and contextualized introductory narrative of Dolly's life. In addition to benefitting from more than thirty years of path-breaking scholarship since Robertson's edition, I have made ample use of family letters written mostly before Dolly began her diary in 1848 and after she stopped writing regularly in her journal, to tell the story of Dolly's life and provide a more complete introduction to her text. Throughout the introduction, as well as in the diary's annotations, I have employed court records to reveal conflicts Dolly had with family and neighbors that could not be settled informally and that made their way into the diary's pages obliquely, if at all. Extensive genealogical studies and local histories written during the last two decades helped me identify and describe many more of Dolly's friends, adversaries, and slaves than earlier publications could provide. Preceding the introduction is a list of family members and other principals that provides biographical and genealogical information on Dolly's and her slaves' families.

The version of the diary presented here is the closest transcription of Dolly's volume possible, while still allowing for easy reading. Like many antebellum diarists and correspondents, Dolly often wrote hurriedly and without apostrophes, commas, periods, proper capitalization, or correct spelling. She sometimes used dashes instead of periods, indicating, I believe, that her thoughts about a subject continued after the entry ended. As often as not, she omitted periods and capitalization between sentences, revealing perhaps her busy routine, or the way one thought triggered an-other. When she turned to a new page, she wrote the full date and some-times her residence. For most other entries, she wrote only the day of the month. To respect the integrity of Dolly's original hand, I have reinstated all of the punctuation errors and misspellings that other editors corrected.

I have, however, employed two general editing interventions for the sake of clarity. First, I have inserted a period wherever Dolly finished a thought and began a new one with a capital letter. If, however, she did not capitalize the first word of what appears to be a new sentence, I omitted the period so that we might follow the flow of Dolly's thoughts and appreciate the fluid nature of her journal writing. Second, at the beginning of each entry, if Dolly did not provide them herself, I have added the month and year in brackets. Finally, I have limited my use of the term *sic*. Although she was a well-educated woman and a teacher, Dolly, like many of her contem-poraries, occasionally misspelled words or alternated spellings of a person's name. Her most common error was reversing the letters *i* and *e* in words such as *receive, piece,* and *field*. She also consistently misspelled the words *privilege* and *weather*. She occasionally left out apostrophes, interchanged *too* with *to* and *peace* for *piece*, and omitted the *e* in *ed* endings, such as *sheard* for *sheared*. In all of these instances, I have left the idiosyncrasies intact.

Because Dolly offers us such an unusually rich and detailed glimpse of her community, I have endeavored to identify as many as possible of the approximately four hundred people and places she mentions. Drawing largely on census, legal, local, and institutional histories and records, I pro-vide biographical information in notes, particularly about those individuals she names more than once. By following Dolly and her circle of acquaint-ances, the reader can glean a sense of the communities in which she lived and the people and personalities with whom she interacted. Most sources used for annotation are listed. Occasionally, local historians or family re-membrances provided the only available information, and for those refer-ences no printed source is listed.

ACKNOWLEDGMENTS

This project began as my first graduate-level research paper at Emory University, but it developed into its present form thanks to many generous individuals who offered me their time, efforts, and expertise. I thank first this project's initial director and my dissertation advisor, Jim Roark, whose unfailing encouragement and accessibility, impressive breadth and depth of knowledge, and thorough editorial critiques are legendary. His kind assistance was fundamental. Other Emory faculty were also wonderfully supportive and helpful. In particular, Elizabeth Fox-Genovese and Mary Odem critiqued early versions of the introduction, and Jonathan Prude offered valuable insights regarding the daguerreotypes and photographs. My fellow Emory graduate students, whom I have watched ably dissect the best scholarship in American history, eagerly read versions of my work and offered gentler, kinder, though no less exacting criticisms. In particular, I am grateful to Ellen Rafshoon, Diane Mutti, Naomi Nelson, Stacey Horstmann, Peter Martin, Jeff Young, and Anthony Clay. I am also deeply grateful to Jacqueline Jones, my thesis director then at Wellesley College, who continues to inspire me.

At Emory's Woodruff Library, Linda Matthews, Beverly Allen, and Marie Nitschke offered invaluable assistance. The special collections department at Emory owns Dolly's diary and most of the family papers I have used, and kindly gave me permission to use these sources. I am indebted also to Theodore Davis and Mary Landt at Oxford College, and Dale Couch at the Georgia Department of Archives and History, for their suggestions and investigations on my behalf. Rosalyn Page, Patsy Stockbridge, and Becky Herring in the Emory History Department office offered consistent moral support, along with their crucial administrative assistance. Key financial support came from Emory University Graduate School of Arts and Science, the Department of History, and the National Society of the Colonial Dames of America in the State of Georgia.

Outside academia, I discovered a wealth of interest in, and contributors to, this project. Marshall "Woody" Williams's expert sleuthing in the documents of Morgan County, Georgia, provided countless annotations for Dolly's days in Madison. Judy Winograd, a leading historic costume designer in Atlanta, magnanimously offered most of the descriptions of the daguerreotypes. Individuals at Emory University Photography cheerfully handled the many photographic reproductions. Dolly's descendants dug into family records, retrieved photographs, retraced genealogies, and jogged their memories to answer obscure biographical questions and offer the rich collection of photographs in this edition. I am especially grateful to Betsy and Sandy Morehouse who provided all of the family daguerreotypes and photographs, along with their helpful suggestions and moral support. I thank also other Burge descendants, including Jack Bolton, Evelyn M. Gray, Mary E. Gaut, and Dorothy Lee. An able genealogist and the great-great-grandchild of Burge slaves, Mildred Diane Baynes provided detailed genealogical information on slaves and freedpeople from the area. Her research has added immeasurably to this study and resulted in a more complete and accurate portrayal of Burge plantation and its inhabitants before and after the war.

I am very grateful to Malcolm Call at the University of Georgia Press for his continued support of this publication and to Kristine Blakeslee for her expert editorial assistance. Carol Bleser, series editor of Southern Voices from the Past: Women's Letters, Diaries, and Writings, provided indispensable editorial advice and endorsement. John Inscoe at the *Georgia Historical Quarterly* expressed early interest in the project and carefully shepherded an early version of the introduction through his journal.

I would like to thank also my friends and family for their thoughtful and unwavering encouragement. Allison Towne and Karen Watkins heard more than they ever wanted about this project over E-mail. Sandra Jacobson has been a steady source of love and support, as well as a constant reminder of the world outside my work. Rob Carter has known my "Dolly project" as long as he's known me and has generously offered his keen editorial eye, high standards, loving support, and refreshing sense of humor to more aspects of this project than I care to admit. Finally, I am eternally grateful for my parents, whose countless efforts on my behalf even included a grueling week of transcribing this text, letter by letter. They first taught me to study history and believe in myself.

INTRODUCTION

Dolly Lunt Lewis, a young widowed schoolteacher in a small Georgia town, penned one Sunday evening in 1848, "Have been thinking for sometime past that I would every day put down the incidents thereof thought feelings, &c. &c. in other words keep a regular journal." Although she found herself "much inclined to neglect these every day matters &c. to pass them off as trivial concerns," she reflected, "do they not make up one's life? Of what trifles are life composed & yet when called to render an account of them will they then be as trifling & unimportant to us as they now seem to be?"[1] For over thirty years, Dolly recorded these "trifles," chronicling her life as a wife and widow, mother, schoolteacher, plantation mistress, planter, and witness to the Civil War. These personal entries amount to an epic story of one nineteenth-century woman's efforts to serve her God and her family through a myriad of personal challenges and a national crisis. Surviving three husbands, several children, and a nation divided, Dolly told not only her own remarkable story but also the story of countless other white southern women of the planter and professional classes. Her diary provided a place for lengthy personal reflection as well as brief notes about tasks accomplished on her Georgia piedmont plantation. On its pages, Dolly revealed the details of her courtships, marriages, and widowhood; her children being born, growing, and sometimes dying; family ties and feuds; crops grown and lost; and slaves who labored under slavery and eventually secured their freedom.

Although she spent nearly all of her adult life in Georgia, Dolly was a northerner by birth. On September 29, 1817, she was born in Bowdoinham, Maine, a small town along Merrymeeting Bay on the Atlantic coast and northwest of Bath. Dolly's father, William Webb Lunt, was born in 1788 and worked as a local merchant in this New England village. Dolly's mother, Ann Matilda Sumner, kin to the famous abolitionist Charles Sumner, was born in 1795. She died in childbirth in 1825; Dolly was seven and her three siblings, Orrington, William, and Sarah, were nine, six, and four.[2] Their father remarried and his second wife, Priscilla Purrington Lunt, in 1828 gave birth to the first of four children. A memoir written much later by Orrington's daughter Cornelia suggests that Dolly and her siblings disliked their new stepmother.[3]

Beyond Cornelia's recollections, little more is known of Dolly's childhood and adolescent years, and she never reflected on them in her diary. Courtship letters to Dolly, however, indicate that when she was about sixteen years old, Dolly met her first husband, Samuel H. B. Lewis, who was about eighteen at the time. Within a couple of years, Samuel felt deeply committed to their relationship and hinted that he hoped for more from their special friendship. "How good it is to have a *friend*, and how rich is that individual who possesses a *true* & real *friend*, one who would be willing to share his joys and *sorrows*—& strive to lighten every burden which might oppress his *heart!!*" he wrote her. "Is it possible that *Lewis* is highly favoured as to have such a *true friend?* How strong is his conviction that this *is the case!*" None of Dolly's letters remains to elucidate her response, but two years later, Samuel continued to plead his case. He reminded her of "the days of our *First Love*" but worried that she had "been a little influenced by others. For I know I have enemies." Nothing exists in his correspondence to Dolly to explain who these enemies might have been. Nevertheless, in this same March 1837 letter, Samuel boldly proposed, "Pardon me for this once, and allow me to say what is *true, I love you. . . .* This *one* question then and all will be sat at rest—*Will you give your consent to be mine? to the chosen, the bosom friend of Lewis? Can* you Love *him* & *him alone* with *due* affection?"[4]

Dolly was not easily persuaded, for some reason, perhaps because she had other offers to consider. Samuel was forlorn, thinking that she might choose another. Still, he pressed her, "If your heart is his, give him your hand. If you *love* him and your feelings are enlisted on his behalf, let the name of *Lewis* die, yes let my *poor name* be forgotten & cast into the receptacle of things forgotten." "With regard to myself I will always love you even while another has that bliss which I was in hopes to possess," he cried; "perhaps you had better accept Mr. H's offer. . . . It will be a year before a connection can take place between *us* and *possibly* more." Samuel continued to cast about for a profitable means of supporting himself and a family, but Dolly evidently was willing to wait for him. Learning this, he wrote quickly to express his gratitude that she reciprocated his affections. He exclaimed, "My Heart is entirely yours. It has been this four years and it shall always be yours while Life [*sic*] lasts . . . when I love it is with *entire devotedness, with constancy and fervor.*" Unfortunately, however, Samuel was about to leave for an eight- to ten-month trip, to bolster his "pecuniary affairs" and allow him "to see some of the world, and learn much which will be useful to me."[5]

Whatever Samuel learned on his travels, he never found a successful career or vocational identity. He explained on Christmas eve in 1837 that he had recently traveled west, trying to "find a place if possible to locate and commence in the Mercantile business, but times how changed and I am sadly disappointed & the year has been nearly lost." Undoubtedly thwarted by the financial panic of 1837, Samuel returned to Maine and tried to begin a business there. Poor Samuel disliked his transient lifestyle and worried about Dolly's perceptions of him. "You can see my faults better than I can discover them myself," he told her; "tell me what they are and, as I love you, I will correct them." By this time Dolly was teaching school in Rhode Island, presumably to support herself and wait for Lewis.[6]

Eventually Lewis returned, and in October 1838 the couple married. Dolly was twenty-one and Lewis, twenty-two. In the first year, a son, Samuel Lewis, was born, but died in infancy. A year later, in October 1840,

Dolly gave birth to their first surviving child, Susan. Perhaps because Samuel still had not found a viable career, the young family moved in 1842 to Zebulon, Georgia, about forty-five miles south of present-day Atlanta. Dolly's sister had moved there earlier with her husband, Isaac Comings, a physician of the Thomsonian system, which was a nineteenth-century homeopathic approach to medicine. Samuel took classes at a medical college in Forsyth, Georgia, and may have tried to establish a practice in Zebulon. Probably because the town could not support both him and his brother-in-law, Samuel moved to Madison, Georgia, about sixty miles northeast of Zebulon, where he set up a new practice and planned to send for his family as soon as possible.[7]

Dolly waited in Zebulon with the Comings, where she had begun teaching school to a few students in the vacant room of her sister's house. When she finished her first quarter there, the trustees of a nearby academy offered her their school, commensurate with a salary of three hundred dollars for the school year. Dolly accepted the offer, thankful that she could support herself and their daughter while Samuel established his practice in Madison. Some of Dolly's wealthier southern contemporaries may have disdained this kind of wifely support, but Dolly never expressed any embarrassment about teaching or her husband's financial difficulties. Perhaps due to her northern roots, their financial need, and a relatively supportive social climate for married schoolteachers, she took pride in her ability to assist her husband and support herself.[8]

During this period, Dolly became pregnant again. Unfortunately, the new baby, Orrington Lewis, died within hours of his birth in April 1843. After his son's death, Samuel complained bitterly about his family's separation. "[Y]ou have no idea what a kind of sickly lonesomeness comes over me at times daily . . . ," he wrote Dolly longingly, "when I retire at night . . . —no soul to speak to—no one to chat with, nothing to keep off the blues . . . —I tell you it is the most trying [time?] I ever had in my life." A few months later, he urged, "You have no idea how anxious I am that we should get settled here—you do not know how much I want your company, nor how much I miss you since you left." Samuel took comfort that his wife similarly "never missed [him] so much" and exclaimed, "'Tis just so with me!" At least Dolly's teaching contributed to the family's financial stability and Samuel appreciated her work: "I feel glad your school is so large because the larger the more money & the more money the better. I regret that our pecuniary circumstances are such as to render it necessary to impose such a burden upon you but never mind *let us save every dollar we possibly can and we will get out of this before many years*." "I am sick of Georgia," he proclaimed, "& just as soon as I can pay my debts & get funds enough to carry us [we will move]." While Samuel felt disillusioned with Georgia and the practice of medicine, Dolly seemed to assimilate easily into her new southern setting, enjoyed her success as a teacher, and reflected later that, "[t]o assist him [by teaching], was a pleasure and I willingly complied."[9]

Samuel became so depressed over his failure as a physician that his self-assured brother-in-law offered his advice: "[Take] some good Cogniac [*sic*] brandy, or . . . still better . . . *Anticipation of future success*, & a contemplation of [your] situation if it was *ten times* worse than it is." Isaac Comings would hear nothing of Samuel's plans to quit Georgia. "Just as long as you keep this idea in your head, you *never will* be contented & will always be troubled with the blues," he admonished. "The fact is, we must be determined to get rich before we go home we must skin these lazy Georgians . . . overcome the prejudice of the community . . . [and] ultimately see The Thompsonian Practice triumphant." Dolly added a postscript to this letter, expressing her hopes to see him soon and offering some cheery advice: "Do all you can and don't get them well to [*sic*] quick." A couple of months later when Samuel's practice had picked up a bit and he had met some prominent Madison men, he felt more confident and happily promised his wife that in only six weeks he would bring her and Susan to Madison.[10]

Regrettably, Dolly would never join Samuel in Madison or anywhere else on earth. Dolly's "cherished idol of [her] school girl days," the person "upon whom [her] whole earthly happiness centered," died that September 1843 of what they termed congestive fever. He was twenty-seven and Dolly, twenty-five. Other losses quickly followed: Dolly and Susan remained in Zebulon, but Susan soon developed bronchitis and Dolly had to give up her school. The two then moved to Madison as guests in the home of Charles Baldwin, an attorney and friend of Samuel's before he died. Susan made a temporary recovery and Dolly secured a new teaching position in Covington, about twenty miles east of Madison, but Susan died in April

1844 at the age of three. "I stand alone apart from all," Dolly recorded in verse shortly afterward. In another poem, entitled "My departed Husband and children," she prayed,

> "Father Divine, at thy decree
> My heart surrendered its dear idols up
> Thy holy will be done—but grant to me
> Thy grace to drink the bitter cup!"[11]

During this period of mourning, Dolly's brother-in-law Isaac Comings offered a steady stream of advice, some money, invitations to visit, and the management of her deceased husband's debts. "I feel a deep interest in your welfare & prosperity & will do all in my power to make you happy," he assured her. "I & my dear wife will give you a home while we have one for ourselves, and be assured too that you *never can be burdensome* to us." Perhaps because she did not want to impose herself on them, become dependent, or subject herself to her brother-in-law's paternalistic counsel, Dolly refused to live with Isaac and Sarah, who had recently moved to Forsyth, Georgia, where he was teaching at the Botanic Medical College. Still, Isaac urged her to visit them during her vacations. Shortly before July 4, 1844, he wrote, "you *must* come down here & spend the short recess you have."[12]

This familial support soon turned to strife when Isaac and Sarah made plans to leave Georgia. It is not clear what ensued between Dolly and the Comings, but family letters indicate that the Comings thought Dolly objected strongly and childishly to their move from Georgia. Isaac complained of her "*hard & severe* letters" and reprimanded her: "I reply; as a *deserved* reproof just as I would *punish* my *child* which I *tenderly* love." He hoped she would soon "feel a little *more reconciled* to our leaving Georgia," and her sister added, "I do not have hard feelings against you as you imagine. I love you as ever & wish to have all these little difficulties settled—."[13]

Fortunately, Dolly had never lost the emotional support of her father in Maine and her older brothers. They kept her informed of family news during these difficult years and encouraged her to visit Maine whenever possible, which she did briefly during the fall of 1846. Yet Dolly chose to remain a permanent resident of Georgia. No remaining records explain this decision, but perhaps she enjoyed her community, the teaching opportunities, and the distance from her stepmother. Back in Madison, she wrote her family that she was doing well, finding her school quite pleasant, maintaining friendships, and remaining financially solvent. Indeed, by Christmas 1847, she assured her sister-in-law in Maine, "The negroes even, did not enter into its festivities more heartily than myself, the firmness of the whether [*sic*], the efforts of friends in my behalf, And [*sic*] all combined gave me an elasticity of spirit to which I have long been a stranger." Dolly seemed to have integrated herself into a community of supportive, like-minded religious folk, and she expressed no qualms about the South's "peculiar" ways.[14]

During these years, Dolly took pride in her ability to provide for herself through teaching. There were a number of academies and colleges scattered throughout the county and surrounding areas, but it is impossible to determine precisely at which schools she taught and the nature of her experiences there. More than likely, she taught in small schools that maintained separate male and female departments, offered instruction in geography, mathematics, English grammar, composition, and moral philosophy, and operated with tuition funds, lottery proceeds, and denominational support. The principal "gives me the same as I got in Covington," she told her sister-in-law in January 1847, "and again it is my duty to be doing for myself while I have health, strength and the use of my faculties. . . . I *know* I *was* wanted." Most likely, her principal was a teaching entrepreneur who operated the school under the direction of a local board of trustees that provided the necessary buildings.[15]

Like many other northern-born women, Dolly found a real demand for her skills and her willingness to teach in the South. Often she complained of the "cares and toils of the schoolroom," but she enjoyed her students and her work. In the evenings and on weekends, she dutifully attended Protestant church services. During this period, she boarded in the town of Madison with friends who offered her companionship and guidance. Yet, in marked contrast to most of her southern contemporaries—and perhaps due in part to her northern background—Dolly still retained an unusual degree of autonomy from familial and financial constraints.[16]

It was during these years that Dolly began the diary that would span the next thirty-one years and document the rest of her life. She turned to its pages initially and primarily to record her feelings about God and her frustrated efforts to serve Him. Indeed, Dolly was a deeply committed Christian and a faithful churchgoer, which she may have learned from her Methodist family in Maine. As her diary attests, she found that her faith both sustained and frustrated her, especially during these independent years. At length, Dolly described the church meetings she attended, who spoke and what they said, and how she felt she was, or in most cases was not, living as a Christian. In her first entry, she revealed her inspiration to keep a journal: "[an] unusual spiritual enjoyment" and "an increased desire for an entire consecration of self to the service of God." However, this would be one of the last sanguine reports on her spiritual state for the rest of the diary. While she always struggled to do God's will and consecrate herself to Him, Dolly typically disappointed herself and rarely experienced spiritual satisfaction.[17]

This frustrated desire for religious contentment was typical for women of Dolly's class and race during the antebellum period. The evangelical faiths in particular demanded this sort of self-scrutiny, driving many women and men to painful self-denial and self-discipline, followed by guilt and shame when they failed to meet exalted standards. Without mentioning specific misdeeds or sins against God, Dolly, like many other white antebellum women, felt overwhelmed with a nebulous sense of her sinfulness and lamented her failed efforts at complete submission to God's will. Yet, being a Protestant woman and participating actively in a church community were central to Dolly's sense of herself throughout her life. Arguably, the struggle over sinfulness in itself gave her a semblance of meaning and direction, but especially during these early years, religion did not give Dolly the fulfillment she sought.[18]

In addition to her religious frustration, Dolly felt lonely without a husband and children. Although she could devote herself to her church, classroom, and home and enjoy the attendant independence, paradoxically she missed having someone to work *for*—someone to give her work a purpose. "It has been quite lonely to day at home. This keeping house without a man I don't like much," she complained in February 1848. Several months later, she grieved, "This world is truly & has ever been a dark sad lonesome place to me." But before long, Dolly found herself in the midst of a courtship and then engagement to a man who offered her a busy life and a family that needed her.[19]

Thomas Burge was a forty-four-year-old Methodist, recently widowed father of four, and successful planter from neighboring Newton County. Although Dolly felt a genuine interest in Thomas, her diary testifies to her strong misgivings about her suitor and the life that she might lead as his wife and stepmother to his children. "Little did I think when I penned the last that when I next wrote I should so soon be the betrothed of another," she anguished. "What have I done? . . . Why these heavy forebodings?" Dolly clearly recognized the risks involved for white women who were considering marriage in the antebellum South. She had been married before, but she likely realized that the master of a southern household enjoyed often mythic power over all aspects of his family's life. In North and South alike, didactic literature and advice manuals for women warned of the real possibility of disappointment and even misery in marriage. Describing marriage as a gamble and a lottery, these authors, and shared wisdom, told women that marriage not only bound man and woman together for life, but also subjugated her desires to his. While a very few women rejected marriage and motherhood altogether, most who chose it, as Dolly did, understood what was to be gained and lost.[20]

Dolly worried also about the holy oaths she would take as Thomas's bride and the spiritual union they would need to form. "Do I love him to whom I am about to commit my all of earthly happiness? Can I take upon myself the most solemn of all oaths to Love Honour & Obey one to whom I am so utterly a stranger!" she prayed. "How can I tell . . . that I may be sowing to myself thorns and briars that may afterwards sorely sting and annoy me." As an evangelical woman, Dolly understood that both sexes were supposed to commit themselves to a spiritual union of mutual support, obligation, and responsibility. Yet, women were thought to possess the more developed spiritual capacity and it was their responsibility to foster what some historians have termed the nineteenth-century "companionate marriage." Especially in Dolly's native North, where industry increasingly separated the sexes and rhetoric allocated them different "spheres," women and men attempted to divide household responsibilities in a way that valued a wife's domestic labor and her special moral contributions to the home. Even southern evangelical women, especially those like northern-born Dolly, might assimilate expectations about mutual respect and collaborative piety that placed them at an even greater risk to be disappointed.[21]

Dolly recognized also that she was leaving behind her familiar classroom to assume the myriad responsibilities of a mother to young children and mistress of a several hundred-acre plantation with thirty-odd slaves. In all of her efforts, she would be answerable to her new husband, a man she knew only from their occasional meetings and by his reputation. "Should I dislike him after the solemn vows are pronounced. What unhappiness What Misery awaits me?" she lamented in her diary. Her fears regarding Thomas seem to have been incited by at least one of her woman friends, who planted upsetting suspicions in her mind and delivered an anonymous note about Thomas. Eventually, Dolly felt more assured and on the eve of her wedding, she reflected, "I have no fears for my happiness if I only have the love of Him Who is to be my husband!" It is rather striking that Dolly referred to Thomas as "Him Who" in capitalization. As a woman in the antebellum South, she understood that the relationship she could develop with her husband was similar to the one she was supposed to build with her God. Her happiness lay in her submission to him, his generosity to her, and any control she could negotiate through this uncertain relationship.[22]

Upon marriage, Dolly experienced an immediate sense of relief and new purpose, but remained aware that she was no longer an independent individual; now, she was a planter's wife. "[Y]esterday I took upon myself the most solemn of all obligations to be another's no longer my own," she recorded in her diary on January 23, 1850. Clearly, the rewards were more than adequate enough to offset any losses and her "heart approve[d]" even if she still wondered about her ability to succeed in her new role. Most importantly, she realized that Thomas himself was a conscientious Christian and pious companion. And although her diary entries were more brief and sporadic after this life change, now she wrote to record her unbounded happiness and thankfulness for her "happy family circle."[23]

With her marriage to Thomas, Dolly began her duties as a Georgia plantation mistress without any apparent moral or practical difficulties about the use of enslaved labor. Apparently, Dolly observed that slavery was simply a way of life among her new friends and family, who were, after all, upstanding Christians. If she had any objections, she may have assumed there was little point in expressing them. Indeed, until the Civil War, Dolly mentioned the Burge slaves only occasionally in the diary, usually to record tasks completed, births, deaths, and illnesses. Fortunately, she kept a list at the back of her diary which outlines the three slave families that included most of the Burge slaves, and later freed people, on the plantation: Elbert and Julia had twelve children between 1830 and 1856; Lewis and Martha had ten children between 1835 and 1852; and Franklin and Hannah had eleven children between 1839 and 1861. Julia, Martha, and Hannah were sisters whom Thomas Burge had bought, probably in the 1830s.

While teaching had often been tiresome for Dolly, she found her plantation duties more varied and rewarding. She no longer complained about her responsibilities but, much like male planters, recorded them briefly, as if not to forget what had been accomplished each day. In fact, her diary shifts in many ways from a primarily religious and personal reflection to a planter's hurried account of weather, crops, slaves' health, and work. She performed or (more likely) supervised the sewing, gardening, preserving of foods, attending to sick slaves, and tending to the dairy and farm animals. And Dolly was also an astute observer of most of the other male-led activities that took place on the plantation, noting wheat sown, cotton ginned, and land fenced. Historians have debated the extent to which southern women participated in plantation management, but it appears that Dolly's active participation was neither typical nor unique.[24]

This record of farm activities, plus the narrative of family activities, shaped Dolly's diary for the next ten years. Between 1850 and 1855, Dolly experienced two more pregnancies, one of which produced a daughter, named Sarah Cornelia, or Sadai, who survived. She also suffered another great loss with the death of her husband, Thomas, in 1858. Despite her grief, which she expressed in her diary, Dolly's work on the plantation as a widow continued much the same. She oversaw the ploughing of swamps, spaying of pigs, improving of her kitchen, and hiring and firing of overseers. Indeed, Dolly seemed to maintain a level of production and profit roughly equivalent to that during Thomas's management.[25]

Although a widow again, Dolly now had a family that needed her care and guidance. Her fourteen-year-old stepdaughter, Lou, attended Macon Female College. Extant family letters supplement Dolly's diary and demonstrate Dolly's persistent concern about Lou's education. She reminded Lou of why she had gone to college: "[for the] cultivation of your mind and the improvement of the talents given you." Perhaps showing her northern roots and her Methodism, and setting herself apart from other, elite plantation mistresses, Dolly admonished, "I trust you have a [more] noble ambition than to strive to out dress others, that dressing the body, arraying it in all the finery of the eye is not *your* aim." Dolly recognized the practical benefits of a good education as well: "A good education will fit & prepare you to adorn the station your wealth will call you to occupy," she advised. Later, Lou got into some sort of disciplinary trouble at school and Dolly scolded her for using "profane language," as the neighbors were gossiping about it. All family records indicate that Lou was an especially opinionated and fiery young person, but Dolly may have appreciated her independent spirit.[26]

While all records indicate that Dolly ran the plantation confidently, and relatively independently of male assistance,[27] Dolly did face some difficulty as the executor of Thomas's estate, an episode that illuminates the diary although she veiled it in her narrative. Thomas's will, written while he was "feeble in body, and feeling that [he] must shortly depart this life," left Dolly "the sole and entire control of [his] whole estate both real and personal, with as free powers concerning the same as [he himself] had in [his] lifetime." Thomas's final decrees differed from those of most antebellum southern patriarchs, who typically named one or two male friends as executors either exclusively or along with the widow, and divided property very painstakingly among the children and widow. The only specific distribution Thomas willed was a division of his slave property that favored Dolly and Sadai, and which was to occur six years after the will was probated.[28]

Obviously unsatisfied with these terms, Wiley Burge (probably Thomas's son rather than a nephew by the same name) and Mathew A. Mitchell, Thomas's eldest daughter Rebecca's first husband, filed suit against Dolly shortly after Thomas Burge's death.[29] They charged that Thomas was "not of sound disposing mind & memory at the time of executing" his will, that he "was under undue influence of his Wife Dolly Burge not only at the making of said will but for a long time before." Furthermore, "Dolly Burge from fraudulent and improper motives towards [W. Burge and Mitchell] unduly influenced [Burge's] mind against them for her own interest." After an untold amount of aggravation, Dolly eventually won the suit in September 1873.[30]

Similarly to these challenges as the estate's executor, Dolly encountered complications with the guardianship of Thomas's children. Much like the executor of an estate, a guardian managed minors' inheritances until they came of age but could not sell land or spend the principle without special permission of the court. In his will, Burge appointed Dolly guardian of their daughter Sadai, but made no mention of his two other minor children, Louisiana, fourteen, and Eliza, twelve, an omission that was not unusual for men in the antebellum South. Dolly again entered the court system to petition for guardianship of Eliza, but this time she was unsuccessful. In 1864, eighteen-year-old Eliza chose as her guardian Augustus I I. Lee, the second husband of her sister Rebecca. Indeed, Dolly seemed to have strained relationships with both Rebecca and Eliza, but again, she was fairly circumspect about recording the details of these interpersonal conflicts.[31]

In addition to these family-related legal tangles that dragged on through the Civil War and Reconstruction, Dolly, as sole executor, faced all the typical challenges of settling an estate, particularly paying creditors. Many southern widows, some less adept than Dolly, painfully realized their husband's sizable debts. Planter husbands, in particular, often kept their financial affairs in notorious disarray, tied up their capital in land and slaves, and generally remained cash-poor. Frequently unaware of their husbands' finances, widows in the old South were considered easy prey for scheming merchants, peddlers, or creditors. Women found themselves at a significant disadvantage in the male world of business, and not infrequently, they became embroiled in lawsuits to settle these debts. Dolly spent several years embroiled in a lawsuit filed by a carpenter, William Stanton, who claimed that he held several unpaid notes against Thomas's estate, one of which amounted to $664. Dolly insisted she had no knowledge of the debt and did not believe Thomas had incurred it. Her diary and letters to Louisiana reveal her ongoing concern that she not wrong Mr. Stanton, but also that she not be duped.[32]

During these years of widowhood and legal entanglements for Dolly, the country was plunging into civil war. Although she made little comment on sectionalism during the 1850s and her unique perspective on it all, all evidence indicates that Dolly consistently sided with her southern ties over her northern roots. For all practical purposes, she had accepted the southern slave system and when she felt moral qualms about it, she comforted herself that her slaves were well cared for and content. A niece remembered that Dolly defended slavery to her northern relatives by explaining, "if you could only hear [the slaves] singing while they work or when they sit in their own cabins sometimes, you'd know they were happy and taken good care of." Dolly supposedly continued, "There are cruel and wicked people everywhere all over the world, but down South we don't any of us know such terrible ones as [Harriet Beecher Stowe in *Uncle Tom's Cabin*] writes about."[33]

While a niece's memoir must be considered carefully, Dolly's diary too suggests that she believed that slavery was a necessary, if flawed, system that provided essential labor for farmers, and proper Christian direction, industry, and care for slaves. Indeed, upon Lincoln's reelection in 1864 she reflected, "I have never felt that Slavery was altogether right for it is abused by many," but she saw little alternative in the South and no scriptural prohibition against it. After all, even pious Thomas, who "would not sin for his right hand," said that if he believed it sinful to own slaves, he would take them where he could free them. She minimized her role as a slave owner, perhaps for future readers, explaining that she had neither bought nor sold slaves, but made life as pleasant as possible for those bequeathed her. She also made it clear that she was not leading a life of leisure because of them.[34]

The last half of the war was especially difficult for Dolly, as casualties, food shortages, and inflation increasingly affected her. Additionally, she buried yet another child and, only a few months later, learned of the deaths of her parents. Meanwhile, Union forces moved closer to her home. In a dramatic series of entries beginning in mid-1864, Dolly described at length in her diary the news she heard of the oncoming Yankees, the terrifying sight of smoke rising from buildings throughout the countryside, and her fruitless efforts to conceal food, clothing, and slaves. Indeed, these passionate and exciting passages have made Dolly's diary famous.[35]

By November 1864, Dolly and her neighbors learned that a large force of Yankees, the left wing of Sherman's army, was headed for their own Newton County. "[L]ike Demons" and "famished wolves," she wrote in her diary, they rushed in, shooting livestock, devouring food, taking money and clothing from her and her slaves, stealing her beloved horse, burning her buildings, and taking away her "boys," young male slaves who begged and wept to be left at home. When the Yankees finally departed, they left her "poorer by thirty thousand dollars . . . And a much stronger rebel," she surmised.[36] The war's end brought its own complications, but by the end of the year, Dolly and her former slaves had made the transition to free labor and sharecropping relatively easily. Many of the Burge freedpeople remained as laborers and tenant farmers.[37]

After seeing her family through the tumultuous war years alone, Dolly married in 1866, a third and final time. Reverend William J. Parks was a widower, father, successful farmer, and prominent minister in the area, to whom Dolly and her family had long referred as "Uncle Billy."[38] But when this longtime friend surprised Dolly with a proposal, she initially resisted his suggestions. Perhaps one of her concerns was that upon marriage she, like most other wives of the time, would forfeit all of her property to her new husband and, possibly, his heirs. Consequently, in an atypical move that Dolly omitted from her diary, William and Dolly signed a prenuptial contract that protected the property she and Sadai had inherited from Thomas Burge. The couple married in September 1866, when Dolly was nearly forty-nine and William nearly sixty-seven. They lived in the Burge home until late 1867, when they moved to William's Oxford home, a few miles away, managing Dolly's farm and its renters in absentia.[39]

Again, Dolly apparently enjoyed a warm loving marriage. Letters from William when he was away at Methodist conferences attest to his devotion. "[N]ow about 469 days of our married life I admire you more and more and love you better and better," he assured her one Christmas. During these years, Dolly cared for her aging husband, oversaw the management of the Burge farm, and looked after the students from Emory College who boarded with her in William's Oxford home. Although Dolly wrote in her diary less frequently then, she did return to its pages in 1873 to mourn the death of her last husband, who died at the age of seventy-three, and to rail against the discriminatory laws that stripped her of many of their shared belongings.[40]

William Parks's last will, written in May 1872, carefully parceled out money and gifts to his various children, daughters-in-law, and grandchildren. Dolly received $1,000 (which was more than the other beneficiaries received) and the use of the house and lot for two years. William named her co-executor, along with his son and two sons-in-law. After the two years elapsed, as Dolly bemoaned, the house and much of the household furniture was auctioned and sold.[41]

Dolly then returned to the Burge plantation, where she set about fixing it up, entertaining family, marrying off Sadai in 1875, and managing her land and tenants, several of whom were former slaves and their children. Sidney and George Gunn, the daughter and son-in-law of Lydia, a freed-woman who married freedman Frank Burge, were especially helpful to the white family in managing the farm from the 1870s into the 1920s. However, while her servants offered Dolly assistance and continuity, family letters suggest they also caused her a fair amount of aggravation. "I declare I get so bothered with [the servants'] wants & ways sometimes that I want to run off & never see or hear of them any more—Dink is 'worser' than Aunt Lydia & so slow," Dolly complained to Sadai. "Mattie is the waiting girl & she is right provoking some times—She needs a whipping badly—." No doubt, former mistress and slaves were wrestling with how to define their new relationships to one another. The legacy of slavery must have colored Dolly's appraisal of her servants, and undoubtedly, theirs of her.[42]

One of Dolly's greatest joys in later life was seeing Sadai and her growing family. Initially, Sadai and her husband, Methodist minister John Davis Gray, lived in Eatonton, Georgia, close enough for frequent visits. Later, when Sadai and her family moved to Hawthorne, Florida, because John's health was failing, Dolly gladly kept some of Sadai's five children in Newton County. "His health must be the most important consideration," Dolly advised Sadai about John. "I do not think though it would be well for him to move us all down & have the care of a family again until he is stronger." In 1887, John died at the age of thirty-five. With Dolly's help, thirty-two-year-old Sadai purchased and tried to run a two-hundred-acre orange and tangerine farm in Hawthorne, Florida. Dolly remained at the Burge farm, managing her tenants and overseeing the land until shortly before her death on October 26, 1891. She was seventy-four years of age. Part of her legacy is this compelling diary, which provides us with a moving and important story about life in the nineteenth-century American South.[43]

FAMILY MEMBERS AND
OTHER PRINCIPALS

William Webb Lunt (1788–1863)
    married Ann Matilda Sumner (1795–1825) in 1813
        they had four children who survived to adulthood:
            Orrington Lunt (1815–1897)
            Dolly Sumner Lunt Lewis Burge Parks (1817–1891)
            William H. Lunt (b. 1819)
            Sarah Ann Lunt Comings (1821–1881)
    married Priscilla Purrington (1795–1863) in 1827
        they had three children who survived to adulthood:
            Mary Matilda Lunt (b. 1828)
            Stephen Purrington Lunt (b. 1831)
            Caroline E. Lunt (b. 1833)

Dolly Sumner Lunt (1817–1891)
  married Dr. Samuel H. B. Lewis (1816–1843) on 10/7/1838
    their children:
      Samuel Lewis (1839–1839)
      Susan Littlefield Lewis (1840–1844)
      Orrington Lewis (1843–1843)
  married Thomas Burge (1806–1858) on 1/22/1850
    his children by Mary Clark (1813–1848):
      Rebecca Jane Burge Mitchell Lee (b. 1830)
      Wiley C. Burge (b. 1835)
      Marguarett Louisiana (or Lou) Burge (1844–1863)
      Eliza Graves Burge (1846–1867)
    their child:
      Sarah Cornelia ("Sadai") Burge Gray (1855–1892)
  married Rev. William Justice Parks (1799–1873) on 9/13/1866
    his children by Naomi Pricket (1796–1856):
      Osborn B. Parks (1823–1855)
      Harwell Hodges Parks (1825–1895)
      Elizabeth C. Parks Pendergrass Thompson (b. 1827)
      William S. Parks (1829–1831)
      Wesley F. Parks (1831–1864)
      Martha S. Parks (b. 1833)
      Mary E. Parks Gunnels Harris (b. 1835)
      Henry F. Parks (1837–1864)
      Sarah N. Parks Harrison (b. 1840)

DOLLY'S SIBLINGS

Orrington Lunt (1815–1897)
  married Cornelia A. Gray (1819–1909) in 1842
    their children:
      Cornelia Gray Lunt (1843–1934)
      Horace Gray Lunt (1847–1923)
      George Lunt (1850–1895)

William H. Lunt (b. 1819)
   married Susan P. Littlefield (d. 1870)
     their children:
       Etta Lunt (d. 1874)
       Sunie Lunt
       William "Will" Lunt

Sarah Ann Lunt (1821–1881)
   married Isaac Miller Comings (d. 1889) in 1839
     their children:
       Ann Matilda Comings (b. 1840)
       Lewis Baldwin Comings (b. 1843)
       William Lunt Comings (b. 1843)
       Sadie Miller Comings Langmuir (b. 1848; m. 1871)
       Fannie Stone Comings (b. 1855)
       Orrington Lunt Comings (b. 1857)
       Jennie Comings
       Mamie Comings

SADAI'S FAMILY

Sarah Cornelia ("Sadai") Burge (1855–1892)
   married Rev. John Davis Gray (1852–1887) in 1875
     their children:
       Ida Eve Gray Morehouse (1876–1953)
       Fannie Comings Gray (1878–1908)
       Dorothy Lunt Gray Bolton (1880–1964)
       Joseph Howard Gray (1883–1962)
       Davis Burge Gray (1885–1934)

THE AFRICAN AMERICAN FAMILIES

Elbert Leving-Glass-Burge (1806–after 1880)
Julia Clark-Glass-Burge (1813–c. 1878)
     their children:

Sally Clark-Burge (1830–1879)
Lewis Clark-Burge (1832–after 1880)
Elbert Clark-Burge-Pace (b. 1836)[1]
Lucy Burge-Pace (1838–after 1920)[2]
George (1840–1844)
Moses (b. 1842)
Ned (1846–1927)[3]
David (1848–1879)
Ann (1850–c. 1879)[4]
Christopher (also Kit or Thomas) (b. 1852)[5]
Priscilla Hester (1854–1930)[6]
William (1856–after 1870)
Elbert's other child:
James Arnold (1838–after 1900)
married Tilitha Zimmerman in 1879

Lewis Burge [later took surname Maddox] (b. 1814)
Martha Burge (b. 1819)
their children:
Lilla (b. 1835)[7]
Henry (b. 1837)
John [Maddox] (b. 1838)
Newton (1840–c. 1879)
–Oliver [Maddox] (b. 1842–after 1870)
Fanny (1844–1844)
Middleton (b. 1846)
Sanford (b. 1848)
Ueole (1850–1879)
Winnie (b. 1852)

Franklin Burge-Mitchell (b. 1819)
Hannah Burge (1819–1864)
their children:
Jack (b. 1839)
William (1840–1856)
Jane (b. 1842)

Robert (b. 1844)
Rachel (1846–1872)
Corene (b. 1851)
Lydia (b. 1853)
Isaac (1856–1856)
Floyd (b. 1857)
Milly (1859–1878)
Margaret Elisabeth (b. 1861)
married Lydia (c. 1823–after 1920) in 1866

OTHER BURGE SLAVES

Charles (b. c. 1789)
Peter (c. 1790–1850)
    his daughter:
        Betsey (1833–1847)
Milly[8]
    her children:
        Adaline (d. 1844)
        Howard (d. 1844)
        Lydia (b. c. 1823–after 1920)

The Diary of Dolly Lunt Burge, 1848–1879

CHAPTER ONE

A Madison Teacher
and Faithful Christian

Madison Morgan Co, Georgia Feb. 6th 1847![1]

Feb 6th [1848]

 Sabbath evening. Have been thinking for sometime past that I would every day put down the incidents thereof thought—feelings, &c. &c. in other words keep a regular journal. I find however that I am much inclined to neglect these every day matters &c. to pass them off as trivial concerns. But do they not make up one's life? Of what trifles are life composed & yet when called to render an account of them will they then be as trifling & unimportant to us as they now seem to be?

"There is no time for trifling here" says the Poet And if we could feel his sentiments we should be more watchful that 'time' did not run to waste. 'The fragments would indeed be gathered up that nothing be lost—

The commencement of this New Year brought to me feelings somewhat differing from those which have preceded it. If I mistake not my feelings there has been an increased desire for an entire consecration of self to the service of God. The last hour of the old & the first of the new found me pleading that this might be the case with me. The midnight hour was one of consecration. And Oh that these desires may be increased. May I indeed as I have resolved pray twice where I have once. May I seek not my own but the will of my Heavenly father.

The past week has been one of unusual spiritual enjoyment. It has been easy to pray. God's ear was not heavy he *did* hear, & answer the petitions, which I put up, & sent His blessing upon my soul. For the week I have been alone, Mr. and Mrs. Kolb[2] have been at their plantation, & yet I was not alone for I felt truly that a Friend was near to me one that sticketh closer than a brother! Praise the Lord for His Goodness & His wonderful works to the children of men—

I have listened to-day to an interesting discourse upon the Atonement by Brother Hebbard from Hebrews 9th 22. For without shedding of blood is no remission. The first I knew the nature of the atonement. 2d its necessity & Lastly its effects—

The different divisions were not much enlarged upon, owing to the inclemency of the weather only eighteen present—This has been an exceedingly cold day one unusual for this climate—Called upon Sister Hebbard[3] who is quite unwell, with Mrs. Kolb spent an hour agreeably glad to find her much better than when in the morning hope that she may soon recover her usual health,—

This cold & inclement night how thankful night how should my heart warm with gratitude for the blessings which surround me. How many widows are exposed to its cheerless blasts? How many are suffering for the necessities of life. How many are stretched upon beds of languishing and pain. And suffering for what I enjoy. May I be grateful. O that my heart may be filled with the praise of God for His exceeding goodness to me.

Read an interesting sermon from Jay's discourses upon despising small things. May I feel that nothing coming from His Hand is small that all is noble like Himself—

[February] 7th [1848]

Noon. Returned from morning's school a pleasant session pupils inclined to study consequently, lessons perfect still remains cold. Recieved invitation to C. J. Baldwin's a party given in honour of his marriage.[4] Shall not probably attend.

Eve. Spent this evening at Mr. Cook's in company with Revd. H. Hendee & Hebbard, Mr. & Mrs. P & daughter & Mr. & Mrs. K.[5] Had an interesting conversation with them respecting the personal pronoun He. Company does not promote one's growth in Grace. One that is so volatile as myself. Retired late—

[February] 8 [1848],

Another very cold day & the night promises to be the coldest of the season. Been through with all of my school duties pleasantly & I trust profitably to my pupils. Walked down town to see Mrs. Shaw,[6] who has been quite unwell a cold windy walk. Reflected or attempted to upon the events of the day, the motives which have governed &c. O me how unlike what I ought to be. Wil Kolb a nephew of Mr. K came down from Marietta[7] last evening to attend school. A pleasant little fellow he is, & right glad am I that he has come. This was our class meeting evening but it was quite too unpleasant for me to go out I thought. Brother Kolb went three out only—

[February] 9 [1848]

Much milder to-day called upon Mrs. Floyd[8] early this morning her daughter is quite unwell. She encouraged me to go out to Mr. Baldwin's. Left school at three o clock to make preparations. Mrs. Saffold sent her carriage. & I went in company with Mr. Porter G. Saffold and Mr. Graves.[9] Met a very large party, felt solemn & little in accordance with the gayety of the scene. Ah how little we can tell of the future. Not long since I spent a week with Mrs. Susan his former wife there. The last time I was there she met & greeted me cordially how different, the scene tonight. How prone to prove the old adage "out of sight—out of mind"—Returned home at ten 15 minutes past, feel little like writing so I'll to bed—

[February] 11 [1848] [10]

Another day with all its accounts has passed duties have been performed as usual but with not that alacrity which I love to have. I feel somewhat the effects of last night's dissipation.

Went to prayer meeting but felt care worn & weary but found it good to wait upon the Lord my soul was refreshed. We not only had a prayer meeting but a class—Bro. Porter's [11] heart was full of love joy & thankfulness. Called upon Sister Hebbard who still remains poorly—

[February] 11th [1848]

Friday evening. School day duties for the week are over & have I striven to do my duties to my pupils in the fear of God? We have had a pleasant week. A shower this evening with thunder & lightning quite warm people all busy in their gardens. Some seeds up pease &c. &c. Read but little to day & that nothing to profit. Rev. Mr. Irving [12] visited our school this evening been reviewing all day. No letters this week friends must have forgotten me—

[February] 12th [1848]

Received letter from Mrs. Round [13] happy to hear from her. Spent the day idly, done something in the way of Valentines went down to Mrs. Shaw's & called upon Mrs. Floyd on my return. Ah this has been an unprofitable week. May the next be better spent—written a letter in Spanish this evening—

[February] 13 [1848]

A bright & beautiful morning. Every thing in Nature calls loudly for praise to the maker of the Universe. 'Tis Sabbath too "the day of all the week the best Emblem of Eternal Rest." Sermon from Matthew 11 2 to

6—Listened to a most excellent Rev L. Wittich.[14] Of two suppositions he took the one John himself doubted & sent two of his disciples to Christ to inquire concerning him. He spoke of the appropriateness of the manner which he took to have his doubts dispelled. The reasons for his having those doubts & The reply of Our Saviour. This was dwelt upon at some length. The miracles which he had wrought & was now doing. Go tell him said he of these things. Refer him to my baptismal scene &c—And lastly of the inestimable gift of the Gospel to the poor. Upon this he dwelt with all of the eloquence of *himself.* Twas *Godlike* said he with a gesture as peculiar as the expression.

Afternoon called upon Mrs. Hebbard spent an hour returned home found company Mr. C. & F. After a while Mr. Wittich came in & stopped to tea had a pleasant time with him talking over last year's scenes. He was very much afflicted with his throat. Went to church again at night some remarks made by him upon Adam's fall & the two motives that were constantly at work in the human heart one inclining them to good the other to evil & our proneness even as Adam & Eve to lay the guilt upon another or to excuse ourselves.

Not been a day of much religious enjoyment. O my heart my heart is so unlike what it ought to be so easily satisfied with the vanities of this world famishing for the want of spiritual food & yet content to feed upon the husks of what it needeth—A foolish chit chat this evening has more passion on my mind [than] the sermons of the day. God forgive my follies—

[February] 14th [1848]

This is the day celebrated or dedicated to St. Valentine but for the reason not well understood. Many are the love tokens which find their way into a lady's boudoir. Many are trembling anxious thoughts which possess the minds of the fair ones but enough. This has been a pleasant day one well fitted to the choices of the feathered mates. School duties have been performed with ease & pleasure recitations not as correct as they might have been. Mr. & Mrs. Kolb have gone to the plantation & to be gone for the week. Miss Catherine is with me to-night. May pleasant dreams be ours as we lie down to rest & prepare for repose. May a review of the actions of the day give us no uneasiness & may the care & protection of Our Heavenly Parent be extended over us.

Tuesday [February] 15 [1848]

No class meeting to-night quite wet & sloppy been in school all day dined at Mrs. Walton's[15] had a pleasant visit & a fine dinner. Quite lonesome at home been reading 'Neal's' Gazette.[16] Had company, Mr. B[17] the same as usual. One new story staid untill [*sic*] nearly nine. I am sleepy so to bed.

[February] 16 [1848]

Very wet this morning, did not rise untill very late & was late at school &c. &c. It has been quite lonely to day at home. This keeping house without a man I don't like much. Ah me how unlike past times, but away with these thoughts. I am gloomy enough children all rude & idle today heard a most interesting peice of news concerning myself which I almost wish was true to night if it would add to my happiness—Very warm for the season. Little religious enjoyment. Oh, why am I so cold & hard-hearted—Wish Mr. & Mrs Kolb would come home.

[February] 17 [1848]

The day has again passed & I am seated to pen its events so far as I am concerned. It has not been very pleasant yet quite warm fine growing weather vegetables are coming up. Dined at Dr. Howard's.[18] Spent a very pleasant noon with them. Been to prayer meeting a good meeting. The Spirit of God was there. Sisters Saffold & Walker[19] both joined in prayer—O that they may be answered that God would hear the prayers that are raised to Him for a reformation.

[February] 18 [1848]

Rainy all day. Staid in school untill 1/2 then dismissed for the day. Called in to Mrs. Walton's & Cook. While at Mrs. C's heard that our folks had returned. Glad of it. I do not feel as well as usual—

[February] 19 Saturday Eve [1848]

Is it not well at the close of the week to look over the past & see what has been our progress. What we have done for Him Who hath made & redeemed us & what too we have left undone. What we have omitted that we have had opportunity to do. I feel that the account is not balanced on the side which it ought to be. It has been a week of levity & of little spiritual enjoyment. And tomorrow is the Sabbath. Tomorrow if health & life are spared I again participate with the children of God in the blessings & privileges of His consecrated board. How ought I to examine myself & see that there be in me the right spirit that I eat & drink not unworthily. May I have proper faith true repentence & a firm resolution to do better. Received a letter from Orrington & Cornelia.[20]

[February] 20 [1848]

Went to Love feast this morning few there but the presence & power of God was there—nearly all spoke. Brother Hebbard requested all who were resolved to seek for holiness of heart to come forward & kneel on the front benches while prayer was made for the descent of the Holy Ghost. So I have once again pledged myself openly to seek for a purer life. Ah if I go to hell my way will surely be paved with broken resolutions. I sometimes fear that I am not honest that when I pledge myself to do thus, &c., I do not in reality intend to do it. O My God thou knowest my heart. Have mercy upon me & let this last resolution be put in practice.

I came home & as it was very rainy no preaching was had have spent most of the day in my room have tried to read, tried to pray. O that my desires could reach the ears of the Lord of Sabbath that he would hear and answer, but O I have so long disregarded his calls. Why should He hear me. Why should He now listen. He will, I feel certain, that He will because He has said that He is as a tender parent always ready to listen to the calls of his children, & He has given us so many tokens of encouragement to ask, & *recieve* the things for which we ask.

Merciful Parent give O give me a clean heart, A copy Lord of Thine. Let me feel the life giving tokens of thy Love. O let me feel from this day forth to seek more earnestly honestly & humbly for thy mercies. O what am I a poor worm of the dust that I should ask such great favors. Ah I am too sinful too unlike those in practice & faith & every good work to recieve the blessings for which they glorified God & sang praises to Him with a holy & clean heart—

[February] 21 [1848]

Another rainy day been to school. Wrote a letter to bro O & sister. Read a little & idled a good deal more. So ends the day—

[February] 22d [1848]

Still the clouds pour down their contents. Its rain rain, rain, a continual rain. Been out to school & have been wet through every day for some days but my health remains good. Recievd letter from cousin Mary.[21]

[February] 23d [1848]

A little sunshine this morning but raining now right merrily. Mr. Russell here to spend the night. Had a fine present of books today from an agent of Appletons. Am I striving for holiness of heart?

[February] 24 [1848]

Still rainy been out all day. Not in my usual health, (done but little studying to-day).

[February] 25 [1848]

Closed another scholastic week & a very wet & unpleasant one it has been too & it still remains so. "But shall a living man complain." Had a pleasant interview with brother Hebbard. Mr. Kolb has gone so I go [?] to mind.

[February] 26 [1848]

I have been very busy all day. Rose early this morning & commenced work took a walk at five this evening with Miss Richards. Spent an hour after tea below, since then have pronounced some "french' & written a

German exercise. Am now to perform some Saturday night ablutions & prepare for bed. Weather about the same a little more appearance of "fairing off."

The week has been one of pleasantness to me. I hope that I am & have made some improvement but it is so slight, hardly perceptible. But I thank God that I have a desire to do better that I am not altogether without feeling upon the subject of my soul's salvation.

[February] 27 [1848]

It is somewhat more pleasant this morning. Commended myself to the care & protection of my Parent in Heaven. Read a portion of His Word & a sermon. 1/2 3 Went to church this morning & heard the Rev G Lane[22] preach the 19 ver of the 3 chap of Hebrews. So we see that they could not enter in because of unbelief. He first gave us a review of the wanderings & journeyings of the children of Israel, the report of the spies concerning the promised land, The anger of the Lord at their unbelief of His protecting care, their punishment. The proposition was then laid down that Faith & unbelief were the two opposing principles of the human heart. Unbelief had lead [*sic*] to all the sin of the world. He made one startling assertion *viz* that he believed every man was just as good & holy as they wanted to be. Proof: God was willing & had done all that He could do for their salvation, & if men sincerely desired & hungered & thirsted for a likeness to God the promise of God was for them. But they did not want to enter into that rest, For it required them to lay aside every weight & sin which so easily beset them.

This "rest" typical of the rest of the christian: To obtain it, We must sincerely believe it, must earnestly strive, making no excuses for the deceitfulness of the heart. Satan had *perfect* servants why should not Christ have the same. And lastly, its application. Again he referred to the children of Israel being brought to the borders of the promised land & not permitted to enter.

Those mourning souls, said he, that have laboured for holiness of heart will be brought in sight of heaven & be shut out because ye have not believed.

9 o clock   Heard another discourse from the same speaker. Words of the text If any man will come after me let him deny himself. The natural deprevity [*sic*] of the human heart. Self denial was necessary to attain wealth any eminence in intellectual pursuits & the greater the object the more self-denial was necessary & as intellectual predominated over temporal or sensual desires so the spiritual was higher than either therefore requiring more & greater self denial. The christians path was marked out as a plain self denying one. May the influences of the day which I trust have been spiritual be carried into the week with me.

[February] 28 [1848]
   A delightful morning & a pleasant day. have for the greater part of the day felt that my desires were ascending to God for a clean heart. O that My God would hear & give me the faith which alone can claim the blessing. Have put in practice today or last evening one little piece of self-denial. O that I may deny myself more & more of this worlds pleasures, &c &c. Heard of the death of J. Q. Adams—the nation's loss!![23]

[February] 29 [1848]
   Attended to my duties as usual, have sufferd extremely with the head ache consequently have not studied any. Went to class to night & had a good meeting. A goodly number out—A fine pleasant day.

Madison Geo March 1st, 1848.
   This the first day of spring has not been very pleasant though mild in the morning it has been succeeded by a cold drizzling rain been out as usual. Had company this evening a long foolish chat. Recieved a letter from Bro & Sister Comings.[24] They have arrived in New England. Well of my headache!

[March] 2d [1848]
   A very mild pleasant day but few out to prayer meeting to night, been writing to Sarah.

[March] 3d [1848]

    Rainy day.

[March] 4th [1848]

    A delightful springlike day. Mrs. Kolb returned from plantation about noon. Miss M Porter, G Wade and Virginia Jones called upon me this evening.[25]

    This closes up another week and what progress have I made on the way to Heaven. I have enjoyed some precious seasons of prayer & have tried to live & do the duties of a christian. But o I lack watchfulness.

[March] 5th Sabbath morning [1848]

    A damp cold unpleasant morning. looks very much like snow. Went to church. Bro Wittich preached from the text. Why stand ye here all the day idle several verses of the preceding chapter were dwelt upon as explanatory remarks. They were first the self complacent question of Peter the maner [*sic*] & cause of the question, & the whole parable was the reply of our saviour.

    The question Why stand ye here idle was used as an accomodated question & put to the congregation. The different answers considered & the application—

Evening

    Bro Wittich preached again from the words Fear not, Little flock it is your Father's good pleasure to give you the Kingdom. Explanatory remark the cententiers[26] brother that wished to make him a judge over them. The comparative smallness of the church, its duty to "Fear not" for all its trials & its divers temptations. The imbecility & unstableness of its membership notwithstanding all it would yet overcome; The principle of Faith was dwelt upon[,] upon which the church acts & beautifuly illustrated by the words of our Saviour. 3d the reward of the church. It was not only in the Future but even here it had the ministrations of angels the approbation and smiles of God & the Good man had that within him which might be called a reward even here. Illustrated by his communings with his Father in Heaven when no eye but His could see & no Ear but His hear his petitions. Then the reward hereafter. The Kingdom given. He closed by an earnest appeal to all to seek the reward promised—Have not enjoyed so much the exercises as if I had not such a trifling spirit & wandering mind. Very pleasant this evening.

[March] 6th [1848]

A pleasant but cool day attended to my daily duties as usual. Went this evening to monthly concert for prayer held at the Presbyterian Church. But few of either denomination out. O for more feeling upon this great & momentous subject—

[March] 7th [1848]

Just returned from the fair of the Ladies P Sewing Society.[27] Assisted in selling. A lively crowd present & all went off right merrily not as many goods sold as there might have been. A very pleasant evening—& now to bed for it is near the witching hour of night—

[March] 8 [1848]

Wearied from last nights dissipation. I am retiring early. Warm pleasant growing weather—.

[March] 9th [1848]

A rainy day, been out to school & to prayer meeting this evening, but 3 whites out and the same number of blacks. Do not feel that I am striving mightily for that straight and narrow way which alone leads to God. Ah me I feel in my heart a love for the world & the vanities thereof quite inconsistent with my desires & intentions for a holy life—

[March] 10 [1848]

Another evening of dissipation merriment & mirth. I have broken a resolution formed from convictions of its inappropriateness for a christian viz not to be found in such scenes. This is me it is myself, myself!!

[March] 12 [1848]

Yesterday was running about all day. Had my daguerreotype taken to send to my father.[28] My mind was forcibly impressed while sitting careful of every motion of the importance of maintaining that carefulness as to my present life that no wrong impression may be found daguerreotyped in Eternity. This is the Sabbath. O may it be a Sabbath to me
Evening—

Bro Hebbard preached this morning from Prov 15-32—He that refuseth instruction despiseth his own soul. He spoke of our advantages of spiritual improvement & showed the consequences &c. we neglected them.

This evening the text was Watch ye for ye know not the day nor the hour when the Son of Man cometh an impressive solemn discourse—

[March] 14 Tuesday Evening [1848]

Quite unwell last evening but about. A cold day *this* for the season spent nearly all of the noon recess at the church they were cleansing it. Instead of being at class tonight have spent the evening at Dr. Wingfields.[29] The Johnson's Jones's Mrs. Stoke Colbert &c., were present a very nice supper & a pleasant evening—but my heart was at the class room & my desires were that God would bless them by His presence and Love shed abroad in their hearts—

[March] 15 [1848]

A very cold, windy day.

[March] 16 [1848]

Still cold & windy. Mr. & Mrs. Kolb at the plantation. Been at prayer meeting only two or three out & spent an hour since at Mrs. Howards.

[March] 17 [1848]

A pleasant day. And moreover it is Friday which makes it still more so. It has been our church fast but I have not kept it as I often do.

[March] 18 [1848]

This has been a week of little religious enjoyment to me. O that the Good Spirit would come down even at this late hour & prepare my heart for the exercises of the morrow. Listened to a sermon from the P. Elder Mr. Pitchford Acts 26, 29 verse. His introductory remarks were of the natural impulse of the man to seek for happiness. His different ways of seeking it. Paul his character for firmness. For decision & Perseverence Applied to christians of the present day. This evening the Rev. W. J. Parks[30] preached from the words, "Rejoice evermore" 'be kind of joy, spoke at some length of Levity inconsistent with strong mental powers & The christian character injured & destroyed by it. Reasons why people did not always rejoice. The true Christian would reioice &c.

[March] 19 [1848]

Love feast this morning interesting. Services of the morning conducted by P. Elder. The text Lord remember me when thou comest into Paradise. The crucifixion scene. 1st the way to get to Heaven considered. Approach by prayer. Public Private Social & Ejaculatory prayer considered. Repentence for sin & a restitution of unjust gains or the undoing of those things which ought not to have been done inconsistent with the law of God. The denial of the Holy Ghost. This was not satisfactorily explained. The answer then of prayer. At the close of the morning services the Lords supper was administered.

Evening

Bro Parks preached. Hebrews 3d 12 verse—Take heed brethren lest there be in any of you an evil heart of unbelief in departing from the living God. But exhort one another while it is called today lest any of you be hardened through the deceitfulness of Sin. Reference to the unbelief of the Jews. 1st The advice contained in the text signifying that we should be careful. A remark here upon Perserverence & falling from Grace. If we keep Gods law He will keep us, Faith considered. We must believe in the truth of what we are required to have faith. Instance a Parent promises a child a toy if he will do thus and so. The child believes him & yet does not the thing required can he claim the reward? If he does He does it not with confidence. Neither can we exercise faith to believe that God will hear our prayer if we disobey His commands. Backsliding not always in the closet. We do what we ought not & then go to our closet & find that we cannot exercise faith & that God does not bless us from that the duties without the approbation of our own conscience are irksome. The duty enjoined & maintained. Exhort one another. The latent the excuse for the lack of it considered. We can exhort a daughter & father can a son. Brethren & Sister's meeting together at fault in this matter &c, &c. The deceitfulness of sin of our own hearts. The blessings attendant upon exhortation. Give not up your confidence. The example of the children of Israel in their journeyings to the promised land. An exhortation to the unconverted—One knelt at the seat for prayer—This has closed a Quarterly meeting occasion.

[March] 20 [1848]

Spring like weather very warm but cloudy. Lettuce for dinner to day. School duties all attended. Called upon Mrs. Floyd—Spent an agreeable evening chatting with the home folks.

[March] 21st [1848]

Another day has carried its accounts into eternity. I am still in health & the blessings of life are multiplied about me. God grant that I may possess a thankful heart to the Giver of every good & perfect Gift—

[March] 22d [1848]

Have been busy as usual. Mr. B spent the evening with me—

[March] 23d [1848]

A lovely day & it closes this the first quarter of our scholastic year. Have not been out to prayer meeting tonight busy with sewing.

[March] 24th [1848]

This has been a holiday with me. Been down town purchased two fine dresses &c. Mrs. Robson & Burnet[31] called this evening. I am destitute of religious enjoyment tonight unhappy & discontented. O where am I & what am I doing—

[March] 25 [1848]

Had Radishes Asparagus & Lettuce for dinner.

[March] 26 [1848]

A delightful morning. O that the son of righteousness was beaming upon my heart as the natural sun is casting its broad beautiful & fertilizing light upon the earth.

Opened our Sabbath School. Rev. G Lane preached to us to day 2 chap of Philippians 15 verse That ye may be blameless & harmless &c. He first spoke of the indisposition of Christians to believe the full extent of the blessings which the Gospel confers—One excuse If we but lived in former times we might have been blameless for society was different—We think we must conform at the present day to the present age in some respects to gain friends to our cause. But what God makes necessary He gives strength to us to perform accordingly. We are to live blameless as the sons of God. It is impossible as such to please the world. We must please God having an eye single to His service. Reference to Mrs. Fry. This disposition rests upon our love to God. To be harmless, not only in words, but in actions others are looking toward us & often following our example. Two great principles to be observed to do no harm but to do all the good that we can. The expectation of the world in that respect, former errors often spoken of without sorrow. Why blameless? Because we are the sons of God. The obligations we are under to Him. The importance of maintaining our character as His sons. Ref—to world affairs without rebuke a building of ourselves to the Lord. Is it possible? Tis Gods word. & command therefore it must be true. Christian Influence abroad in the world—

[March] 26 Evening [1848]

The same speaker spoke tonight from Galatians 6, 7 verse. Be not deceived God is not mocked for whatsoever a man soweth that shall he also reap.

[March] 27 [1848]

Another beautiful day. Mr. Hendee very joyful in being a *parent*. Heard of Mr. Browne's death. Took a short walk this evening.

[March] 28 [1848]

Pleasant morning but rainy evening. These spring showers are refreshing—

[March] 29 [1848]

Quite unwell for a little while this morning. Report came into town this Evening that Thomas Saffold's wife[32] had put an end to her life. She was at her mother's in Athens and ate a hearty breakfast apparently cheerful & happy. As she got up from the table she took from it the carving knife & went to her room & with her innocent babe sleeping by her she bared her breast & stabbed herself twice & when discovered was a corpse. Her husband was here in town having left her but yesterday morning. The news was immediately brought him and none but the merciful Parent above can tell the feelings of his Heart. The agony which he endures. O how thankful ought we to be that our minds are not often left to their own vagaries— She was a Christian so far as we could judge!

[March] 30 [1848]

Engaged as usual. Mr. Hendee has left the school in my care for tomorrow & a part of this evening. Been to prayer meeting twenty three out.

[March] 31 [1848]

A pleasant day but very much fatigued.

[April] 1 [1848]

Somewhat cooler to day. I am very hoarse whether from talking so much yesterday or not I cannot tell. Have been down to Sister Wittich's to see Clara who is very ill of the measles. Received a letter from cousin Mary.

[April] 2 Sabbath day [1848]

Been to Sabbath school & attended church all day. Brother Hebbard spoke this morning from the words Broad is the way that leadeth to Death & many there be that find it &c. A solemn service. I do not feel that I have much Religion. The vows that I have made are forgotten or not put in practice. O my soul! my soul! Why is it thus? Why live at this poor dying rate?

[April] 3rd [1848]

Not as pleasant or warm as it was last week have not felt very well or in as good humor as usual to day. Had a long conversation with Mr. Hebbard & Hendee upon Mrs. Saffold's death upon temptation &c.

[April] 4 [1848]

Wrote cousin Mary. Been to class to night.

[April] 9th [1848]

I have not written for several days in this my journal for I have been very much engaged sewing nothing new however has transpired. We have had a few days of rainy weather & vegetation looks really beautiful.

Bro L Wittich preached to day as usual two excellent sermons. The morning's text was from the 2d Epistle of Timothy—3d chapter 16th & 17 verse, All Scripture is given by inspiration—He attempted to prove that the religion of nature unaided by the revealed law would never lead a man to God—

This evening 'twas from Hebrews 2d from the 14 to 18th—It has been a day of little religious enjoyment. I feel gloomy this evening. O for the company of the loved ones who are at rest. Why all these warm yearning affections given me to be thrown back upon myself—

[April] 10 [1848]

A pleasant day went into Miss Jones to have my dress fitted busy all day in school. Called upon the sick at night Mrs. Floyd's children. Circus in town. Mr. B spent the evening with me. Five years to day was the birthday of my little Orrington[33] and its last of earth.

[April] 11 Tuesday evening [1848]

Our usual class this evening. I've not attended for I felt unprepared. Been with Sister Kolb down town purchasing summer goods. Met one that I would like to have spoken with.

[April] 12 [1848]

Mr. Hendee has again left me with a double duty to do—

[April] 14 [1848]

Tired out. Mrs. T Baldwin[34] and Mr. K from the country dined with us to day—

[April] 15 [1848]

Received letter or package from cousin Mary to day been out & purchased her a beautiful barage silk &c. Sewed this evening upon my muslin.

[April] 16 Sabbath morning [1848]

And a rainy one it is. Lay in bed late for me. Before eight the sun came out & I went to Sabbath School & have attended services in the Presbyterian church. Mr. Allen a colporteur[35] spoke upon the necessity of laying aside every weight that doth so early encumber us. He held a meeting this evening in the Methodist church where he presented the claims of his society to us quite lengthily. I feel this evening that I have gone far astray from God. I do not feel spiritively as I want to feel. I have not that spirit of prayer that I had weeks ago.

[April] 17 [1848]

A warm pleasant day. Been in school all day. Have not done any sewing wrote a letter this evening to Miss E. Brentwell & now to bed.

[April] 18 [1848]

One of our neighbors Mrs. Heard died today a great affliction to the family! Been to class to night & had a good meeting though my thoughts wandered much about a trifling circumstance which happened to day with some of my pupils—& which caused me to write a note to my neighbor Mr. H.

[April] 19 [1848]

We dismissed school for this morning and attended the funeral of Mrs. Heard. Mr. Hendee preached from the words Blessed are the dead that die in the Lord &c. Mr. & Mrs. Harris[36] dined with us. Recieved a letter from cousin Mary called upon Brother Hebbard who is quite ill of a cold. After school, went in to Mrs. Cook's & spent the evening or untill after eight. When I returned home found that Mrs. Robson had sent for me to come over there & see Mr. & Mrs. Round my old friends, who are on their way to Indinia [*sic*]. Went over immediately & spent the night.

[April] 20 [1848]

Came home to breakfast & saw our folks leave for the plantation & went back & spent the time with them untill it was time for them to leave which they did in the freight cars for Oxford. Thus have I bidden adieu to dear ones again never expecting to see them again they have three fine children & a little daughter that much reminds me of my beloved Susan.[37]

Eve 20

Attended prayer meeting but few out. O that the spirit of prayer was more with us. O that my own heart was deeply imbued with it & that the command Pray without ceasing & in everything give thanks was by me obeyed. Spent the night at brother Porter's.

[April] 21st [1848]

Arose early this morning & listened to a heartfelt prayer by brother Porter. After school in the morning dined at Judge Saffold's. A pleasant interview with them. Called in to Bro Hebbard's & there learned that our folks had returned. Came home & found them well. Had green peas for dinner.

My mind this evening goes back to four years since when my darling Susan lay contending with her last adversary Death. O the bitterness of that night. How hard to give her up & am I still unreconciled still murmuring & wishing her back forgive me O forgive these selfish feelings.

My head aches severely & that I too was at rest. O how pleasant will be the rest promised to the people of God. May it be mine.

[April] 22 [1848]

A cold wet morning but corresponding to my feelings. My head still pains me & I feel lonely & gloomy. Made me a cape. Very unwell this evening.

[April] 23d Sabbath morning [1848]

Feel much relieved. Kept Radish leaves on my neck all night. A wet morning but went to Sabbath school & church. Judge Longstreet[38] preached from the words My peace I leave with you &c. A heartfelt sermon. He has recently lost an only son & he felt in his own heart the consolation of that Peace which he preached to others. Mr. Veal at the close of the exercises knelt for the prayers of God's people. O may he find peace & joy in believing. May converting grace be abundantly showered upon him & may he speedily rejoice in a sin-pardoning saviour. Come O my Saviour & visit us in mercy. Revive Thy work. Oh revive it in my cold barren heart.

Evening.

A full house to night text.

[April] 24 [1848]

A delightful day. Mr. Hendee did not return from Greensboro until the freight train came up so I took in school &c. Went to Presbyterian prayer meeting to night. Some 30 or 40 out. Sent letters to Boston & Worcester.

[April] 25th [1848]

Again have I met with my dear class & not alone with them but I trust the Lord was with us. O that His presence may continue to be with His people here. And may converting power rest upon Sinners. This has been a delightful day. We have had new potatoes for the first time this year. Several were in class to night that do not profess religion Mr. Veal Campbell &c.

[April] 26 [1848]

Nothing new.

[April] 27 [1848]

Found it raining when I awoke this morning but it cleared away early. Duties performed as usual in school. Called in to Mrs. Hilsman's & invited her to take a class in Sabbath School. Then went to Mrs. Vanlandingham's[39] upon an errand for Mrs. Kolb. Been to prayer meeting this evening more out than usual with us & consented anew to pray for a revival. Mr. Delona present a converted Catholic.

[April] 28 [1848]

A foggy unpleasant day. Went to school this morning. But this evening Mr. H gave a holiday, until Tuesday morning. It seems a long time to me now, but it will soon pass away. Went to purchase some things for cousin with Mrs. Howard afterwards called to see Sister Porter. Met several there & spent an agreeable hour.

[April] 29 [1848]

Mrs. Kolb not well this morning but [out?] nearly all day but went to depot & saw the corpse of Montgomery Wingfield's child landed here for interment [*sic*]. A dull day. Green apple pie the first this year.

[April] 30 [1848]

Went to Sabbath School this morning a good many out. No preaching at the Methodist as it is a fifth Sabbath. Went to the Presbyterian and heard Mr. Delauny on the cause of Protestantism. Spent the evening in my room mostly.

May 1s [1848]

This was given us as a holiday by Mr. Hendee but the rain in the morning prevented us from enjoying it in the manner we wished. I sewed some this morning on a muslin dress. Went to Mrs. Shaw's with my bonnet & this evening plied the needle industriously until five o clock when I went to Mrs. Swifts[40]—spent an hour with her & from there to Mrs. Cooks where I took tea & went to concert prayer meeting from there. A good meeting & a goodly number out.

[May] 2d [1848]

Again have I to bless God for His goodness toward me for His long suffering & mercy to one of the most wayward of human creatures the most erring of mortals. Here I live day after day feeding upon His bounty upheld by his gracious hand & Oh what a thankless heart? What a cold selfish mortal. God have mercy upon me. Been in school as usual dined at Mrs. Waltons. After school this evening called upon some young ladies at Sister Vanlandinghams invited them to come to class & did not leave them until they promised to do so & they were there & blessed be God others were there also. O' Lord revive Thy work. Revive thy work. May every heart there feel thy Presence & rejoice in Thy love & that right speedily.

[May] 3d [1848]

Mr. & Mrs. Kolb gone to plantation dined at Mrs. Cook had green apple pie & a pleasant visit. Walked with my Botany class in the woods after school. Mr. Bissell called & spent evening with me.

[May] 4 [1848]

A day of business. Went down town before school time bought Cousin Mary a pair of boots edging & prepared her box to send her this evening. At noon dined at Bro Hebbard by special invitation. Returned home immediately after & wrote a letter to Mr. Holden of Philedelphia [sic]. Sent my watch to him for repairing by Miss Virginia Walton.[41] After school hastened home & packed the box to send to cousin then took it to Depot or Ike took it for me & went to see it properly labelled & directed. Hope Cousin will be pleased with her dress.

Mr. & Mrs. K. returned about dark took supper & went to prayer meeting. A goodly number present much serious feeling in the congregation I should think. Meeting appointed for tomorrow morning at sunrise as it is fast day.

[May] 5 [1848]

This morning at sunrise went to prayermeeting felt that it was good to wait upon the Lord. But Pride was humbled upon attempting to lead in prayer being called upon I could scarcely find words to express my desires & the embarrassment took away all enjoyment. Mr. Hendee unwell & did not come in untill late. went to the depot expecting to meet Bro & Sister Wittich. Did not come down however.

[May] 6 [1848]

A very warm day busy sewing all the morning late in the evening took a class of little girls to walk into the woods enjoyed ourselves finely. Attended a phrenological lecture this evening rather amusing than otherwise.

[May] 7 [1848]

Thus again has another Sabbath come round 'tis a delightful morning attended Sabbath School early then to class where I felt my heart softened by the influence of the Holy Spirit. Thence to church where Bro Wittich preached from Acts 24, Chap 24 & 25 verses. A good sermon. Spent the afternoon mostly in my room. Company below Major Warren[42] &c., &c. A large congregation out to night. O may some heart be reached three joined the church Mr. Veal Mrs. Walker & Miss Woods.

[May] Monday 8 [1848]

Felt this morning like living more for God than I have done had some conversation with V. Heard upon Religion. May God bless & comfort her sorrow stricken heart.

[May] 9 [1848]

Received package from Worcester. Mrs. J Wittich T Floyd Bro & Sister Hebbard dined with us to day. Had a pleasant interview. Went to class meeting to night. A good meeting. Feel more & more resolved to live for God to serve Him all my life.

May 14 [1848] Sabbath Evening

The last week neglected writing much as I was away with the sick two nights & felt wearied & sleepy the others. To day which is the Sabbath have suffered with a derangement of my stomach &c which has unfitted me for the duties of the sanctuary have been on the bed most of the day. Reading Guide to Holiness.

[May] 15 [1848]

A very warm pleasant morning feel better than I did yesterday & though weak must attend to my duties. Evening, had company which I ought not to have had in the absence of Mr. & Mrs. Kolb. Little enjoyment in religion. O that the work of the Lord might be revived in my heart.

[May] 16 [1848]

Mr. & Mrs. K. returned late this evening no meeting to night on account of heavy thunder shower.

[May] 17 [1848]

Delightful weather. Been to Baptist prayer meeting a good meeting.

[May] 18 [1848]

Friday evening has come again & I am again free from school duties for the week it has been one of hard labour & yet I find that my happiness is increased by being constantly employed. The mind needs employment to be cheerful & happy. God has been exceeding good to me. So many blessings as I enjoy. While I am so ungrateful so unmindful of Him & His commands. A protracted meeting has commenced to night in our church first sermon by our pastor from Luke. Take heed how you hear. A very appropriate & feeling sermon. May the Good One bless us & preside Himself over our meeting & get to Himself a great name!

[May] 22d [1848]

Saturday & Sunday attended preaching. A discourse in the morning from Bro Wittich. The Bishop arrived in the evening & stopped with us. Mr. Veal from SC & son supped with us. Mr. W text this morning was Shall a man rob God? Bishop Andrew[43] Saturday evening, While we look not at the things which are seen but at the things which are [not] seen, for the things which are seen are temporal but the things which are not seen are eternal. Sunday morning the 29 & 30 verses of the 5th chapter of Matthew. They were both plain pointed practical sermons. In the afternoon Bro Wittich preached from the words Seek ye the Lord while He may be found. Call upon Him while He is near. Judge Longstreet at night My peace I leave with you not as the world &c.

Thus have closed a series of most excellent sermons. Sermons which have been listened to by large & attentive audiences but there has been but little good seen.

My heart was melted in Love feast this morning by hearing Judge L experience.

O who can hint the power of the most High. Every thing here is apparently against the Spirit of God. My own heart is not in the right state for a blessing & yet I earnestly desire it.

Sabbath Evening May 28 [1848]

Prayer meetings have been continued during the week & well attended yet no one says "Pray for me." On Thursday I was quite unwell & unable to be at school. Have not yet felt as well as before my sickness. Spent all day yesterday & to day at home.

To day it has rained incessantly. No meeting although the judge is here to preach. I have named the name of God. I have placed myself among his children. I feel that I love them & yet I have but few evidences that I am a Christian. O shall I thus pass through the world a doubting unbelieving child? Is it never for me to say Abba Father. Is it never for me to rejoice with all my heart in the knowledge of sins forgiven. Well be it so. I'll try to serve God as well as I can & though often I may have no enjoyment therein I'll try to do my best & leave the event with Him. It's my fault it lies somewhere in me & when it is overcome I know God will bless me with a knowledge of pardoned sins.

[May] 29 [1848]

A pleasant day had cucumbers for dinner attended school as usual. Been to Presbyterian prayer meeting this evening.

[May] 30 [1848]

School duties have been unusually tiresome. Went to class to night.

July 2d [1848]

The last month I have neglected writing the first & second weeks being much engaged preparing & attending our examination which was held the 7 & 8 of June. Some of the classes did very well others was [*sic*] a failure. The house was crowded most of the time. Friday after I went out visiting all day & at night to the girls party at the Academy.[44] Saturday went to Buck Head to church with Mr. & Mrs. K Mr. & Mrs. H Mr. Porter & Wittich. A very good & pleasant time. Sunday attended church. Monday went to plantation. Spent Monday night with old Sister Bentford returned home on Tuesday. Wednesday went out visiting. Thursday prepared to go to Covington which we did the next day & I remained there until Wednesday. The remainder of the week was spent at home & Mondy [*sic*] school was again commenced. I have and am more pleasantly situated in school now than I have ever been.

This is Sabbath morning & how unlike the quiet and peace of the scene is my heart full of disquiet & an uneasy conscience & little prepared for the holy duties of the Lords Day.

Aug. 5 [1848]

Every day I am getting more & more averse to writing.

Sept. 29 [1848]

This is my birthday a standing point from whence I can look back over the past & recall the scenes of bye gone days. O the days of the past how bitter their memory scarcely would I recall any of them unless it might be that I could live them over better than I did. This world is truly & has ever been a dark sad lonesome place to me. Whatever of its scenes I have seen but few again I wish to see.

> "O happiness most blissful sacred name
> Sacred to every mortal mind
> Thee have I sought in every form
> But searched for what I never could find

'Tis not for me to know full well
Stern's the decree & fixed my fate—
I in a dreary wild must dwell
Firm's the decree & fixed my state—

Oct 2 Sabbath Eve [1848]

A wet & cold morning not much prospect for a full attendance. Went to church found many more there than I expected. Heard a fine sermon from Bro Wittich. Called upon Mrs. Swift—met Miss Hixy & Sister Hebbard. from there went to Mrs. Cooks & took tea. Went to church & heard Colonel Foster a gentleman who has recently been converted.

Nov 11, Sabbath Eve [1848]

Still backward about writing in journal but my Heavenly Parent does not forget me as I fear that I do Him. His blessings are still multiplied about me. Still am I blessed kept and Sustained by His unceasing care. Been a gloomy day. Sister Kolb says yet nevertheless it has been a pleasant one to me. Went to church this morning but few out. Bro Wittich made a few remarks. Spent the evening with us & we have had a social chat about matters & things in general. Well it is bed time & as all friends must part so I must say good night & retire.

Jan 1st 1849

Monday   I desire to bless God for being spared to see another year. May it be better spent than was the last! Have a headache from being out late at watch night. Called at Col. Walkers, Mrs. Walters, Killins[45] dined at Mrs. Cooks & supped at Mrs. Swifts with Bro Hebbard & wife. Went back to Mrs. Cs. Met Mr. Boning from Mass & from there to concert prayer meeting & then home. Now for bed. Mr. Kolb gone.

[January] 2d [1849]

Went down town early this morning & settled account with Cohen & Robson.[46] Went again with Mrs. K to Mr. Burneys store[47] & bought more goods for two dollars & a half than I ever did before. Lord [*sic*] came home while we were gone & have all been busy the remainder of the day & until

1/2 past Elevin [*sic*]. I went to class few present & turned it into a prayer meeting. Quite warm weather.

[January] 3d [1849]

Much cooler today attended a party at Dr. Hugh Oglebys given to Dr. Crawford honour of his marriage.[48] Returned home after twelve.

[January] 4th [1849]

Feel like I had been dissipating right smartly have done work of any account this week poor beginning for a new year. Went to prayer meeting had a church meeting to decide upon a station preacher.

[January] 5th [1849]

Prepared for company this morning & had several of our friends in to take tea with us[.]

[January] 6th [1849]

Called upon Mrs. Dr. Crawford & others. Went in the carriage with Mrs. K & Mrs. Wittich. Very cold. Miss Virginia Warren arrived here this evening from Macon.

Feb 19th [1849]

We have had a week of excessive cold wheather. Mr. Kolbs brothers have been on a visit to him the eldest left in the cars for home this morning. Many interesting things have taken place since I last wrote. I have been very remiss. Been engaged in school since the 8th of January fine school & everything goes on pleasantly. We have pease up & trees in bloom but I fear this cold will nip them all.

Recieved news last week of the death of my Grandmother Lunt aged 95.[49] Dear old lady she has gone to her rest. O what a long time did she have to buffet the waves of lifes troublesome sea. But the haven is gained at last. She is safely moored in the mansions prepared for her. Farewell dear old Grandmother. I shall never see you again till I meet you in that world where we are to recieve our reward.

We have for a preacher Caleb W. Key[50] on the circuit. Meetings not well attended. My own heart cold hard & unthankful. Oh Me, O Me!! I feel *very very* sad to night.

Feb 20 [1849]

A delightful day as balmy as June. Mr. K gone to the plantation. Mrs. K. been with Mrs. Key to Mrs. Porters. I called at Mrs. Waltons after school saw two beautifully ornamented cakes which she is going to send to Virginia W. Been to prayermeeting an excellent meeting prayers by brothers Porter Wittich Allen & Shaw with some remarks by Brother Key upon the faith of Joseph—pleasant day in school—

[February] 21 [1849]

Been in school as usual. Mrs. K quite unwell with a cold—

[February] 22d [1849]

Saturday been out visiting called upon Mrs. Allen Mrs. Burr Sherman Willy, Norton, Seymour, Shaw & Wittich. Recieved calls from Mrs. Cook Walton, the Mrs. Robsons Mary Cook the Misses Durdens Mrs. Harris &c. &c. Went to Mrs. Porters early this morning in company with Mrs. Floyd. So goes the day. Mr. K returned from Plantation.[51]

[February] Sunday 24 [1849]

A pleasant morning. Went to church heard Bro Wittich from the parable of the rich man & Lazarus. A most excellent sermon. Bro Key at night from Jacobs Ladder—Called upon sister Key this evening—also at Mrs. Cooks.

[February] Monday 25 [1849]

Still pleasant weather school full and pleasant.

[February 26] Tuesday [1849]

Day spent as usual in school went in to Bro Wittichs at evening recess met Mrs. Rees[52] & Floyd there. Mrs. K been out visiting all day. Went to class to night.

[February] Wednesday 28 [or 27th?] [1849]

Pleasant day. Spent evening in company with Mr. Cook & lady at Mr. Paulettes—

March 1st [1849]

Spring has come again & found me in possession of heavens best blessings of a temporal nature—But O my heart is insensible to the goodness of the Giver of all these benefits. Prayer meeting at night—Worked until late upon calico dress. Mr. Kolb gone to plantation.

[March] 2 Friday [1849]

The rest day has come at last. Walked down to Dr. Oglebys with Miss Chandler & Eugene Wittich. Sewing all the evening. Mrs. Kolb dined at Lancelot Johnstons.[53]

Friday March 10[54] 1849

It has been a week since I wrote any last Sunday the 4th Dr. Ogleby & lady Dr. Saffold Mrs. Rees & Clay were recieved into full connection. A very good discourse & the exercises altogether very solemn. Monday Tuesday & Wednesday were not pleasant yet I was out to concert prayermeeting the only lady present also to the other meetings of the week.

Yesterday we had some Indians in town a holiday in consequence. A poor show—

to night was invited to a party given to Mr. William Burney. Did not go in consequence of the distance—Spent the evening reading foolish chatting & actions. God forgive me for my sins—

[March] 11th [1849]

Mr. Kolb nephew & neice came early in the cars this morning. He has been North. She spending some weeks in Augusta busy making & icing cake all the morning while she slept dressed this afternoon & went out with her to return some calls staid until late tired out & unprepared for Sabbath exercises.

[March] 12 [1849]

Went to church. Mr. Wittich preached. Company as usual Phinny Lane Miss Dawson &c. The day not spent as a Sabbath should be—

[March] 13 [1849]

Mr. & Mrs. Kolb gone to Plantation our company left in the cars this morning. Spent an agreeable evening.

[March] 14 [1849]

Attended duties as usual. Class meeting at night good attendance—

[March] 15 [1849]

Went down town early this morning bought material to alter dress. Jacenot muslin. Went to Mrs. Killins to have it cut. Spent night—

[March] 16 [1849]

A rainy morning to come home dined at Mrs. Waltons—feel unwell to night—

[March] 16[55] [1849]

Very sick vomiting nearly all night. Went to school intending to come home directly. Found Mr. Wittich sick & expecting me to go on with school done so but did not feel strength sufficient—

[March] 17 [1849]

This is a day that has been set apart as an anniversary of the Sons of Temperance. The Ladies of Madison by Miss M J Rees present them with a banner— [56]

House was crowded good address fine dinner at the Male Academy &c &c. Picnic at night enjoyed myself right well—

[March] 18 [1849]

Feel dull this morning don't think last evening a fit preparation for the Lords day. Bro Key preached a full house. Maj. Warren & Williams came up. I dined at Mrs. Cooks & in the evening witnessed the baptism of their darling boy Edgar. Oh he looked lovely. No wonder that Christ said Of such is the kingdom of Heaven. For what could be more pure & holy than such innocence. He smiled sweetly at Rev. Mr. Baker[57] when he was consecrating him so sweetly that angels could but have joined him. Miss Mary is with me to night. Came in late after service—She leaves in the morning for the country.

[March] 19 [1849]

Mrs. Dyer here all day nothing new.

[March] 20 [1849]

—still here. Chloe not very sick. Went to class few there.

[March] 21st [1849]

A hard storm this evening got wet very wet coming home—

[March] 22 [1849]

Mr. Kolb gone to plantation. Mrs. K & I alone.

[March] 23 [1849]

To day ends the first quarter for '49 close with upwards of seventy. We shall have a weeks recess—

[March] 24 [1849]

Went down town this morning after cleaning up a little with Mrs. Cook. Looked at Dr. Wingfields new goods some very pretty. Called at most of the stores. Afternoon went to Lancelot Johnstons the Mrs. Peavy' Mrs. Jesup' & Oglebys with Mrs. Kolb & Key—Another badly spent day.

[March] 25 [1849]

Been to Sabbath school this morning few out a wet morning have scarcely got organized. Dr. Means[58] preached two good sermons to day no company to day cleared off & quite pleasant. Chloe the cook has a fine boy—

[March] 26 [1849]

Went down to Wingfields store purchased napkins for Mrs K & a lace visette for self been busy all day preparing for a dining tomorrow very tired & weary 'tis vacation week at the close of the first quarter—Frost to night.

[March] 27 [1849]

Mr. & Mrs. Key Mr. & Mrs. Irwin L. Johnston & wife Mrs. Pullain & some others dined with us to day pleasant visit had radishes for the first time this season—Was invited to Bro Wittichs to tea went quite a large party & a good time. This is dissipating quite smart for one day—Staid all night as Bro Wittich is in Oxford. Gardens much blighted from last nights frost.

[March] 28 [1849]

Spent all the morning visiting with Mrs. W & Floyd at Mrs. Reeses & the afternoon shopping so ended the day. Spent night at Wittichs again.

[March] 29 [1849]

Made calls with Mrs. Cooke this morning bought blue barage—Afternoon shopping & visiting.

March 30 1849

Here is a new page but nothing new to write. Invited to dine at Dr. Oglebys. Wrote letters to Miss Brentwell & Warren this morning some callers, dressed & went to dining at twelve fashionable dinner very much so large company present. Visited the Gallery of Paintings by Mr. Jackson & Daguerean rooms of Leigh & Co. What an art thus to convey the lineaments of friends to canvas & plates. Spent a pleasant day. Mr. Kolb returned from plantation to which he went yesterday. I was disappointed in not being able to go—Bissell spent evening with me.

[March] 31st [1849]

Shopping & making calls all day this completes the week & I am very weary & little prepared for the exercises of tomorrow.

April 1st [1849]

A bright & beautiful morning arose & took my bath. O that the Good One would cleanse my heart even as I cleanse outwardly. Went to Sabbath School at eight Lovefeast at nine & at half past ten preaching after which was administered the Lords Supper. Resolved anew to do & live better. God help me. Finey & Lane with us to day. Good sermon to night. Word of discourse "Shall these dry bones live"—

& now for the duties of another quarter—

[April] 2d [1849]

Commenced a new quarter with upwards of eighty pupils this has been a delightful day, commenced making green gingham. Been to concert prayer meeting held to night at the P church.

[April] 3d [1849]

In school all day went in to Mrs. Cooks & took tea & from there went to class a good meeting & many out. Mrs. Harris & Mary Fannin[59] dined here to day—Bought chip bonnet.

[April] 4th [1849]

Showery morning been to Baptist prayer meeting. B came home with me—Sent letter to Cousin Mary—[60]

[April] 5th [1849]

Written to Mr. Graves. Went to Robsons at noon recess with Mrs. K got trimming for bonnet. Prayer meeting at night after meeting wrote Sister long letter.

[April] 6 [1849]

In school all day & done nothing else. Walked after school with Miss Chandler to the Graveyard. Sad & serious thoughts yet is a place I love to go to for there are buried my dearest hopes. Went after tea to Mrs. Keys & sat until nine o clock—Have a head ache—

[April] 7 [1849]

Awoke unrefreshed had nightmare & also coughed badly. Went down town. Maj. Warren dined with us. Had long chat with him privately— Called on Miss Hixy. Went early to bed feeling badly—

April 8th 1849

Arose unrefreshed this morning having spent a bad night coughed a great deal & slept but little. Really don't feel able to go out to day but were it week time should feel obliged to go to school. Went to Sabbath School full school. Arranged classes & hope next Sunday to go to work—Came home & laid down & then prepared for church. Major Warren Lane & Merrit with Mrs. Merrit & Mr. & Mrs. Harris.

Had a good sermon from Bro Wittich upon faith being the substance of things unseen yet hoped for. A pleasant day & a great many out. Feel some better have taken a large dose of Paragoric & hope to sleep well to night.

[April] 9 [1849]

Very warm thermometer standing in the shade at eighty.

[April] Friday 13 [1849]

I have been very busy all the week upon a dress. Wednesday & Thursday our folks were gone to plantation to day we had Miss Warren to dine; had peas also for the first time this year finished dress spent night with Mrs. Cook. Mr. C out late at Lodge.

[April] 14 [1849]

At home all day attempted to make sunbonnet failed however feel dull have a very bad cough sort of sympathetic one. Whooping Cough all about!

[April] 15 [1849]

It has been until yesterday very warm & dry & dusty to day it is quite cool a fire necessary. Indeed it is like wintry weather. Went to church this morning. Mr. Key preached. Sorry I did not go to Presbyterian & hear Mr. Hendee as he does not preach at night. Mr. Lane here to dine.

[April] 15 Evening [1849]

Mrs. Lewis did not go to church went with wife. Bro Key preached and Mr. Irvin concluded with prayer. It is now clear & very cold. May expect frost in the morning. Mrs. Lewis has a bad cough, is taking Brother Keys drops in hopes she will rest well to night. Mr. Bissell was standing in the vestibule looking so doubtless was disappointed at not seeing Mrs. L.

The above was written by Mr. Kolb who is a joking dear old fellow. He has gone to plantation to day. Weather moderated some frost last night. Mr. B called this evening to invite me to concert did not go with him—O dear me, me, me.[61]

[April] 17 [1849]

Still continues cold windy & dry it has been a month since rain of any amount fell. A dreary prospect ahead for farmers. Went to class again to night. Mrs. K quite unwell.

[April] 18 [1849]

Wind blowing yet no rain but dust aplenty. Very unpleasant going to school. Mr. K. still at plantation.

[April] 19 [1849]

Cold & windy. Been to prayer meeting

[April] 20 [1849]

Still cold but some appearance of rain. Feel unpleasant tonight in regard to a little money affair with my old friend L did not fulfill my engagement upon account of sickness.

[April] 21st [1849]

Spent morning with Mrs. Cook assisting her to make cake. It is very nice.

[April] 22d [1849]

Sunday. Attended church as usual. Dr. Means preached. Feel gloomy & sad. The Past O the Past. five years to day little Susy died.[62] Walked to her grave this evening.

May 1st [1849]

We have had rain since I wrote & everything is much revived. Went out to Harmony to church last Sabbath a dull tedious time to me. Had new potatoes beets & peas to day for dinner. This is doing quite well when we consider the backwardness of the season. Mr. Kenan Mr. & Mrs. Key dined with us.

[May] 2d [1849]

A pleasant shower this evening.

[May] 3d [1849]

Very warm & pleasant been to meeting to night. Do not feel just right—

[May] 4 [1849]

Been in school all day. Mr. & Mrs. Kolb returned from plantation this morning. I have been alone this past day & night. Took tea at Mrs. Robsons large party of ladies fine supper & a pleasant time. Came home & went to the hotel to call upon Dr. G with Mr. Cook pleasant walk saw Dr. G upon business relating to Henry L Graves.[63]

[May] 5 [1849]

Have felt unusually dull all day. Picked strawberries for a long time this morning. Mrs. Willey & Morton took tea with us pleasant visit from them. Called at Mrs. Cooks & saw Miss Mary. Do not feel sufficiently prepared for the Sabbath.

[May] 6 Sabbath Evening

Arose this morning with a sense of suffocation could scarcely breathe left my room & went down into the open air. Went in to prayers felt very nervous & unwell sitting awhile before breakfast. I became very sick & faint was entirely prostrated. Revived after a little though unable "went" to Sabbath school for I do not like to miss my class though I feel I am doing them but little good. Had apple pie for dinner for the first time this year.

for a long time I have said nothing of my religious feelings & indeed what have I to say for I am making so little improvement in the Divine life that I am ashamed & take the confusion of fear to myself. Gods goodness toward me is unbounded. Without number are his mercies & they alone should lead me to love adore & serve Him. But my whole heart is not His glued yet to earth & the things thereof it does not soar Heavenward un-trammeled. O that I was just such a Christian as I ought to be & as God would have me be. Lord Jesus search me & help me to see myself as I am seen by thy all piercing eye. O for a new life in Christ Jesus for a sprinkling of the baptismal blood, for holiness of heart.

[May] 7 [1849]

Health much better to day been in school all day. After school called upon Mrs. Reese with Mrs. K. & then went to monthly concert instead of prayer meeting we had a very interesting lecture from Mr. Lanier upon Jerusalem & its environs—

[May] 9 [1849]

Rain last evening no class meeting. Mr. K returned from Augusta where he has been since Sunday evening. Brought me a present from Major in the form of a dress pattern. A heavy shower this afternoon.

[May] 10 [1849]

Morning still raining but I must to school.

[May] 11 [1849]

Took supper last night at Mrs. Waltons with Miss Mary & Cook spent night with Mary.

[May] 12 [1849]

Went early this morning to call upon a sick child belonging to Mr. Few.[64] Found her very low with Whooping Cough & measles combined. Promised to stay with them to night—

[May] 14 Sunday Morning [1849]

A gentle shower is refreshing the earth this calm Sabbath morning. O that the showers of Divine Grace may be sent down upon us a dry & thirsty people. I spent the night as promised. Child very sick called again to day to it & witnessed its departure to the Land of Spirits. Innocent Lamb by the merits of Christ ye are prepared for the joys of Heaven. We should not wish to call them back to the sins & strife of life. Better that they were folded in the fold of Christ & secure from every danger. But I know well how to sympathize with the distressed & bereaved parents. May another warning have its influence on my own heart & may this Sabbath be spent as it should be spent.

Evening May 14 [1849]

Been to church & listened to an excellent sermon from Bro Wittich Ps 5, 3d[.] When I consider the heavens the work of Thy hands &c The Power & Infinitude of God & his tenderness & care of Man were dwelt upon at some length. I have spent one more Sabbath upon calls & yet I know not that I am any better prepared to spend an everlasting one in the presence of my Maker. O for deep repentence & humiliation before Father in Heaven.

[May] 15 [1849]

Mr. & Mrs. K going to plantation & I go to spend night with Miss Killian.

[May] 16 [1849]

Feel much happier to night than usual had a long chat at Mrs. Cooks to day noon she called me in to see————her cupovanka.[65]

[May] 17 [1849]

Had company to night. Mr. Bissell has not called before since his return from La Grange. A rainy evening.

[May] 28 [1849]

Some time since I wrote but have been well but much engaged in school & various matters—Have been for several evenings attending a course of Phrenological Lectures been much interested. Dr. Means has been with us had a pleasant visit from him.

[May] 29 [1849]

Attended another Lecture upon the different organs how situated & their influence one with the other. Do not feel very well.

[May] 30th [1849]

Intelligence was brought us this morning of the death of Sister McKee a young married lady of this town died in child bed. We went in immediately. Walked up to Miss Jones' with Miss Chandler & Cook, been to a meeting of the committee of Sabbath School preparing for fourth of July celebration.

June 1st [1849]

Wrote letter this morning to V Warren. Called upon Mrs. Walton been to prayer meeting this evening.

June

This has been a month of excitement & I have not written in my journal. The first of it very busy in preparing for examination. Then came vacation which was spent in visiting. Went to the Stone Mountain[66] & spent two days enjoyed myself finely. Saw a good deal of company no religious enjoyment.

July Madison 1849

4

We commenced school again with but few scholars. Had a pleasant celebration of the "Sons" & Sabbath schools & Each school with its own regalia looked beautifully. Fine dinner at the Grove. Dr. Conger & Lizz are with us. Went at night to a pic nic given by the young men at the Male Academy had a pleasant time.

Thursday [July] 5 [1849]

Bro Key commenced this morning a series of religious meetings. If I should judge of others by myself &c. There would be but little good done but I hope the good spirit may waken me up to Zeal in the Divine Cause. Have felt exceedingly dull & stupid. Went to church after school in the morning did not go to prayer meeting this evening. Took supper at Bro Porters in company with the Dr. & Lizzy went to meeting at night. Bro Hebbard preached.

Friday [July] 6 [1849]

Bro F Sanders preached in the morning & Bro Arnold at night, good congregation. Feel sick & worn out.

Sat [July] 7 [1849]

Presiding Elder present & preached but not acceptably. Bro Key at night at the close of the sermon the Elder got up to exhhort, he saw some one whispering. Stop! said he "till I get done talking then you may talk."

Sunday [July] 8 [1849]

I fear for the exercises of to day cannot think the rough manner of our Elder calculated to win souls to Christ. Had a large & attentive congregation this morning but no seriousness the sermon was not one calculated to promote it text The truth shall make us free. He explained truth or divided it into two kinds logical truth & moral. The sermon was anything but appropriate for the occasion. Before the administration of the Lords Supper many left which called forth some cutting rebukes he was not justified in them for a portentous cloud overspread the heavens & made it necessary for many to leave.

I don't know that I ever had more serious feelings than I had while kneeling during the consecration prayer. The thunder pealed forth shaking the house the lightning glared & altogether it seemed that our Heavenly Father was angry with us.

Madison Sept 19th 1849

Six years ago to day since my dear Samuel[67] left me for a better & brighter world. Ah the stroke the bitter bitter cup can I ever forget it. Little did I then think that I should have remained so long separated from him. But this unfaithful heart though it does not forget often puts out of mind these sad memories & it is well that we are thus constituted for the burden of grief that was first upon me I could not have long borne. How dark & dismal everything looked & though I cannot now penetrate the future yet from the past a light beams upon & illumines it. Will another year find me in Madison. Can I look upon my *darlings* grave upon this time next year as I have looked. But why attempt to penetrate the future. Enough Enough is the present. I have been a great sinner affliction has not eradicated all seeds of the wicked one. O God purify me & make me a good & humble Christian prepared to die or prepared for whatsoever thou hast for me to do—May I never forget the scenes of Sept 19, 1843.

[One and one-half pages left blank.]

CHAPTER TWO

A Happy Family Circle

Madison Dec 29th 1849

I have turned over from the other page. Not that time has been a blank altogether to me for very many things of deep interest have occurred but O I feel that it is wrong to write what I now have to say. Little did I think when I penned the last that when I next wrote I should so soon be the betrothed of another. What have I done? Am I not dreaming? What means it all. Why these heavy forebodings? Oh, my Father Who art in Heaven give me the assurance of a right heart in this matter. Let me feel that I am under thy Heavenly Guidance and direction in this ["affair" is crossed out].

I have often joked & laughed about marrying & though I have when asked always refused yet I am caught this time. Is my heart truly interested? Do I love him to whom I am about to commit my all of earthly happiness?

Can I take upon myself the most solemn of all oaths to Love Honour & Obey one to whom I am so utterly a stranger! How can I tell but that my feelings & affections may prove recreant to my Judgment. And that I may be sowing to myself thorns and briars that may afterwards sorely sting and annoy me.

Can I add to the happiness and comfort of Him who offers me his name? Will I not be as a dark shadow in his pathway obstructing the sunlight of his household Gods: Is he not mistaken in my character and disposition. Can I be to *His Darlings* all that his departed one was? Can I in any supply her place but in name? 'Tis a fearful task a great responsibility. It has never been brought so close home to me before. And I shudder at the contemplation of it. Well it is near midnight and I must to bed but sleep the sweet soother of all cares has forsaken me. 'Tis Saturday night tomorrow is the Lords day how can I put on the semblance of worship when such confusion reigns within. Oh that He who calmed the troubled waters may speak peace and quietness to me.

Sunday Evening [December 30, 1849]

Went to church twice to day thoughts and feelings wandering from the place they ought to have been in these privillages will soon be over and how I shall mourn that they have been no better improved.

Dec 31st 1849

The last evening of "49 how swiftly the wheels of time roll onward bearing their records upward. What have I done this year for the Glory of God & the promotion of His Kingdom nothing absolutely nothing in comparison to His exceeding good & great benefits to me. What am I that He should spare my life and thus crown it with blessings. O help me to consecrate myself renewedly to thy service for another year. And may I recieve aid & support from Him Who knows my many infirmities to bear the new cares & trials that this coming year may involve.

Midnight I alone of all the family have watched the departure of the old & the coming in of the New Year. For the last three hours I have been trying to hold converse with my own heart & its Maker. The past year with all its errors has gone into Eternity. May the coming be indeed a new one void of faults & may I if I see its close have nothing to regret.

1850
Jan 2d

Am greatly troubled concerning my engagement of Saturday. I do not wish to recall it but O how much do I wish it deferred. I am a creature made up of prejudices & they often more or less influence my judgement. Suppose then my next meeting with my friend should prove against him. How am I to act? Should I dislike him after the solemn vows are pronounced. What unhappiness What Misery awaits me? I fear that he has been influenced by others that I am not his own free choice—Yet I ought not to think so unworthily of him. I know he is every thing that is good & true & I should not doubt him, but I will beg him at least to put off this to a more convenient season—

1850
Jan. 3d

I have written him calmly & seriously my feelings. I do not know how he will take it but I trust kindly as it was meant. I feel relieved in this matter & hope that I am right in it—Been down town settling up accounts find myself to have been more extravagant than I ought to have been. When shall I learn prudence & economy—

Madison Georgia January 6th 1850

Been to church again the first Sabbath of the new year. Services appropriate to the occasion. Felt while listening that I could indeed give all up to the care of my Heavenly Father leaving him to work for me knowing that whatsoever he doeth will be for the Best.

Major Warren & William both spent day with us—Mrs. Kolb is lying on the sofa asleep. Mr. K sits by the opposite side of the stand reading. I really wish that I could draw his portrait that I might ever have the good man recalled to mind when I open these pages by seeing his noble countenance. How shall I ever repay the debt of gratitude I owe him. Heaven alone can only repay such kindness & Love as I have recieved at their hands.

And as true as there is a rewarder of Good & Evil so true will they recieve compensation.

The future I cannot fathom but the Past I know & shall ever love its memory.

[January] 7 [1850]

This was to have been my bridal day had I not begged a postponement. But a gloomy day it is. I should have feared it ominous of a gloomy future. Bro Key read me a letter from my friend. O how I wish that he would have come along & asked me of its meaning. I fear that he does not take it as I meant it should! Well I wished a test of my affection. I believe that I have it or I would not be so troubled by his feelings & opinions of me—O that I had more firmness and decision of mind.

Bro Wittich called & I gave up the school after the first week—In this I may be hasty for I may never hear from him again. Well good friends are about me & God will not forsake those that trust Him—

[January] 8th [1850]

Been busy sewing all day—

[January] 9th [1850]

Making fruit cake. Mrs. Porter Saffold Robson & Key came in unexpectedly but prepared supper for them had a long chat about my friend—I don't know what to think. Mrs. Kolbs suggestions are right perhaps that he does not love me & is away with others. What shall I do this certainly renders me unhappy.

[January] 10th [1850]

No news from him yet were I possessed of twenty thousand this would not be—

January 13th [1850]

Hence all worldly & for a day of communion of God for a day spent in His temple. Took my usual bath felt while the liquid shower was pouring over me—that the Holy Spirit might be in like manner be bestowed. Sometimes I think could I as easily cleanse myself from Sin & impurity how holy I should be—but poor human nature cannot do it & it is hard to look up by Faith & claim it. Bro Wittich preached a most excellent sermon subject Samson & the Philistines proving Grace of God sufficient for all things—

Feel willing to trust everything in the future to my Heavenly Parent—

[January] 14 [1850]

Went to school in the morning some forty present. My friend arrived at noon. So I sent in an apology for my absence. We have spent the evening together & again made arrangements for our future. I feel better satisfied than at first for I know that there is a degree of reciprocity of feelings between us—

[January] 15 [1850]

To day noon I felt calm & contented with the future before me hoped that I was at length in the right path & the way to happiness. Came from school in the evening & Mrs. Kolb handed me a letter. I opened & found it anonymous warning me of the addresses of Mr. B—What does it mean? Not a doubt before has ever crossed my mind but that he would prove the kind & affectionate husband and Protector—Well it is too late now but did I believe it I could "stop & think before I farther go"—

[January] 16 [1850]

Thought busy thought kept me awake all night. What does that letter mean? May it not be Providential? And yet I cannot doubt him. Have a mind to send it to Judge Floyd & make inquiries.

[January] 17 [1850]

The above thoughts I know unworthy of me & the confidence I have in him who is to be my future Protector—

Rainy day full school—Had some little trouble with Kolb about the matter of Monday Evening—

[January] 18 [1850]

Been writing to Bro Orrington & Sarah. Still continues Raining. Called at Bro Key had a chat about the letter.

Madison January 19 [1850]

I came out of school last night for the last time. O I did feel sad to give up the dear children that I have watched over and taught and had so deep an interest in for so long a time. How I wanted to press them to my heart and tell them to be good.

I did not go to the party to night for I did not feel like mingling with the giddy and the gay—

Have been busy all day packing and preparing for my departure! Am going to spend the night with my friend Mrs. Cook. feel sad why I cannot tell a cloud seems resting upon me that I cannot dispel—Many friends have called to day to bid my good bye—

[January] 20th [1850]

This will be the last evening that I will in all probability write in this under my present name.

Tomorrow dawns upon me anticipating my bridal. O my treacherous self decieving heart help me to discern the right & walk therein.

I have no fears for my happiness if I only have the love of Him Who is to be my husband!

[January] 23d [1850]

Many things of importance have occurred since writing the above changes which will tell upon the future for well or woe—The 21st being very rainy Mr. B did not come in town but yesterday I took upon myself the most solemn of all obligations to be another's no longer my own. We were married directly after dinner & left town immediately for his home in Newton. Arrived soon after dark.

Evening   It is nearly bedtime & here allow me to record my thanks to the Giver of all Good for His loving kindness toward me in thus providing me a protector & a home. O what a pleasant home a loving companion & beautiful children I have. Praise the Lord O my soul & all that is within me give thanks for His wonderful goodness to the children of men—

[January] 24 [1850]

Contented & happy. Had a pleasant visit from Mrs. Hays also from Dr. Shaw & lady.

Newton January 27th 1850

This is a new heading for my journal & the journal will probably of itself take quite a different statement of facts & things to which it has taken. New events, new scenes & household changes will be the order of the day. My heart approves & tells me that I have done right in this matter. I only trust & hope that God may give me Grace to enable me to discharge my duties in a manner creditable to myself & the station I occupy. He has given me a man after His own Heart One who looks to Him & acknowledges Him in all ways—I humbly hope that I may be no hindrance to his onward path. I feel the need of a strong decided Christian to help me onward for I am weak & faltering. My heart has been melted within me in prayer to God that he would render me sufficiently grateful for all His mercies. What a comfort to know that He heareth prayer.

Mr. B gone to church to class am alone & yet not alone—

Jan. 30 [1850]

Sewed peas &c.

Feb 3d Sabbath Evening [1850]

A week of cares has prevented from writing perhaps I am growing careless. I find much to take up & employ my time, but withall [*sic*] I find myself happier & more contented than I expected. Heard Bro Hebbard preach from Deuteronomy, 29.

Feb 21st [1850]

My journal shows bitter things against itself but I have excuses which I never had before. This morning & yesterday I feel a peculiar depression of feeling. Why or what I cannot tell something gloomy & dark apparently hangs over me & I cannot penetrate the mist. Is it true that coming events cast their shadows before if so I fear grief & misery await me. Still with a reconciled heart all will be well. Whatever my Heavenly Father ordains that ought I to be pleased & satisfied with. But O My God visit not my transgressions & sins upon me nor upon those are dear to me. Cast them from the book of thy remembrance & bring them up no more before me. Lord have mercy upon & forgive them me I entreat Thee Help me by Thy Holy Spirit to be all that thou would have me to be—My husband is not well—

Saturday Feb 23d [1850]
   Been busy all day but happy took short ride on horseback accompanied by Mr. Burge.

Sunday [February] 24 [1850]
   A wet & gloomy day after the duties of the morning were over selected several good books to read. Employed my time with them & in chatting with Mr. B.

March 8 [1850]
   I find now that the Sabbath is my time to write the week that has passed has found me enjoying all the blessings of health & happiness made a visit to Mrs. Slopes & been sewing wrote to Mr. & Mrs. Kolb Mr. & Mrs. Cook & Miss Chandler sent for my things in Madison & have recieved them they come to me like old friends. O the Past the Past how its memory comes thronging back upon me. The days & scenes of other times happy moments as well those of joy & misery come rushing over the mind like a turbulent sea often times disturbing its serenity & for the time making me miserable—Such were my feelings to day when seated in the church to which my lot seems to fallen. O how unlike any that I ever attended the places the people all all [*sic*] were strange & in my lonliness I almost forgot that He who is in all places could be there as well to bless & Save as in others of a more fashionable exterior. When will my poor proud heart learn that it is the lowly & contrite that recieve the blessings.
   Do I enjoy the love of God in my heart? Do I know that I am accepted

of Him? My poor, decietful heart. The fruits of the tree must bear witness of its worth. And O how little moral worth how little of the essence of Christianity is about me. God of truth of Mercy & Justice help me to live & love thee with a pure & devoted Love. O I pray Thee that in the Gifts thou hast given me I may not love them better than the Giver.

[March] 17th [1850]

Bro Thomas[1] spent the night with us & has gone to his appointment this morning but a rainy wet time they will have of it. Mr. Burge has been planting corn this week when the state of the weather would permit.

Newton March 24 1850

This has been a week of rain it has literally poured most of the time. No ploughing nor planting. I have been making mattresses & I find as much as my poor hands can do to be done. Been down to church this morning on horseback called in to Mrs. Vasons[2] they feel like kinfolks almost to me had class meeting.

[March] 28th [1850]

Mr. Burge has been in town thus far all the week acting as juror. I have been having the house cleaned. Mr. R left home yesterday. Found plenty of snow when I awoke this morning (an inch deep I think) reminded me strongly of home & of times when the heart free from cares & responsibilities basked in its own quiet happiness sending forth no thoughts for the future unless gilded with the bright hours of hope & never calling up the Past—wishing again to be amid its scenes.

April 2d [1850]

Went March 31st to Lanes meeting house[3] to hear Bro Hebbard. Met & dined at the carriage with Iverson Graves & lady. Mr. Bs Nephew Wiley came up from Augusta & returned again this evening.

Mr. Burge had me up this morning by daylight—it was trying to this slothful disposition I have so long indulged in. I would fain cry out with the sluggard. A little more sleep &c.

We have had an addition to our stock of a colt this morning though it is blind of an eye &c. Mr. Burge has been working in the garden all the morning sticking peas & planting others (marrow fats). We have had asparagus & I eat a radish this morning. Vegetables are very back ward indeed. The season is And it is now cold & windy with every appearance of rain.

I have been cutting out a pair of pantaloons for Mr. B & commenced making. It is something new under the sun for me to do but I reckon I can come [to] it. Well Julia has sent in for oil for her negro baby[4] & I must attend so good bye Journal. Mr. B. has gone to sleep after all. I meant that he should have staid up all day to have fixed him for waking me up this morning.

Newton Co April 11th 1850

It still continues wet damp & unpleasant weather commenced planting cotton to day the garden does not look as forward as usual for the season. Bro & sister Hebbard spent last Saturday night with us—I have suffered thus far this week with a bad cold & am otherwise quite unwell—

[April] 12th [1850]

Still wet & unpleasant weather feel better myself but Mr. Burge is complaining. We are going to Covington to day if we can muster force enough.

May 5th [1850]

April 24th went to Madison found friends all well dined at Bro Wittichs &c. The past week been very busy sewing for the children but visited Mrs. Perry[5] Rossmore Glass[6] and yesterday went to Lanes church to attend the quarterly meeting heard Mr. Stansill preach[7] dined at Mr. Rakestraws.[8] This morning woke from a sweet pleasant nights sleep found it raining & therefore unable to go to Lovefeast felt sad cannot take hold & claim the promises as I wish to.

If I know my own heart I desire to Love & serve God to do the duties of a christian to bear their crosses & to be ever found in the right paths.

Heard Dr. Means preach a most excellent sermon from these words: And He is the propriation for our sins & not for ours only but also for the sins of the Whole World. He first dwelt upon the necessity of this propriation then upon its character & finally upon its efficiency. 1st the inability of man said he Man could no more do it than he could move into the sea with a hair the stone mountain from its base. Other comparisons were as appropriate & forcible—I always feel deeply interested in hearing the Dr.—After the services were over the sacrament was administered. I fully intended to be of the number that commend the dying love of the Saviour but by waiting lost the privillage. It may be all for the best—I know that I am unworthy & it might have brought a wound upon the cause of my blessed Redeemer—

May 11th [1850]

Went again to Lanes & heard Bro Bonnell[9] preach a missionary sermon—

May 18 [1850]

Yesterday Mrs. Perry called & spent the evening the girls have all gone down to the convention at Augusta quite lonely she says. Mr. Burge is looking better than she ever saw him. I say it is because he has so *good* a *wife*—

Raining hard to day absolutely pouring. We have been truly favoured with an abundance of rain this season. Crops are suffering very much from it—Mr. Burge has had an unpleasant case of discipline with Martha the cook.[10]

[May] 14 [maybe should be 19] [1850]

O how greatly do we need Grace from on high to enable us to discharge our duties aright to keep accounts justly balanced with High Heaven & ourselves. Mrs. Glass visited me this evening. Louisiana[11] behaved badly & I have had to punish her. It is a hard task for me but I find it must be done.

May 20th [1850]

Started to church at eight o clock with my family in service for Sabbath school after which we had Bible class. Bro Thomas from the words My Spirit shall not always strive with man. Mr. Burge stopped to attend Negro

Class[12] & consequently I have been alone this evening. We have been having some difficulties with servants—Very cold for the season.

[May] 27 [1850]
At home all day yesterday which was sabbath had a lonely & gloomy day been laughed at about a coat I have been making for Wiley[13] which has mortified me exceedingly. Bro Thomas our preacher came in on the 24th. Lovick Wittich dined with us also on that day. We took a strawberry hunt in the evening & got a good supply. Heard bad news from Conference the death of Bro J. Boring & the consequent adjournment of conference—
We had snap beans for dinner to day.
My husband sits by me enjoying a cigar & telling me a long tale of Zac Glass. He looks quite happy & whether he is or not with me I find myself quite so with him. I did not expect so much happiness as I find myself in the possession of—

[May] 28 [1850]
Been putting up red under curtains making preparations for two days meeting. Mr. B gone fishing—Very warm thermometer stood yesterday 88 in shade, 110 in sun. Everything looks interesting in the fields now. Walked over to Mrs. Glass yesterday evening with Miss Frances & the little girls—

June 7th [1850]
— —
Je ne pas la enfin en la couche.[14]

June 10th [1850]
Went to Covington yesterday & heard Dr. Means from the words Why stand ye here all the day idle dined at Judge Floyds[15]—

[June] 17th [1850]
Staid at home by myself yesterday. We are having very warm weather now & every thing grows finely. Commenced this morning making preparations for my northward journey.

July 8 [1850]

Just packed & sent off trunk for New Eng. trust & pray that we may have a safe & pleasant journey & be returned to our home in safety.

Sept 7 [1850]

Returned.

Newton Sept 29 1850

Another year has passed & finds me numbering my 33 year & O what a miracle of Grace that I have been thus long preserved. Even the year that has passed I have been very near the threshold of Death very near my final home either joy or woe.

Yes, Yes, a year of blessing this has been notwithstanding it has given hitherto untried cares & duties to me—When I look over the past & remember what sorrows I have undergone what trials suffered & mercies granted I feel that I ought to be very grateful—

[October] 18 [1850]

Had frost.

Oct 24 [1850]

Recieved from Augusta 100 lb of Coffee & 236 lb of Sugar & sack of Salt—

Been to Mrs. Glass to day with Miss Maria Hebbard & V. Vason they have been staying with me this week—

[October] 25 [1850]

Mr. Burge gone to town to listen to speeches from Judge Cone & Esq. Foster upon the Union.

Nov 1st [1850]

Sowed wheat. Went to town yesterday many sick with billious fever there had letter to day from Wiley Burge [16]—

Nov 27th [1850]

Went to mill with nine bushels of wheat.

W & I took a dose of tartaric acid[17]—

Dec 8th [1850]

A very cold day thermometer standing at 30—None of us went to church this morning. Mr. B has gone to his Negro class the past week I have had Bro Thomas with us most of the time been rainy & wet. Made bed curtains dresses for myself & children—

Nov [probably December] 11th [1850]

Je ne enfin.[18]

Jan 22d 1851

One year to day I with trembling & fear took upon myself vows again to Love & honour another & to be to that others children a mother. Yes it was with fear but could I have [seen] thus far ahead I should not have had them—

O it has been a year of happiness a year of *heartrest* for after striving & toiling alone for years in this cold hearted world thus to find a heart that truly loves & a home full of every comfort—"O How my heart expands with love to him that has thus taken me to himself.

Feb 1st [1851]

Filled the sugar chest. A cold unpleasant day expected the preacher but was disappointed—

[February] 2d [1851]

Went to church.

[February] 6th [1851]

Sent to mill nine bushels of wheat. Making pillow cases—

[February] 7th [1851]
    Planted potatoes & sowed oats.

[February] 17th [1851]
    Cold & uncomfortable day. expected Bro Key last night but the rain prevented. None of us have been to church to day owing to the unpleasantry of the day. Mr. B has rode down to Mr. Harwells.[19]

[February] 28th [1851]
    Hannah sick.[20]

March 10th 1851
    Commenced planting corn—

[March] 14 [1851]
— —
    Roasting ears beans cucumbers squash & watermelon planted delightful weather peach trees in full bloom—putting up meat—Going to Sandtown this evening. Making Louisana pantelettes.

20 March [1851]
    Sowed seed wheat from Maine which came in a letter.

[March] 28 [1851]
    Wheat up.

[March] 30 [1851]
    Rainy Sunday all at home been reading "Judahs' Lion."

[March] 31st [1851]
    Last day of March feel well continues rainy everything looks like making crop.

April 6th [1851]

Sabbath morning. A pleasant day after a rainy night. Have been at Oxford the last week to visit Bro Keys family—To day is the first quarterly meeting for the year—

[April] 7th [1851]

Monday morning. A pleasant morning. Mr. Burge commenced planting cotton. The heavens soon became overcast with clouds & rain commenced pouring in torrents. Such a rain has not been known for years it continued during the night one thunder cloud after another passing over & discharging its watery burden. O such a night—

[April] 8th [1851]

Morning found many a fence prostrated mills washed away &c. &c. Road around the plantation to observe some of the effects—

[April] 9 [1851]

Not well to day, but have made pillow slips.

[April] 21st [1851]

Finished planting cotton. 16, 17, & 18 house cleaning & whitewashing 19th Bro Key spent the night with us expected bro Wittich.

April 1851 24th

After a rainy night it has cleared away pleasant & warm indeed it is warmer than any day we have had I think. The season is very backward though we have had no severe weather yet we have had none that was warm three nights this week we have had a slight frost—My own health is good but chronic complaints are very troublesome how it will end with me I cannot tell. God only knows. Let the result be what it may. May I be prepared to meet it—Have made four pairs of "pants" this week one each day—thus far.

May 6th [1851]
frost had peas.

May 12th [1851]
The second day of this month was taken *sick* & after several hours of severe pain [gave] premature birth to a daughter. True I had all along feared it would be thus but was not resigned to the dispensation. I would rather suffered on three months longer if then I could have had my living daughter but God knows what is best for us—I have got along very well. My dear husband is kind & attentive to every want—Kindly & cleverly does he watch every change & O I am glad for his sake that I am yet spared. I trust that I shall go from my sick room better prepared for the duties of life than hitherto—Bees swarmed & husband had great difficulty in getting them hived—

[May] 14 [1851]
Very warm. Mrs. Perry & Glass have both sent me some very nice honey they are very kind neighbors indeed every one is kind to me—

[May] 18th [1851]
Dr. Pierce[21] preached yesterday at Lanes. I prepared dinner for them but they did not come bro Key came home with Mr. Burge & spent the night & Dr. P with his little son & daughter came about 9 o clock. I was not able to go out but attended to my home duties. His text "Now the Lord is that Spirit & where the spirit of the Lord is is Liberty."

bro Key preached at 4 o clock from I am a stranger with thee & a sojourner as my fathers were. both of the preachers came home with Mr. B. & spent the night—

[May] 19th [1851]
Very warm thermometer at ninety. I've had breakfast at sunrise & the preachers started for home. I have been on the bed nearly all day. Do not feel quite well yet.

[May] 29 [1851]

Had *Green* Corn.

Newton June 1st 1851

For the two weeks past it has been very warm four weeks to day since any rain has fallen consequently vegetation is very much parched. I have been riding about considerably the last week the 28th spent at Mr. Rake-straws[22] had a pleasant day returned home early & found a little negro (Sanford)[23] badly bitten by a Moccasin Snake his leg was swollen & he had vomited several times though it had been done several hours we sent for Dr. Shaw.[24] He prescribed a wheat poultice saturated with sweet oil gave him hartshorn to allay excitement & turpentine is said to be an excellent remedy applied immediately, so also is Sweet Oil & Lobelia. Gathered our May apples yesterday finished Negro breeches.

Dr. Shaw was up one day last week as a peace maker has not succeeded to his satisfaction but I hope that he may claim the blessing promised to those who act in that capacity—

June 17 [1851]

It has still been very warm ever since the 10th of May. Thermometer scarcely below eighty in the shade & standing mostly at ninety & upwards. Neither have we had sufficient rains to wet the earth since the 4th of May. Last friday night we had a light shower which served to lay the dust & make it rather more pleasant for our quarterly meeting. By the way we went & heard a good sermon from Bro Parks Malachi 3d 18 Then shall ye return & discern between the righteous & the wicked between him that serveth God & him that serveth him not—

A good Lovefeast on Sabbath morning & another sermon from the parable of the ten virgins dwelling more particularly upon the words that the *door was shut.*

Yesterday went to town it looked very much like rain & we had it all the way home as soon as we got here it stopped. Dined at bro Sanders he is quite unwell—bought me a plain muslin dress & several other articles— Set out yam potato slips got in wheat a fine crop.

June 27 [1851]

Just returned from the Madison commencement stopped at Mr. Cooks & had a pleasant time for which I have every reason to be thankful to my Heavenly Father.

[June] 28th [1851]

Mrs. Glass has spent the day with me. Went to Sandtown & called upon Mrs. H Harwell who is sick at Mrs. Bobers with fever. A Mr. Green Agent of a book concern spent the night & following day with us. I did not go to church—

July 4th [1851]

As this is the anniversary of American Independence I ought not to pass it without notice. We have had a Mr. Hunter & Bush from Massachusetts & a Mr. Russell & Allen from Macon to visit us this week. Mrs. Graves & Hinton also called but I was spending the day with Mrs. Pitts. We have had no celebration to day. I have been busy serving but just at night walked over to Mrs. Perrys with Mr. B & Eliza—[25]

[July] 14th [1851]

Thus far the month has been one of exceeding heat & drought two weeks tomorrow since we had any rain & thermometer standing at ninety & upwards in the shade.

We have been to day at Lanes to attend a missionary meeting sermon by G. F. Pierce.

"Ask of me the Heathen & they shall be given thee & the uttermost parts of the Earth for thy possession." He considered these words as a promise to Christ & showed the duty of Prayer. The want of it on the part of Christians & conclusively arguing that if Christians were importunate in Prayer for the conversion of the world that it would soon be accomplished for Christ & God were both for it & we should be all agreed.

One of his comparisons were that all should work all Pray & that God acted as farmers or Planters they bought more "hands" that they might make the more. He converted men that they might work in this vineyard & bring in more laborers. A good sermon.

[July] 21st [1851]

Yesterday went to Oxford and heard the commencement sermon from Bishop Andrew. Words of the text Honour thy Father & Mother that it may be well with thee.

He first proved that God had instituted families & had placed man over them that He & not woman should rule & that her assuming to do so was contrary to Divine Authority as he proved from Scripture.

He spoke of the Union necessary to raise our children right that father & mother should agree that one should not pet while the other punished & that the petted one was always the ungrateful child—

Dined at Bro Keys & met a Mrs. Davis from Savannah there. At ½ 3 Dr. Lovick Pierce preached from the words "If any man will come after me let him deny himself & take up his cross & follow me"—He spoke of the difference of the church now & 30 & 40 years ago—Showed how the spirit of the world had crept in & how christians so-called drank of that spirit. Showed also that if we lived up to the Gospel to its precepts & doctrines that we should find the reproach & cross as difficult as in years gone by. He appealed to the young men before him beseeching them to weigh well the consequences of rejecting this cross of not bearing in all times & places & of refusing to listen to the call of "Go get out & preach the Gospel to all creatures. He gave the reason why many called to preach did not listen that it was not the way to Worldly fame & aggrandizement that Congressmen were not taken from the ranks of the Itinerancy that if they were it would be well fitted. Closed by speaking of the trials & the crosses of the preacher & the reward held out hereafter—We left Oxford at six o clock & got home a few minutes before nine—

Am expecting Mr. Russell & lady from Macon & Mrs. Hicks to spend the day with me—

Have been to commencement exercises on tuesday. Were interesting more so than on Wednesday.

[July] 24 [1851]

The Preaching Elder Bro Parks arrived here this morning—Will remain with us until tomorrow evening. Had washing done for him.

[July] 25 [1851]

Made Pear preserves & pounds. Very warm. Thermometer 98.

[July] 26 [1851]

Been to Morgan Campmeeting dined at Bro Hansons tent a good meeting.

[July] 27 [1851]

Went again this morning leaving home before sunrise disappointed in not being able to take Louisiana. She had severely bruised her arm—Bro Wittich preached this morning Park at eleven & Payne in the afternoon no special interest. A large congregation.

[July] 28 [1851]

Not much refreshed from our C. meeting ride. Rode behind Mr. Burge over to Mrs. Glass found him unwell boys started to school to Graves's Academy. Cotton at Mr. Montgomerys[26] plantation opening a boll found. Hannah & Julia both spinning.

August 1st [1851]

The first rain for several weeks has fallen upon us to day for which I desire to be thankful. Julia is not well. [small drawing of a hand with five fingers]

[August] 3d [1851]

Cloudy all day yesterday & it was really refreshing to have a withdrawal of the beams of the burning sun.

Sunday August 3d 1851 [continued from previous page]

A shower last night. Been to church to day with the girls drove by myself. Bro Littlejohn preached.

[August] 6 [1851]

Heard of bro Sanders Death. Shall go up tomorrow been over to Mrs. Perrys after quilting all the day to see Mrs. Chisolm—

[August] 7th [1851]

Returned from town a little after eight dined at Judge Floyds called upon Sister Sanders & found her much resigned the Lord is her Support & in Him she can trust. Dr. Pierce preached—bought two pieces of homespun—

[August] 17 [1851]

Bro & Sister Key have visited me they have left this morning & I feel very lonesome prospect of rain. Dried peaches last week. Martha got to Weaving tuesday evening. Hannah commenced the wool.

[August] 21st [1851]

This morning commenced another shirt for Mr. Burge have turned & made over his sack this week. Bro Thomas who is now stationed at Atlanta called & spent a couple of hours with us promising to dine with us tomorrow. Mr. Burge went to town after the mail & I rode with him as far as Mrs. Glasss taking the children with me. Mrs. Shaw & Vason came in & we had a pleasant time. Mr. B. is still at work upon his carriage house.

Sept 27 [1851]

A mule folded [sic] by Kitty—

Nov 8th [1851]

Sowed wheat the land next to the branch sowed with Canada! The next peace to it sowed with Meditereanian [sic]. The third place with spring bearded. Commenced sowing the first day of Nov Day after Mr. Burges return from the Macon fair—

December 18th 1851

This week has been unusually cold for the climate. Mr. Burge has just remarked that it is too cold for work—

Killed hogs yesterday. Meat frozen. Thermometer 14. Irish potatoes frozen!!

January 20th [1852]

I have just recovered again from sickness which commenced on the night of the third of January am now about—

We had on the Monday following a change of very cold weather. The following Monday another change which was the 12th of January, the thermometer standing at twenty. And now we have it still colder everything of a liquid nature in my room has frozen hard & my poor flowers are I fear ruined—Hung up the meat yesterday. Our new preacher Normond preached on Sabbath. Wrote letters yesterday to Wiley & Dr. Comings.[27]

Jan 26 [1852]

Old Mrs. Shaw came up to day to spend the week with me. I am getting quite strong again.

[January] 29 [1852]

Sowed peas radishes beets & collards—

[January] 31 [1852]

Our preacher Bro Florence came from Lanes Church with Mr. Burge & spent the night with us very pleasant & mild.

Feb 25 [1852]

Saw the first Peach blossom for the season—

March 5th [1852]

Julia had a boy last night & *the old black cow a calf*.[28] Mr. Burge commenced planting corn.

[March] 13th [1852]

Organized a church at Mt. Pleasant with which Mr. Burge & myself connected ourselves. 8 members only.[29] Came home with sick headache—

[March] 15 [1852]

Mr. Burge went to town & I went over to Mrs. Glasss & spent the day. Met the Sandtown girls there. Did not rest well last night from the fumes of *turpentine*.

[March] 17 [1852]

Set out cabbage plants. Corn sprouted. Twenty four chickens.

[March] 29 [1852]

Planting cotton & swamp corn.

April 5th 1852

Mrs. Cook & Barber from Madison arrived to day. Will spend a week or more with me.

[April] 9th [1852]

Planted new land in corn.

April 14 [1852]

finished planting cotton ladies from Madison returned home commenced ploughing corn. Set the first turkey hen. Had a present this morning. Mr. Burge is not very well.

[April] 17th [1852]

Attended Quarterly meeting at Covington. Bro Parks preached from Keep yourselves in the love of God. He went on to show that it was impossible to have His love in our hearts & not know it. Dr. Pierce exhorted & I reckon many were of the mind expressed by Lawrence Baker, that if they had a Parks to preach & a Pierce to exhort they should know at all times w[h]ere they were! Stopped with Mr. Pace.

[April] 18 [1852]

Lovefeast well attended & a good time. Parks preached again from the words "Quench not the spirit." Dined at Judge Reynolds came home in the evening very cold for the season.

[April] 19 [1852]

Cut out dresses for the girls. Dr. Shaw came in & spent the evening with us set an hen with pheasant eggs still cold & wet—

Cold very cold for the season. Mrs. Phillips came up to-day to give me instructions in warping &c &c. Set the goose eggs.

[April] 20 [1852]

Planted corn peas.

22d of April [1852]

Planted four bushels of Irish potatoes.

June 13 [1852]

Yesterday went to Oxford to preaching. In the morning heard Bishop Andrew from the words How long halt ye between two opinions. Evening Mr. Stancill from "Why Stand ye here idle" & at night Dr. Pierce.

[June] 19th 1852

We were this morning called to the death bed of Mr. Jackson Harwell whose first wife was the sister of Mr. Burges mother. Since her death he has twice married. Uncle Harwell was a man that all delighted to honour for his piety sincerity & worth was widely known.

Some years since soon after coming to Geo I heard of him as a doctor who cured rheumatic complaints by burying his patients in warmed earth and leaving their head exposed. Then again as "Old Hundred" who blew the trumpet at Camp meeting—By this name he was generally called originating [from] the number of Camp meetings that he had attended—He would never allow one to pass that he could attend for there he felt that he could Honour & serve his Master who had called him to this service. By singing prayer & exhortation to the mourner much good has resulted—

My personal acquaintance commenced with him the 16th of February 1850 just after my marriage. We walked down to his residence & I was introduced to him by my husband. The old man says Cousin "Tom" you done right & now you will feel settled again. He talked over old times. But his mind had lost the vigor of earlier days & he was as but a child in intellect. The occupations & incidents of early life were (as is often the case) more familiar to him than the things of yesterday & he would tell of simple occurances of years long gone by with the minuteness of the present hour. He was sick about five weeks literally wore out with a complication of diseases which his old & enfeebled system could not withstand—We were with him most of the time during his sickness to the interrogatories of my husband in the first of his sickness as to his hopes of Heaven he said that "all was well & that when he thought of the joys awaiting him there he could hardly wait." Much of his time he was delirious. A few nights before his death he prayed earnestly & long that we might live Holy lives that we might die happy deaths &c &c & sung his favorite hymn "What wonderous love is this O my Soul O my Soul." This song was one that he sung with great effect & Mr. Burge has expressed the idea that if emancipated souls are allowed their entrance into Heaven with song & praises that this song of his will be his & will be recognized by hundreds who have gone before & who will join with him in that Spirit world in the praise of Him who hath redeemed us & through Him who hath gotten us the victory—He would have been seventy nine the last of July 1852.

June the 27 [1852]
    A pleasant rainy Sabbath—

Sept 29 [1852]
    Been to camp meeting. Wiley Burge here.

Oct 11th [1852]
    Rode to Sandtown in the morning with big Wiley. Evening rode over to see Mrs. Morse who is down with billious fever—Mr. & Mrs. Wallace staid here all night on their way to Alabama—
    Mr. Burges   Trunksbag 50lb. 106

[October] 17 [1852]
    Dr. Means preached Uncle Jack Harwells funeral sermon from I have fought the good fight &c. A good sermon. There was a very full house.

The Dr. & old Mr. Lane dined with us & a Col. Bates from Charleston a friend of Wileys with some dozen more.

[October] 18 [1852]

This morning Wiley went to town. John Davis spent some time after breakfast with me & old Mrs. Callahan[30] came over. We had got well to warping when Martha coming from the garden says Mistress somebody is at the gate. I peeped and there saw Dr. Comings & his cousin Miss Frances Stone. O how glad I was to see them.

Nov 1st [1852]

Dr. left this morning for Macon. Fannie stays with me—

[November] 9 [1852]

Attended Bro Bellahs funeral he leaves a distressed family. Very [un?]pleasant. Called to see Rebecca went with big Wiley.

[November] 10 [1852]

Wiley left for Charleston shall miss him very much.
Making Negro clothes.

Newton Dec 1st 1852

Went to Madison the 29 of Nov. Miss Fannie & Wiley accompanying me. Miss Barber returned with me. We had a pleasant visit. Made the acquaintance of Mr. Clark. Saw Mrs. Dr. Howard Mrs. Jessup & many others. Came home & found Martha quite sick. Sent for old Mrs. Neely.

[December] 2d [1852]

Martha has another daughter.[31] I am busy with my friends.

[December] 11th [1852]

Fried doughnuts with Miss Fannie built a fire in the parlour & looked for a beau for Miss Barber but he didn't come.

[December] 15th [1852]

Killed hogs & dried up the lard in the rain. O such a rainy time lay awake most all night have since heard that brother Joseph died that night—

[December] 17 [1852]

Killed again to day.

[December] 18 [1852]

Miss Barber went home to day drying up lard.

[December] 23d [1852]

Dr. Comings & Dr. Chalmers arrived to day wet & rainy.

[December] 24 [1852]

The Misses Perry came down & spent the evening till bed time quite lively for us filled the stockings for Christmas.

[December] 25 [1852]

Rebecca & her husband[32] have spent the day with us. Children look happy with Santa Claus gifts—

[December] 26 [1852]

Still raining & has been for the last three weeks. Mr. Barnes another Medical student arrived this evening.

[December] 27 [1852]

Before breakfast Vines Harwell from Walker County arrived which makes our family party quite large.

[December] 28 [1852]

Commenced "Uncle Tom's Cabin."

[December] 29 [1852]

The Drs. have all left for a few days.

[December] 31 [1852]

Dr. C came back from Madison.

Jan 1st [1853]

A New Year. What will its end be how little we can tell—Killed the remainder of our hogs. Went to Mrs. Glasss & brought over Rebecca & her baby.

Jan 3d [1853]

Miss Fannie & the Dr. left for Macon. I after attending to my lard went to Mrs. Perrys & dined had a nice good time—Very cold & a little snow—

Jan 4th 1853

Took Rebecca to Sandtown this morning. Very muddy & cold done some shopping.

[January] 5 [1853]

Went down to Aunt Rhodas.

[January] 10h [1853]

Mr. Mitchells family left for Heard County their new home. Last week made drawers pantaloons & a dress for Eliza.

[January] 14 [1853]

Went to town had our dagauereotypes [sic] taken.

[January] 15 [1853]

Sowed or planted Peas. Went over to Uncle Davis found Margaret comfortable—

[January] 16 [1853]

Came home very tired rode horseback.

[January] 17 [1853]

Cut out four shirts. Having my meat washed preparatory to being hung up. Mrs. Glass spent the evening with me.

[January] 18 [1853]

Stitching & plaiting bosoms feel very unwell—

[January] 22d [1853]

The anniversary of my marriage with Mr. Burge three years to day & thus far it has been a happy one. Been quite sick all the week with a cold, thought of Death & how stands it with me—

[January] 23r [1853]

Neither Mr. Burge nor myself have been to church to day it is so very unpleasant.

[January] 31 [1853]

Sowed cabbage seed & beets.

Feb 2d [1853]

Mr. Burge went to town & brought home with him a Mrs. Alford of Marrieta.

[February] 3d [1853]

Spent the day with Mrs. Glass with Mrs. Alford Mrs. Perry Mrs. Pitts[33] & Robert.

Feb 7th [1853]

Commenced sowing oats delightful weather peas up.

[February] 22d [1853]

Attended the burial of George Brooks a neighbor & friend who died in Augusta from the effects of the removal of a tumour from his leg. A very cold day.

March 8th 1853

[March] 9th [1853]
   Commenced planting corn but very wet ground cold rain almost every day. Hen came off with 10 chickens first this season. Hannah sick.

[March] 13 [1853]
   Planted corn but two days on account of continual rains.

[March] 18 [1853]
   No church to day. In the evening rode around the farm everything seems overflowed with water—18 chickens. Peach trees in bloom nothing scarcely done in garden yet—

June 22d [1853]
   First cotton bloomed, sugar corn for dinner very dry no rain on our farm for 8 weeks of any consequence. Harvesting oats—Martha sick.

[June] 28th [1853]
   Tuesday noon. I have been having whitewashing done & feel very tired from working so hard have ironed & put up parlour curtains. No rain yet every thing looks gloomy & disheartening—
   Recieved a letter from Wiley he is sick at the Indian Springs. We had no rain for 9 weeks.

August 26th [1853]
   A shower last night the girls have gone to Dr. Perrys. Wiley is in college & Thomas in Warrenton so Mr. Burge & I are by ourselves. He is clearing up the gin house preparatory to putting in his cotton. We go if nothing prevents to Morgan Camp meeting tomorrow.

Newton Co Sept 29th 1853—
   Again has passed my birthday. Oh what a greatful [*sic*] heart ought I to have that so many returns of this day have found me enjoying so many

blessings. Every year accumulates mercies untold showered upon me who art so unworthy of them—

Casting my thoughts back over the years that have flown how very many returns of this day can I distinctly call to mind. How varied have they been. Upon what different scenes have they looked. And now how unlike many of the past are my prospects—At the other side of the table opposite me sits my husband & how very dear has he become unto me. Such kindness & Love such devoted affection calls up my hearts warmest love & my earnest desire to be worthy of him—Here too are our *little* girls the eldest knitting & the baby Eliza teasing to go to bed. A happy family circle. O may it not be broken into by affliction disease or Death. And yet why should we be exempt. 'Tis only Gods goodness that has kept us thus far. And whatever he wills in the future will be for the best—

I have been cutting & making a calico dress to day it is very pleasant weather but somewhat cool to night. A meeting commences tomorrow evening at Sandtown to be protracted—

Was at Oxford last Sabbath. Heard Dr. Pierce preach from the words Grow in Grace & in the knowledge, of our Lord Jesus Christ. He said that Christians should live in this world as one in a cave that could see nothing [but] only by looking up—The attractions cares & concerns of this life should not take our attention from above—A very good sermon— Some thirty or forty students requested prayers by going forwar[d] to the altar—

I wish that I could say of a truth that I know that I have grown in Grace that I am a better Christian than my last birth day. I grow older but I fear no better—

Oct 24 1853

After a most pleasant month for gathering in the crop the weather has at length changed last night there was a heavy rain & it has cleared away very cold. Rebecca came in Saturday & Wiley Mrs. Perry & Mary Jane called as did Dr. Perry & Mr. Roberts—We shall have frost to night I think. Killed a beef to day. Picked out thirteen bales of cotton—

Oct 25 [1853]

Frost. We have had last night a heavy frost which I think must kill all vegetation—

Nov 2d [1853]

Commenced sowing wheat—getting in swamp corn peas &c &c!

[November] 3d [1853]

Old Sawny the buggy horse was found dead in his Stable this morning. Poor old horse. Mr. Burge remarked this Sabbath as I came from church with him & was complaining of his want of spirit as a traveller. Well Well I always feel so easy about you when you are away and Sawny has to pull you for I know he will bring you back safely—Spent the day with Mrs. Glass. Walked over with Rebecca.

[November] 5th [1853]

Went to town a cool windy day everything is killed by the late frosts— Rebecca left us for town to day—

Nov 20 [1853]

Martha sick.

[November] 28 [1853]

M very sick last night called in Dr. Perry.

[November] 30 [1853]

Father & mother & Sis Caro arrived unexpectedly to day. O how glad I was to see them.[34]

[In margin:] Killed hogs week before Christmas.

Dec 23 [1853]

Very rainy but Mr. Burge & father started by private conveyance for Macon to spend Christmas & to attend Conference.

[December] 25 Sunday Morning *Christmas* [1853]

Yesterday the rain ended by snow & this morning we find the ground covered with [snow] looking for all the world like New England—the negroes have all come in for Christmas gifts & a right merry time have they had—Mild & pleasant not very cold.

[December] 26 [1853]

Snow melting pleasant but sloppy clear overhead.

[December] 27 [1853]

Still pleasant cloudy towards night rained about ten & continued raining hard all night.

[December] 28 [1853]

Ceased raining but cloudy & cold. Dr. Perry & John Davis came up. Davis staid all night.

[December] 29 [1853]

Clear but cold father & Mr. Burge returned had an unpleasant ride—

[December] 30 [1853]

Again raining—Servants cannot get about.

[December] 31 [1853]

Still bad weather commenced snowing about eleven & so continued during the day—

Jan 1st 1854

Clear but cold very much such a day as last Sabbath. Snow melting fast nearly all gone had a Pea fowl for dinner boiled custurd &c. Cousin Ransom took dinner with us & left immediately after.

[January] 2d [1854]

Very mild wet & sloppy but clear sky.

[January] 3d [1854]

Pleasant washing to day. Walked in the woods with Caroline gathered moss. Very mild & warm. Mr. Burge in town attending sale—

[January] 4 [1854]

Packing cotton. Warm & pleasant. Ironing doing up shirts. Went up to Mrs. Shaws in the evening rode horseback. She was not at home. Stopped at Mrs. B Perrys. She has a fine boy—

[January] 5 [1854]

A foggy morning rainy day towards evening ceased raining. Mr. Burge has been at the circle[35] looking up a lost mule—

[January] 6 [1854]

Servants all going to the swamp this morning. Not quite clear weather yet.

[January] 18 [1854]

Wiley left for college again very unpleasant.

[January] 19 [1854]

Went with father up to Mr. Parkers[36] whose wife I had learned was very sick. Found it untrue. Caroline came back from Sandtown where she has been visiting for a week.

Newton Co January 22d 1854

This is the fourth anniversary of my wedding day as John Gilpin said to his loving spouse but no ride to Kensington though a slice of cold turkey has graced our board to day. O it has been so cold that I am right glad that I have an old man to keep me in wood.

[January] 28 [1854]

A pleasant day after several of rain. Mr. Cheney[37] called this morning been making mince pies. Very good. Went over to Mrs. Perry to see Josephs bride accompanied by Mother & Caroline. We have done no gardening yet. Mrs. Ps cabbage plants are up.

[January] 29 [1854]
A lonely gloomy Sabbath. Mother sick. Mr. B & myself in the parlour the remainder gathered about. Cold looks like snow & O how cold & hard am I in a spiritual sense.

[January] 30 [1854]
Sowed peas cabbage radishes &c. hung up meat—

[January] 31 [1854]
Warm & pleasant. Mrs. Glass called been making crabapple preserves.

Feb 1st [1854]
[February] 10 [1854]
First plum bloom.

[February] 19 [1854]
Went to Sandtown to preaching & all of us dined at Dr. Perrys.

[February] 20 [1854]
Spent the day at Colonel Wilsons. Father mother & sister remained all night.

[February] 21 [1854]
Planting potatoes.

March 20 [1854]
Spent the day at Mrs. Perrys making fly brush. Father & Mr. Burge went to the circle & brought home word of the arrival of Orrington at Covington—[38]

[March] 21 [1854]

Can it be possible that Brother has really come to Georgia. Yes & valuable presents he brought me & the children.

[March] 22 [1854]

Called upon Mrs. Iverson Graves & Baker took a late dinner warm & sitting in the porch.

March 23d [1854]

My friends all left to day we going to the Circle & dining with them— Sold cotton to day 14277 lbs. got 81/4 cts.

[March] 24 [1854]

Feel lonely. Mr. & Mrs. Whitman here.

[March] 25 [1854]

Very cool been to church. Preacher dined with us—

[March] 26 [1854]

Heard Bro Sasanett good sermon very cool killing frost.

[March] 27 [1854]

Bad effects of the frost. Well house took fire—quite frightened. Mrs. William Guise[39] died eight o clock.

[March] 28 [1854]

Spent part of the day with Mrs. Shaw the rest of it at Mr. Guises— Mr. Burge went to town.

April [1854]

Old Mrs. Shaw came down to spend a few days with me—

[April] 10 [1854]

Commenced planting cotton & reworking garden.

[April] 15 [1854]

Quarterly meeting commenced to day at our church. Bro Talley[40] preached from 1st Ps 3d verse dined at Widow J. W. Graves. Aunt Polly Davis with me. Had green peas for dinner.

[April] 16 [1854]

Left home early for meeting. No lovefeast but prayer meeting. Sermon nothing very excellent. Sacramental services after preaching. Dr. Perry & wife dined with us. Sarah Strong joined the church by letter. Very cold & unpleasant—.

[April] 20 [1854]

Planting swamp corn commenced to day.

[April] 24 [1854]

20 turkeys hatched.

[April] 29 [1854]

Went to Oxford Saturday evening the 29 done some shopping in Covington 7 Dollars.

[April] 30 [1854]

Heard Bishop Andrew preach from the words Search the Scriptures. *Very cold & frost last night.*

May 1st [1854]

A colt folded [*sic*] last night. We have named her Fanny Louise.

[May] 6 [1854]

Planted fall Irish potatoes. Mr. Burge not very well. [In margin: 5th set out a few slips of potatoes.]

[May] 11 [1854]

Finished swamp corn.

[May] 12 [1854]

Sheard 13 sheep & turned out 17. Sick to day.

June 8 1854

Been to Sandtown with the girls expected Gus Ski to have got me a basket of cherries from his mothers but found him sick with the complaint which is now so general (Dysentery). Mrs. Roberts has died of it & several others are quite sick—

[June] 9 [1854]

Mr. Burge has just got over his cotton for the first time. Very backward he thinks. Cut wheat the 5th. Quite cool & unpleasant—Had *cucumbers* the 5th.

[June] 10 [1854]

Let out Juno.

[June] 13 [1854]

Commenced planting peas in swamp. Brought home Sallie Perry with me yesterday. Mrs. Maria Harwell & James dined with us.

[June] 15 [1854]

Little Sallie was quite sick this morning & I have sent her home. Mr. James Loyd was buried this evening.

[June] 16 [1854]

Went up to Mr. Guises this morning made quite a long call. Called in to Mrs. Perrys & stopped the remainder of the day. A good shower which still continues.

[June] 17 [1854]

Mr. Stewerd came over this morning to survey our land but it being so rainy couldn't do it. A very good rain which will make everything pleasant & green again. Finished potatoe slips.

[June] 18 [1854]

The first news I heard this morning was The dairy door is open Mistress. Left open & all my cooking for Sunday eat up. These little cares & perplexities how they annoy & perplex me. Did not go to church. Mr. Burge went. Had a class meeting six present. We have just returned from a walk to the creek. Eliza would accompany us & now she sits by me just as loving & uneasy as a little pup.

[June] 19 [1854]

Had my yard cleaned out been cutting a basque waist for Louisiana. Mr. Burge been cutting bearded wheat which ought to have been done before the rain—

[June] 20 [1854]

Whippoorwill peas.

[June] 21t [1854]

Putting up blackberries sunning meat. Wrote to Sister Sarah heavy showers to day plenty of rain now—

Sept 29 Newton Co 1854

Again am I enabled to record another year of blessings of mercies undeserved. Not a really sick day for the year past perfect health I may say that I have enjoyed & thus has it been with the whole family. To many very many this has been a year of affliction & death. Disease has spread all over our land. Death has taken many from our neighborhood yet we have all been spared. Father mother & sister have visited me during the last winter. Everything about is calm peaceful & quiet—We have taken supper. Mr. Burge is reclining upon the lounge having been to town. Louisiana is reading & Eliza laying down with her father. The same quiet family of last year thank God unbroken—

The past week been making them dresses have cut one for myself to day!

Called in to night Newton & Lydia[41] & given them a portion of Medicine—

The little girls are improving some in their studies. Could I see Eliza as anxious to read as her sister. I should be better satisfied about her. They will soon be prepared for other teachers.

The past summer has been an unusually hot one said by the oldest people to be the hottest within their recollection.

20 Oct [1854]

For the three nights past we have had slight frosts but not sufficient to kill vegetation. For the last week been quilting petticoats. After a two months silence have recieved letters from home & Dr. His family I expect, will be here next month—

Rode over to day to the farthest swamp to see the good land Mr. Burge bought last year fencing it in for a pasture for my cows & stock—

[October] 21st [1854]

Have got a ring worm or something similar on my shoulder. Very painful killing a beef this morning gathering in peas. About done with cotton fields nearly clean.

12th of Nov 1854
Sunday.   Dr. Sister two of her children arrived to day. We had been looking for them several days. Dr. Middlebrooks came down yesterday to meet them. Been to meeting to the Baptist Church. Heard a sermon from Iverson L. Brooks upon the occasions of the death of Mrs. Graham [42] & his nephew George Brooks—

[November] 13 [1854]

Trunks arrived to day many a present in them. Quite cool.

[November] 24 [1854]

Finished negro clothes.

Dec 1st [1854]

Yesterday started for Gainsville stopped at Richard Harwells in Oxford the first night. Second two miles beyond Lawrenceville at a Mr. Brooks one room four beds in it. All right.

[December] 2d [1854]
    Arrived at Marys found all well *very* cold.

[December] 7 [1854]
    Started for home. Stopped at a Mr. Bowens. Poor accomodations.

[December] 8 [1854]
    Arrived home found all well glad enough to get here folks ginning.

[December] 12 [1854]
    Theresa sick very much trouble about her.

[December] 19 [1854]
    Dr. Comings arrived. Killing hogs.

[December] 21 [1854]
    Sister & Dr. gone to Madison.

[December] 25 [1854]
    Christmas yesterday went over to Bro Rockmoors[43] his wife died suddenly last evening. A sad Christmas to him.
    Mr. Guise called. He & Mr. Burge went to the burial. Gave them all a good dinner.

[December] 29 [1854]
    Doctor left for Macon. Very warm & pleasant Christmas.

January 1 1855

[January] 2d [1855]
    Killed more meat. Making cloak.

[January] 15 [1855]
    Killed again. Making in all 4700 weight. Mrs. Glass called this evening.

[January] 13 [44] [1855]

(Sowed peas & cabbage seed beets.)

[January] 18 [1855]

Set a hen. The Misses Rakestraw [45] spent the day with me.

[January] 21 [1855]

Went to church very heavy shower which is very much needed there has been no rain this winter scarcely—Wells all dry.

[January] 22d [1855]

Anniversary of my marriage five years to day. They have been calm peaceful contented & happy ones for which I desire to be thankful. Been making me a new silk dress—

My husband is putting up fencing. Wiley left for Oxford this morning. Cold very cold we think the coldest of the season. Slim Bush had a calf last night a ewe a lamb.

[January] 28 [1855]

A rainy Sabbath. Hailed a little towards night have written Cornelia & Caroline took supper by the fire doughnuts & cheese & ginger tea.

Feb 12 [1855]

Sarah & her children left to day went over to the Circle with them though very sick with a headache yesterday bid her good bye & then called upon Mrs. Hebbard to cheer up a little cold ride home & when there looks lonely.

[February] 15 [1855]

Spent day with Mrs. Parker—very cold.

[February] 17th [1855]

Went to town with Mr. Burge sold 20 bales of cotton. Some for the servants making in all 23 bales. Got 7 *cts*. Called upon Mrs. Floyd. Dined at Mrs. Curintons.

[February] 22d [1855]
   Went to Mrs. Glasss with Theresa.

Newton Co Feb 25 1855
   The last Sabbath of the winter of 54, 55. It has been a very cold winter
& the dryest for this country ever known this morning snowed for
several hours so that it prevented us from attending Sabbath school.
Theresa is preparing to leave for home. I feel sorry & yet I cannot urge her
to remain.

March 2d [1855]
   Went to the Circle with Theresa stopped all night with Mr. Low &
family. Came home next day.

[March] 10 [1855]
   Planted corn in garden.

[March] 11 [1855]
   10 chickens the first of the season.

[March] 15 [1855]
   Planted Irish potatoes in patch beans corn &c.

[March] 23d [1855]
   Very cold. Frost last night.

July 15 Sunday [1855]
   This is a lonesome day. Mr. Burge has gone to hear the commencement
sermon at Oxford to be preached by Dr. Green from Tennessee—I not
being well & there being some boys here to get out wheat tomorrow have
thought it best to remain at home. I rode out yesterday to get some wild
cherries first rode down to Aunt Rhodas, but did not get out. Came home
by the old place. Lost my scarf in looking at the corn & had to return &
found it by the creek. Soon after getting home it rained a little.

[October?] 15 16 17 [1855]
    Slight frosts.

Oct 30 [1855]
    Digging sweet potatoes.

[October] 31st [1855]
    Hard & killing frost.

Nov 7th [1855]
    Finished negro clothes for this year. A wet & unpleasant week though not much rain. Ginning cotton sowing oats & wheat.

[November] 12 [1855]
    Bad & painful night. Mr. Burge went to town returned early. Mrs. J. Perry with her little one called & spent the evening with me.

[November] 13 [1855]
    Made Mr. Burge a pair of pants that he bought for himself yesterday.

[November] 16 [1855]
    Finished sowing wheat & ginning the white cotton. Sowed 5½ bushels of the Illinois 11¾ of Fillmore.

[November] 18 [1855]
    Very pleasant & warm but looking for a change. No frost as yet this month heard last Sabbath of the death of Fanny Burge or Mrs. Rutherford. Not learned the particulars. Mr. Burge & the girls gone to church to hear Dr. Smith.[46] Lewis[47] complaining doctoring him.

[November] 19 [1855]
    Banking [*sic*] potatoes. I've got no sewing to do.

Dec 1st [1855]
    Finished sowing oats. No weather for killing meat yet.

Dec 3d [1855]

Mr. Elliot called & paid 200 dollars on his note. Still warm. I never had so little sewing on hand before since my marriage.

[December] 5 [1855]

Mrs. Glass & Mrs. Pitts called & spent the evening. Killed 5 hogs quite cold.

[December] 6 [1855]

Mrs. Perry & Clarissa were in this morning much warmer—

Newton County Jan 1856

With this page commences a new year. On December 11th I gave birth to a daughter. Was quite sick for several hours. Desire to feel thankful for the gift. How greatly indeed have I been blessed & how have my lost ones been made up to me.[48]

[January] 14 [1856]

Mr. Burge employed an overseer at ten dollars a month. Snowed the 11th. Still on the ground.

March 20 [1856]

Peach nor plum trees did not bloom until the 20 of March. Cold & frosty wintry weather. Nothing doing in gardens.

April 9 [1856]

Lost by death William *a good boy* died unexpectedly sick only about 36 hours.[49] getting quite warm & pleasant—

[April] 11 [1856]

Mrs. Hodge & Miss Guise came to see me to day. At night old Father Eli Bennet arrived who baptized our daughter Sarah & eleven little Negroes.

[April] 12 [1855]

Commenced planting cotton very busy.

[April] 13 [1855]

Went to Baptist church in my new carriage thermometer at night at eighty.

[April] 14 [1855]

Spent the day with Mrs. Glass who I heard was very sick found her better but two of her children quite poorly.

July 9th [1856]

Been disappointed in not going to Madison. Had a good rain which was very much needed. My Sarah grows finely. She is a good child can sit by herself has been doing so from five months. She has got no teeth yet loves to eat drinks the most water like a fish.

Putting up front door steps.

August 30 1856

Returned friday the 28 from a visit to Spaulding. We have been spending a week with Mr. Burges sister. Visited Griffin stopped a night with old Bowdoinham out in Mcdonough. Mr. Hatch & lady Eliza & Sada were with us. Sada grows finely & still remains a good baby. She has four teeth & can call kity. Having my house painted & whitewashed. This is a very stormy day, the wind has blown without cessation all day & it has fairly poured. O what a gloomy day & what damage will be done.

Dec 31st [1856]

This the last evening of the year should be one of retrospection & how thankful should I be that I am alive in the enjoyment of domestic blessings. What a happy year I have spent with my darling babe. With what interest I have watched her growth how her little mind begins to expand & yesterday she walked several steps by herself. We were at Uncle L Fretwells,[50] a pleasant visit we had to.

April 10 [1857]

What a long time since I wrote anything the last was of Sada. Well she is still interesting. Can talk & goes about as well as anyone.

Miss Matilda & Hodge spent day with me again. Brother L Baker was buried in Covington to day. Mr. Burge setting out cabbage plants. Quite cold & an exceedingly backward spring. Fruit killed. Commenced planting cotton—

Jan 1st 1858

How swiftly the years slip away. I have not written a line in this but once for the last year.

When I look back it has been one of mercy. Death has not come nigh our dwelling & we have had but little sickness. Peace & plenty have abounded—

To day we have had our last killing of hogs making 4500, forty five hundred & eighty eight pounds.

April 20 [1858]

Mr. Montgomery shearing sheep for us. Sheared 19 turned out 25. A rainy day. Dr. Comings & Anna[51] with me. Set out cabbage plants. Busy all hands in the swamp.

[April] 24 [1858]

Quarterly meeting. Bro Branham[52] preached followed by bro Tally. Mr. Strong[53] & Briggs Perry went forward for prayers. Uncle Davis & wife with Margaret & family are with me.

[April] 27 [1858]

Dr. & Anna have left for Macon in our buggy quite cool.

May 25 [1858]

Left home with my dear sick husband for New England a cooler climate. Took Sada. Sailed from Savannah in the Steamer Alabama 28th.

Arrived in New York Tuesday morning.

June 1st [1858]

Met my brother Orrington there very unexpected. He wished us to go directly to the St. Nicholas with him but we declined as Mr. Burge was so poorly & went directly to the boat & took stateroom. As she did not sail until 5 o clock in evening bro came down for us & we rode around the city & dined with him at the St. Nicholas. I was afraid little Sadai would not behave herself well having been acostomed [*sic*] to a nurse, but she done admirably. Sat at the table like a lady & told the waiter distinctly she would "have ham."

[June] 2d [1858]

Got home to fathers found him at Depot. Very much surprised to see us.

CHAPTER THREE

A Widow Planter

January 2d 1859

    I have no heart to take up my pen to record the events of the past year & yet it may possess some interest in after time to me if not to my darling Sada.

    After two years of failing health indeed my dear husband has had a cough for thirty years but always being active & out of doors most of the time it has at last conquered him. Yet he never took his bed until the last day of his life so fearful of giving trouble that he would scarcely allow me to send for neighbors to see him die. One of the best of men truely [*sic*] said the preacher Bro Stone.

    He had been quite ill all day but before sundown the sickness of the stomach passed off & he sat up in bed & eat supper cheerful & talkitive [*sic*]

& I felt the danger I had feared all day was passed. I had Sada in my arms at one time by his bedside & he looked up at her sadly and said "Bless the child." After preparing himself for the night he solemnly clasped his hands & said

I commit & conjure myself with all that I have & am into the Hands of my Heavenly Father for this night & for all Eternity. Death came to him as sleep. I had sent for friends he welcomed them but said he felt very sick & wished to sleep. I saw signs of dissolution he was calm & composed apparantly did not suffer got up in the bed upon his elbow & took coffee not more than an hour before he died just like dropping off too sleep was his death. Gone to God in the arms of his dear Saviour.

Some weeks before his death feeling that it was nigh he told me how happy I had made his last years how if it had been Gods Will he should have been glad to have staid with his family that in a temporal veiw he was just fixed to enjoy life that for my sake to keep trouble from me he would gladly remain but "My Heavenly Father knows best. I leave it all to Him. He will take care of you & the children. I have prayed for you Dolly that your faith fail not. That in the trials to come your faith & trust may be in Jesus. He doeth all things right *remember that.*"

The next day he took Elbert out over the farm & showed him what to do for the next year. So calmly & cheerfully he gave up all. Bless God that I have been the wife of such a man. Oh yes I thank Thee O my Father that it was for me to make his last years happy ones that it was my privillage to wait upon him until the very last moment of his life.[1]

Newton Co Jan 22d 1859

Nine years ago to night I came here a bride with many misgivings. I took upon myself those sacred vows binding us till Death do us part & death has done his work. Parted to meet no more on earth. O God help me to live so that we meet in Heaven. Here let me record the loving kindness of my husband always thoughtful of my happiness. Always the same never fretful or cross or unkind to me & O how thoughtful of me. God Help me to revere & love his memory as it should be loved. May his prayers be heard for me & for his children. Aunt Rhoda & Cally[2] both with me.

Feb 17th 1859

Finished sowing [oats is crossed out and replaced with] oats planted potatoes peas & cabbage up trees not in bloom broke colts.

[February] 18 [1859]

Saw peach bloom very warm windows & doors open. Hauling out manure & bedding cotton land.

[February] 22d [1859]

Mr. Stanton[3] came to put up kitchen. Four ploughs running.

[February] 24 [1859]

Sent box to Lou, bed mattress & cotton seed to Wiley. Drove a cow that Mr. Turner[4] bought of Mr. Finley to him—Julie[5] worked out peas.

[February] 25 [1859]

Ploughing swamp. Walked down there. Very warm & pleasant everything putting out—

[February] 26 [1859]

Rain this morning thunder & lightning last night. Spaying pigs Mr. Roquemore. Raking manure & hauling rails, only 5 chickens heard that Mrs. Perry had a daughter.

[February] 27 [1859]

Rainy bad wet morning undecided for a long time whether to go to church finally went bro Tally preached from Cain & Abels offering upon faith. Good sermon. Evening went down to Margerets. She has a fine babe her father & mother with her.

[February] 28 [1859]

Uncle Billy Davis[6] dined with us. Mr. Stanton at work upon kitchen.

March 1st [1859]

Dr. Perry called in morning. Ell Brown working on chimney. Afternoon went over to swamp the oats are looking finely rode over & about the disputed ground & then over to the old fence & into the old place to the graveyard. Carks cow had a calf.

[March] 2d [1859]

Drizzy day have promised to go to Mr. Graves to spend the night to have a settlement with him. I learn that Col Wilson died this evening. Thus one after another departs—

[March] 3d [1859]

Rained very hard this morning took down meat yesterday. Sorry that I went to Mr. Graves upon account of rain cleared off in evening & came home with headache. 3 of spaid pigs died.

[March] 4t [1859]

Bright morning up early.

Saturday March 5 1859

Went to Covington to day to see Judge Floyd respecting the guardianship.[7] It has been deferred until the Saturday before court. I leave it all with the great Lawgiver & whatever He does will be right & for the best. Bought peice of osanburgs. Mr. Stanton has finished kitchen—

[March] 6h [1859]

A rainy Sabbath & cannot go to church. I regret it very much. Spent the day in reading & J. Perry & wife came in in evening. A very rainy night thunder storms & rain in torrents.

[March] 7 [1859]

Up early & went to creek to see the rising water. Cannot plough. Sent flour to mill could not get it ground. Water is so high.

[March] 8 [1859]

Lewis clearing about the kitchen boys cutting in the swamp & hauling manure.

[March] 9 [1859]

Bedded out potatoes. Peas which were fine rabbits have eat down. Went to Margerets this evening carried Sadie & Callie. Pleasant day but I feel very sad & lonely.

[March] 10 [1859]

Commenced planting corn the pond place.

Mr. Zacry bought my cotton the 6th gave eleven cents all around thirty five bags two belonging to the negroes.[8]

[March] 14h [1859]

Hauling off cotton clearing up swamp.

[March] 19 [1859]

Went to town to court & found the decision against me.[9]

[March] 29 [1859]

Been settling up bills paid off all I knew of in town. Went up with Dr. Perry. Aunt Rhoda with us again.

It is very warm & pleasant & everything promises an open & forward spring. Wiley came down last night from town with me. Settled off with servants their cotton money. they are richer than I for all of mine is owing. When our debts are paid I shall have none but I feel thankful I have something to do it with how many are left widows with nothing to depend upon & many looking to them for bread. Sada keeps well & is a great comfort to me.

April 2d 1859

Went up to Mrs. Perrys. Settled off a note yesterday. Went to town to get Lou some summer clothing left two skirts with Miss Guise to make am fixing to go to Macon. Rainy &c.

[April] 3d [1859]

So rainy to day that none of us went to church. Everything is overflowed.

[April] 4h [1859]

Expected to have started to Macon this morning but did not upon account of the rain. It is almost too wet to bed cotton ground.

[April] 6th [1859]

Left home early for Macon took cars at the Circle bro & sister Parker with me as far as Atlanta at which place we arrived at half past ten. Left at eleven got to Macon at five. Met children at Vineville depot found all well felt very tired.

[April] 7 & 8th [1859]

Busy settling bills paid out three hundred & seventy five dollars my expenses fourteen.

[April] 9h [1859]

Left Macon at midnight very lonely. Doctor put me aboard the cars introduced the conductor to me. I went in found not a single lady aboard. A few gentlemen all sleeping. Got to Atlanta to breakfast stopped at Thompsons. Went shopping took cars at ten for the Circle arrived there at ½ past twelve found Sister & Sada & the carriage there & soon came home. A warm day & I am about tired out—

[April] 10 Sunday [1859]

Aunt Rhoda & Calla have gone to Carmel meeting. I am sick.

[April] 11h [1859]

Commenced planting cotton the graveyard field. Mr. Glass & some others commenced the 6h. I am quite unwell—

[April] 12 [1859]

took medicine & feel better. None can tell how much I miss Mr. Burge & how gloomy everything seems without him.

[April] 14 [1859]

Carried Aunt Rhoda home. All well there. Met Mrs. Veely there had Sada with me. When I got home found Mrs. Perry & Clarissa here.

[April] 15 [1859]

Settled off with Mr. Guise two hundred & eleven dollars that is the way the money goes.

April 17 1859

Mr. Stone[10] preached to day a very good sermon upon the danger of riches good many out rather cold fearful of frost potatoes looking nicely.

[April] 18 [1859]

Slight frost last night planting swamp the middle one.

[April] 19 [1859]

Finished planting cotton.

[April] 20 [1859]

Went to Sandtown[11] gave in my tax. Spent morning with Cousin Margeret. Servants finished their cotton. Commenced plowing corn.

[April] 21st [1859]

Breaking up swamp & planting corn. Rain to day very much needed there. Severe wind at night.

[April] 22d [1859]

Wind continues expected Mr. & Mrs. Parrington.

[April] 24d [1859]

Went to Hard Shell meeting at Shoal Creek expecting to hear Elder Parrington preach Mr. Montgomerys sons funeral but he did not come.

[April] 25th [1859]

Visited at Mr. Parringtons with Cally left Sadie at home. Still planting in swamp.

[April] 26 [1859]

Commenced shearing sheep. Sheared 25 turned out thirty nine. Rain again & it will do good for the swamp. Some parts of it was so dry they could not plant it—

May 7 [1859]

25 turkeys.

May 10th [1859]

Been over cotton once. Very good stand fine rains yesterday.

Last Saturday went over to the factory carried cousin Margeret & children. Mistook the way coming home & got within a few miles of Montecello [sic].[12]

[May] 14th [1859]

Mr. Roquemore died this morning caused by a fall of his horse he was quite an old man.

[May] 15 [1859]

Funeral preached by Mr. Wallace—Been to church & heard bro Stone.

[May] 18 [1859]

Cleaning house. Had plenty of rain too much if anything.

May 22d [1859]

This is a beautiful morning so pleasant from the rain that fell last night. O could I see my husband. Could it have been the Masters Will to have spared him to us how grateful I should have been. It does seem at times that I cannot still this longing for him[,] for him to be with us. Just a year to day & he was in Covington making preparations for our visit North. He was feeble but how much I hoped from it—

June 10th [1859]

A fine rain last night. Our crop looks finely & this rain will bring it out more & more they have gone over some of it three times. Going to work in swamp corn tomorrow. Miss Amanda Harwell is with me have written Dr. & Lou to day. *3 turkeys left.*

[June] 22d [1859]

Thomas Burge our nephew came here a few days since & has gone with Cally to the commencement at Covington Female College. Very glad she had some one to accompany her. The bridge over the river being gone they have to go by the way of Starrsville. I have been out on the farm this morning. Cotton as a general thing is very small one or two blooms. Potatoes look well had rain several times within the last ten days—Oats have the rust badly.

[June] 23d [1859]

Wiley came home with Cally last evening. Will stay several days.

[June] 25 [1859]

William Stanton called with several notes against the estate one of six hundred & sixty four I have no knowledge whatever of & cannot believe it was given by Mr. Burge. I would not wrong the man in any way & if he is right & I mistaken may it be plainly shown me.

[June] 26 [1859]

Did not go to church to day. Sent Wiley to Covington had a fine rain this afternoon.

[June] 27h [1859]

Commenced cutting oats badly rusted shall make but few. Making Sada a dress.

[June] 28 [1859]

Went out early to the feild. Afternoon put up blackberries have made wine been up to Mrs. Perrys.

Newton County July 2d 1859

Saturday July 2d

Went up to church this morning heard bro Tally from the words We have not a High Priest that cannot be touched by our infirmities &c. He dwelt first on the nature of the Priesthood 2 its adaptedness for Sacrifices &c. &c. A good & comforting sermon especially where he presented Christ as our Priest comforting & consoling us watching over temptations trials &c &c.

He called on his way to Sandtown & I settled with him for the Advocate & paid up until sixty one. Sister Parker I heard was quite sick to day.

[July] 3d [1859]

Went again to church heard a bro Allen [13] the appointed missionary to China from the words Whatsoever your hands findeth to do do it with all your might for there is no knowledge nor device in the grave. The words alone applicable to those that were doing good &c. &c. He was followed by bro Smith in some very good remarks. Got home about two. Had a very pretty rain fell very hard it has cooled the atmosphere which was very warm. Staid by myself last night felt very lonely.

Sept 29 [1859]

Another year of my life has fled & what is the record. I am forty two years old to day. It has been a year of severe trial. Suffice it to say That I have been greivously afflicted. Lou left me for Macon College to day. I have had a pleasant vacation from her & I feel very sad that she has left. It has been very warm to day rode over to the walnut tree & weighed twice to day to night. Waited some time at the gin house for them with William Comings & saw the cotton put away—

Dec 24 [1859]

Finished ginning & packing cotton putting up meat &c. &c. Made 41 bags sold 10. have done very well. Verily the God of the widow hath provided for me & abundantly blessed me. To Him be all the Glory.

[December] 27 [1859]

Attended the marriage of Miss Amanda Glass.[14] Very rainy & unpleasant.

[December] 30 [1859]

Mr. Gresham the overseer[15] came to day rainy. Mrs. Perry called in the evening.

Jan 1st 1860

I am still able to record another year of mercies. We have all been well had no sickness whatever in the family—This has been a very cold day indeed all of the holidays have been not but one pleasant one which was Monday. This evening Callie sits by me questioning Willie & I upon the genealogy of the patriarchs. I have promised Willie if he will read the Bible through this year to give him five dollars—

Feb 13th [1860]

Commenced bedding cotton land & hauling cotton seed for manure. Broke up swamp for corn the last week in January—Peas cabbage up planted Irish potatoes. Martha Mid Sally[16] sick.

April 2d [1860]

Started to Macon in carriage left at twelve got to Hillsboro & stopped with a Mrs. Reese. Sada with me. Returned the last of the week.

[April] 5th [1860]

Commenced planting cotton. Got all through the 13th. Miss Lizzie Dutton[17] spending week with me.

[April] 13th [1860]

Commenced planting swamp corn. Very dry.

[April] 17 [1860]

Went to town.

[April] 19 [1860]

Slight rain. Set out cabbage plants.

[April] 23d [1860]

Sat up all night last night with Mrs. Perry. Very dull to day have been out over the crop. Very weedy. Not managed well. Callie making travelling dress. Miss Amanda with me.

May 3d [1860]

Carrie left for Maine. Sada & I went up to Covington & saw her off.

May 9 [1860]

Finishing going over cotton first time. Poor Stand in most places for want of rain perhaps. A gentle shower falling now. Am going up to Mrs. Perrys to be with them if that operation is performed upon her breast.

[May] 24 [1860]

For the last ten days we have had plenty of rain. Good showers. To day has been very warm & as I sat in my lonely porch tonight how vividly was brought to mind the night of two years since when I had every thing packed & ready to start home to Maine with my poor dear sick husband. How I dreaded the journey how I feared the consequences that might be & how calmly & cheerfully he said I want to go & you must go with me. And when I told him "My fears" he said Well suppose I should die. Will I not be as near Heaven there as here." And you can have my poor dust brought back. And this night two years I was ready & all packed up to go & the same moon that now shines so calmly upon his grave & me in my loneliness shone upon us together in the porch talking it all over. Praise the Lord that he came back & that he lived months afterwards.

June 8th 1860

From a letter received to day I learn the death of Matthew A. Mitchell the husband of Rebecca Mr. Burge's eldest child. I feel very sorry for her.

Her very life was wrapped up centered in him. For him she dared a fathers displeasure for him she forsook home & friends poor child how her very heart must ache as she finds herself a widow an orphan. "No weapon formed against thee shall prosper" came so suddenly into my mind I almost started. 'Tis the Lords doings & marvellous in our eyes. A very heavy rain the most washing one of the season. Commenced cutting wheat yesterday. Mr. W. Stanton sued me to day two writs. Called over to Judge Glasss & gave them to Sanford.

[June] 9 [1860]

There came up a very heavy storm of wind & rain hundreds of trees were blown down corn & cotton much injured. My cotton has not bloomed yet. It does not yet cover the ground. Some stalks look as if they had just come up only a few leaves while others are large & thrifty. They are going over it the third time. Some of the swamp corn is just up a very poor stand. Aunt Rhoda, Sada & I went over to Jackson Harwells this evening got some cherries which I shall put up tomorrow.

[June] 10 [1860]

Sent Rachel[18] up to office. Got a letter from President Bonnell[19] in which he says I need have no anxiety about Lou. She is getting over the measles finely. I hope so but I cannot help feeling very anxious about her. She is so delicate. Ironed Sadas white dresses made plum jelly & put up cherries to day.

[June] 11h [1860]

Went to church two prayers the congregation mostly gone to Covington. Got home early.

[June] 12th [1860]

Rode out early this morning hoeing in the apple orchard swamp before getting down rode up to Mrs. Perrys. She is getting well. Mrs. Chisholm & Eggard both there. Went round the farm in the evening. Our cotton rows are too wide not even. I must look to this in the future especially in manured land. My garden corn is tasseled.

[June] 13th [1860]
   Just commenced getting in Wheat & down came the rain again a great deal of wind.

[June] 27 [1860]
   Laid by all of the corn looks very well but had a bad time getting a stand. The cotton scarcely needs ploughing but it had better be done. Mr. Gresham says it is the fifth ploughing.

[June] 29 [1860]
   Got out wheat by thresher. Sowed 12 bushels gathered 111 which is remarkably good for the season.

July 12 [1860]
   Severe dry wind. Man putting up blinds.

July 13th [1860]
   Lou came home to day by way of Eatonton. I dined at Mrs. Strongs having attended Miss Johnsons examination.[20]

[July] 14 [1860]
   Got through chopping out cotton they have left the weeds on the ditch & will have to get over them few hands splitting rails. Lewis cutting stock. Corn on the upland looks bad needs rain. We have had but little for a month. Cotton is waist high in some patches.

[July] 19 [1860]
   Mrs. Cook & son came from Madison to visit me to day. The hands having got through their weeds have made them put up two pens of manure. Very hot & dry corn suffering severely. Give an holiday until Monday.

[July] 23 [1860]

Rain this evening the first for some weeks for which I desire to be very thankful. How good My Heavenly Master is! Clearing turnip patch. Lewis & John[21] to work for Judge Glass.

[July] 24 [1860]

Went to Covington & bought meat & groceries. Mrs. Cook with me.

[July] 26 [1860]

As we have had several showers I have had them plough again the burnt field & the new ground.

[July] 28 [1860]

Finished turnip patch. Cotton looks promising.

[July] 29 [1860]

Went to Sewells to church to day hard rain this evening.

[July] 30 [1860]

Commenced hauling leaves for the lots & manure for the turnip patch.

August 10 [1860]

It has been very dry ever since I last wrote—There is a good meeting going on at Sandtown. I went down last night. A hard rain came up & it was very dark & bad getting home. Tom Glass[22] came in the carriage with us & carried a lantern. Commenced making baskets. Some few bolls open. Pulled some fodder.

August 16th 1860

Sowing turnips to day. Commenced on baskets.

[August] 22d [1860]

Commenced cotton picking boys cutting down pine thicket been at it four weeks.

[August] 23 [1860]

Thomas & Lou have come back from a visit to Ransom Harwell.[23]

[August] 24 [1860]

Bishop Andrew preached at Sandtown from I am a debtor both the Jews
& the Greeks also. O such a good sermon & then I had the pleasure of
dining with him at Judge Glasss & his parting words were God bless &
prosper you. Thomas & Lou both left to day. She has gone to Uncle Billy
Daviss. The meeting is still going on at Sandtown.

[August] 25 [1860]

Had to have corn gathered to day for bread drying it in the garden.
Got a bag of cotton out. Had a day of trials & cares. My overseer is so
inefficient.

Sept [1860]

Cotton has opened finely & all are busy picking it. Lou is preparing for
Macon.

25 Sept [1860]

Lou left for Macon by the way of Eatonton where she will stop a
few days.

Oct 8 [1860]

On the 6 went to Uncle Lem Fretwells.[24] Met all of his children but two
a good meeting going on down there & all seem deeply engaged. A good
love feast on Sunday several joined. Boys in apple orchard swamp. Killed
beef—

[October] 22 [1860]

Dismissed my no account overseer paid him off. Gathering for swamp
corn waggon [sic] broke having it shucked.

[October] 24 [1860]

Went to the fair. Left Sada at Mrs. Bakers.

[October] 27 [1860]

Got home my new gin finished swamp corn.

[October] 29 [1860]

Turned hogs in swamp.

Ginning & packing & picking cotton. No killing frosts yet.

Nov 3d [1860]

Went to town & sold my crop to Hunter & Harris for 10⅛ all around. I feel I trust thankful to my Heavenly Father that He has enabled me to do so well.

[November] 6 [1860]

The day of Election which may be the last presidential Election Our United Country will ever see—

Digging potatoes.

November 19 [1860]

Mrs. Fanny Cannon & Cousin Nancy Fretwell[25] came today. Rode over to old place with Mrs. Kenner. Went to Sandtown early this morning. Mr. Glass rode home with me. Picking over swamp not leaving much cotton nor many bolls to open. No hard frost yet—

(16 [November 1860] Put hogs up in close pen.)[26]

[November] 22 [1860]

Went to town with Cousin Nancy. "Frank" started at Heard. Met Wiley. He is for Secession bought my cloak. Mr. Thompson[27] went up for me to see about a cog wheel bought one of Mr. Anderson. Very cold.

[November] 23 [1860]

Wiley came & spent the night with me.

[November] 24 [1860]

Still cold. My neighbors are killing their meat. Wiley left for town.

[November] 25 [1860]

Went to church few out. Cousin Nancy with me.

[November] 26 [1860]

Commenced sowing wheat the 21st the gin house feild—Went over to Mr. Rakestraws & spent night.

[November] 27 [1860]

Very Rainy. Left Nancy there & came home in the rain.

[November] 29 [1860]

Mr. Thompson here at work. The Misses Rakestraws & Miss Crowder & Cousin Nancy Mr. Glass & Houton happened in on business just as dinner they staid & ate with us. Had a turkey mince pie &c &c.

Sat 1s Dec [1860]

Eb went to carry Miss Nancy home. Not done sowing wheat yet—

[December] 3d [1860]

Killed 15 hogs.

[December] 13 [1860]

Killed 22 hogs. I went to town in morning.

[December] 19 [1860]

Finished sowing lot feild.

[December] 24 [1860]

Been to town again to see about the suit of Stantons. It has been put off. Had obelisk put over the grave of Mr. Burge. Paid man 135 dollars. Sent off to day also 230 dollars to Lou. Finishing up years business. Made 45 bags of cotton. Thankful for the care of my Heavenly Father yet gloomy & sad in my loneliness. Tis a lonely Christmas Eve. The stocking is hung ready for Santa Claus by darling Sada & she has gone early to bed to give him time to fill it well.

Newton Co Jan 1st 1861

Thus a new year has commenced. I have had a lonely week. Most of the time rainy. Negroes have appeared to enjoy themselves finely. Commenced doing some sewing for myself.

[January] 3d [1861]

Heard Mrs. Perry was quite unwell. Went up early in the morning stopped until dinner time came home & sent for Aunt Rhoda. Folks clearing pine feilds.

[January] 4h [1861]

This is a fast day for our Country that our Great Ruler may restore Peace to our disunited country. Thomas Burge [28] arrived is going to spend some time with me. Aunt Rhoda & I went up to Mrs. Perrys. Still very sick.

[January] 5 [1861]

Curcuit preaching went & met with my old friend Mr. Round brought him home with me. Oh it is so pleasant to meet with old friends, friends of former days. Bro Evans also spent night with us. [29]

[January] 6t [1861]

Bro Round preached for us at Mt Pleasant church text He shall be called Jesus for he shall save His people from their Sins. Spoke first of the significance of names referred to the Patriarchs &c. Very interesting sermon. Bade him good bye again & came home with Aunt Rhoda.

[January] 20 [1861]

Sixteen lambs. Clearing pine thicket.

Feb 19 [1861]

Finished clearing pine thicket. Thomas still with me. Commenced hauling out manure. Martha sick. No chickens & nothing up in garden & no trees bloomed.

[February] 22d [1861]

Wiley [O?] came this evening on his way to Charleston.

[February] 25 [1861]

Just commenced bedding cotton land five ploughs two subsoiling. Other boys making fence & hauling out manure just finished a pair of pants for Thomas. Not taken down meat yet.

March 2d [1861]

Miss Amanda Harwell[30] went home after making me a visit of two weeks. We have had delightfully warm weather the past ten days. The month has come in very warm & many of the neighbors planted corn last week.

[March] 11th [1861]

Finished bedding the graveyard feild looks mellow & nice. Commenced planting corn the apple orchard manured with cotton seed. Mrs. Hatch came on Friday last. Miss Johnson spent Saturday night with me & we went to Sandtown to church & heard George Yarbrow[31] preach. Very cold & unpleasant.

[March] 18th [1861]

Finished planting corn in apple orchard which was subsoiled & broken up deeply. Went to old house place.[32] Heavy frost.

[March] 19 [1861]

Slight snow.

[March] 20 [1861]

Eighteen chickens hatched. Commenced breaking burnt field. Hard & dry breaking with subsoils single feet 3½ foot bed.

[March] 21st [1861]

Nothing in garden. Found turkeys nest. Mrs. Hatch & children left. Sent them to Depot have done no sewing yet for servants.

[March] 22d [1861]

Went up to Mrs. Perrys her garden looks finely. Josiah breaking up cotton field by house.

[March] 24 [1861]

Uncle Parks preached. I came as far as Dr. Cheneys & dined with them. Pleasant day & quite warm.

[March] 28th [1861]

Went down to Cousin Ransom Harwells with Aunt Rhoda found Maria reduced almost to a skeleton. Left Sada at Cousin Margerets. His garden looks backward.

[March] 29 [1861]

Finished my visit & came home in evening found Thomas had got through bedding up burnt field. Put on two tons of superphosphate with the exception of three barrels. It is well broken up & bedded. I hope the good Master will send the rain & sunshine in due season & make it bring forth abundantly. From there they went to the 12 acre peice belonging to the swamp. Put upon that one ton of Phoenix with the exception of one barrel.

[March] 30 [1861]

Holiday for all but plough hands.

[March] 31 [1861]

A long lonesome day but very pleasant & warm. Dr. Perry rode up after Cora. I gave him a cold bite of Pea Fowl & sent Margeret some. I feel the need of more religion to day.

April 1st [1861]

Corn is up. Set out cabbage plants Saturday. We had a good shower Saturday morning the 30. We have had no rain before for over two weeks. My peas & beets are doing nothing. Can get no stand for the moles had potatoes covered with leaves. Set turkey hen to day 18 eggs. Thomas went over to see Bill Elliot about ditching the swamp he says we may plant it this year if we'll ditch it. Boys are ditching the potato patch & hauling out cow pen manure for it. Plough still in middle swamp. Feel very uneasy & sad about Lou. Had several letters from her.[33]

[April] 4th [1861]

Gave in tax. Mr. Thompson called & took it. Evening Mr. Annesley[34] called. Cold & unpleasant. Tuesday it was very warm. Thunder on Wednesday morning since then very cool & cloudy.

[April] 5 [1861]

Ploughs came up & bedded up the patches about the house. Evening Thomas & I went down to the Elliot swamp.

[April] 6 [1861]

Muster in town. Thomas went up. Cold rain half day holiday. Finished the house patches.

[April] 7th [1861]

Sunday. Rainy & cold Easterly wind. Did not go to church morning so unlikely. Rode over to Judge Glasss in evening with Thomas & Sada.

April 1861

9th   Commenced cotton planting the burnt field. Should have done it on yesterday but it rained so hard that we could not begin. Aunt Rhoda came up from Mr. Harwel's. Dick brought her. Cut out 14 pairs of breeches yesterday. Very cold & unlikely.

[April] 12 [1861]

Got into gravevard field to day. Still cool & cloudy. Rain tonight.

[April] 13th [1861]

Hard rain last night so that no ploughing could be done soon in the morning. Went to Quarterly meeting. Heard an excellent sermon from

Rev Thomas Pierce from the words of St. Pauls I count not myself to have apprehended but this one thing I do forgetting those things which are behind I reach forward to the prize & reaching forth unto those things which are before I press towards the mark for the prize of the high calling of God in Christ Jesus. He went on to show that if the Apostles would not look back to his experience to His trials why should we? Heard that fighting was going on in Charleston Harbor[35]—Learned of Bro Hebbards death a good man gone to his reward. Thomas went up to church to night & I am alone.

[April] 14 [1861]

A bright & pleasant morning the Sabbath day. Went early to Love feast had a good meeting bro Graves looked feeble. I fear that he will not be with us long. He talked calmly of his death & future prospects. So did bro Steward. Elder Yarbrough preached Secret things belong to God the revealed to us and our children. Spoke of the natural feelings of men if their private affairs were inquired into & made the subject of remark of Gods dealings with us. Of the present state of our country at War & the soil stained with the blood of our brethren of the natural laws in regard to rain &c. with many pleasant anecdotes & finally wound up with the written word of God as a sheild to all of our temptations.

News came that Fort Sumpter had surrendered to the Carolinians. Dined at Mrs. Strongs.

[April] 15 [1861]

Commenced planting creek patch. Still cool. Aunt Rhoda with me.

[April] 26 [1861]

Came home to night from Dr. Perrys. She has a babe & I spent a day & night with her.

[April] 28 [1861]

The last week Miss Libby Dutton has been spending with me. Have been busy sewing for Lou. Thomas went to town on Wednesday & joined a company of volunteers. Anna Comings our filly died this morning a great loss to me just at this time. We are so behind in our crop. Have not finished planting cotton nor commenced swamp corn. The Young Guard left Covington for Va. yesterday. Had letters from Callie Doctor Comings & Anna this week. 9 turkeys.

May 1st [1861]

Just finished planting cotton commenced ploughing corn apple orchard. Spent day with Mrs. Baker. May party of little girls at Academy at which Sada went.

[May] 3rd [1861]

Commenced shearing sheep.

[May] 4th [1861]

Finished shearing. Sheared 45. Meeting to day. Saturday Bro Evans at M P Church. Met Lou. Bro Parks had brought her up from Macon to recruit a little.

May 5th 1861

Rainy Sabbath. Thomas Lou Sada & I are all at home. Very rainy but we need it.

[May] 6th [1861]

Still rainy morning. Commenced hauling stock for fence & breaking further swamp. Mrs. L Perry[36] had a son to day.

[May] 7 [1861]

Commenced working cotton with harrows. A good stand & looks well but backward. Took Lou out to ride. Went to Sandtown. Ploughing the Pond place & planting the old house place in corn which I have had planted in cotton. My wheat looks well in bloom.

[May] 9 [1861]

Still breaking up swamp. Mr. & Mrs. Parks spent night with me. Little boys chopping out cotton. We are as forward as our neighbors with our cotton but backward with corn.

[May] 10 [1861]

Mrs Graves Henry & Fannie Gresham spent day with. Chicken pie for first time this year. Took Lou home with them.

[May] 11 [1861]

Went to mill.

[May] 15 [1861]

Commenced planting swamp corn.

[May] 16 [1861]

Miss Sallie Parks[37] visiting me.

[May] 18 [1861]

Rev. J Parks called & took Sallie home with them. Miss Z. Glass[38] spent last night with us. Very pleasant rain to night needed very much.

[May] 19 [1861]

Rev Mr. Thomas preached from the words Never man spoke as this man." An interesting sermon but we heard better from the same words. Cloudy & warm day with light showers—

[May] 20 [1861]

Came out of the far swamp to night done planting corn. We have broke up & then planted found it very heavy & hard on the mules. Beck looks badly & gave out as well as Cack & Fox. In future I must try to have breaking up done in March when the weather is cooler & it will not be so hard on the mules. We have got nearly over the cotton with harrow & it looks well four & six leaves. This rain upon it will do it good.

[May] 21st [1861]

Commenced ploughing the pine thicket field of cotton to day. The hoe hands are well up but that is very weedy. Put out potato slips to day & yesterday. The apple orchard corn looks well & the swamp part of it has come up well. We begin to be up with work. Received letters to day from bro William [and] Wiley Burge. How very unlike they are. Hail to night I fear damage done some plantations how thankful ought I to be that mine is spared that my crop looks thus far so promising. The wheat in this lot field looks a little rusty, was not sowed early enough. Hannah is sick to day, two months. My turkeys are not doing well. Sent to mill.

June 1st [1861]

This morning the first news I heard was Mrs. Perrys mule has the colic quick Aunt Dolly give me some Laudnum & camphor. The remedy gave relief but I was troubled unnecessarily & that sense & weight of care did not leave me all day.

I was fretted in getting off to meeting & had to wait there some time & wishing to go to Mrs. Bennets burial I left before meeting closed. She was to have been buried at two o clock & I thought I should not have time to come home & went right from church there found them all waiting & waited with them until nearly sundown for the coffin & finally came home before burial so had my labour for my pains. Boys finishing going over cotton with ploughs first time. Hoes not up. Cotton is very small. Feel very sad & lonely life looks not desirable only as my fatherless child is concerned.

[June] 2d Sunday [1861]

Started to church, got there & some of my neighbors went also but found they had our meeting at the Circle. Lost all of that now by not stopping until meeting closed yesterday. Should like very much to have gone to the Circle to Quarterly meeting. A lost day yesterday was surely when can I learn in Patience to possess my Soul—Slight shower this evening—

[June] 3d [1861]

Commenced cleaning house took up my room carpet. Ploughing pond place corn. Received papers from Charleston.

[June] 4 [1861]

Rain last night putting out potato slips.

[No date, probably late July 1861]

Omitted writing for some time. Crops look small after a dry spell. The rain set in about the first of July. Just as I had got my wheat thrashed out by Mr. Pearson. I had 250 bushels. The crop was injured by the rust. My potato slips finished putting out. We have every reason to be grateful to our Father in Heaven for the timely rains which have continued over a week indeed I may say all of July.

This is a month in the anals of this Southern Confederacy long to be remembered for upon the 21st a battle was fought at Manassas, Va which resulted in a grand victory for our troops. To God be all the praise.

Wiley has been up on a visit left the 27th. I hear nothing from Eliza. 26th commenced work on palings. Worked nine days.

August 1861

2d   Finished chopping out cotton & laid by boys have a holiday until Monday. Charles[39] was taken very sick to night. Sent for Dr. Cheney.

[August] 3d [1861]

Frank & family have gone to Janes wedding.[40] Old Dutch got stung by the bees while I was up to see Charles at Mrs. Perrys & we cut the bridle & he ran home with the buggy but broke nothing at all. Rode around with Thomas this evening. The crop looks finely. Thomas says the corn in the apple orchard is too thick. It was planted four by two. Corn looks well the cotton is bolled & squared well.

[August] 5th [1861]

Martha has commenced weaving. Afraid she will have a bad time with her peice. The hands are all putting up muck for manure. Will continue it all the week.

Nov [1861]

Our beautiful house wherein we praised God has been burned by an incendrairy [sic].

Dec 31st 1861

I had sadly neglected writing when this too has been a momentous year one never to be forgotten in the history of this country. Our once united & prosperous country is in the midst of civil war. Battle after battle has been fought & it still goes on. The enemy has blockaded our coasts so that we can neither export our produce or import our needfuls. Some of the best blood of the country has been spilled. O the horrors of war. The privations the hardships to which our soldiers are exposed. Every thing is very high. Coffee 75 cents & not to be had at that. Salt 18 & 20 dollars a sack & every thing in like proportion bagging 30 cents a yard & rope 25 a pound while cotton is unsalable—

We have only made a tolerable crop of corn it was left too thick & the swamp not properly prepared—

Cotton had done tolerably well. We have only ginned 80 bags. The season injured cotton only the first bolls doing anything—The holidays have passed. Lou Sada & I have been by ourselves most of the time. Thomas has gone to the low country upon business for Mr. Graves. Lou & I dined at Mr. Glasss Christmas day according to invitation. Sada thought the syllabub[41] not good after eating two glasses. We also called at James Harwells & Mrs. Perrys.

Everywhere the war the war is the subject of conversation. O that it might cease & that Peace may again be ours. I have not heard from my parents since April. May God have them in His holy keeping.

Jan 1st 1862

How rapidly has passed another year a year of mercies & blessings to me though of sorrows cares & trials to many. The hands have gone to breaking up the gin house feild preparatory to sowing oats others to fensing &c the women to spinning. My cloth will have to be made at home this year as it cannot be bought. What will the end of Sixty two see. Every thing looks dark & dreary in our country now. The weather all through December has been delightful. I never knew a pleasanter month & more beautiful weather for the holidays. Thomas came home to day. Miss Fannie & Cora Graves[42] brought him down & spent the day with us. I rode up as far as Mrs. Perrys with them to learn when John would be buried. He died in Va in the Hospital.

[January] 4 [1862]

Been to church our Saturday appointment bro Evans made very good remarks on the 7th chapter of Matt. Very few out. Dined at Mrs. Graves he is very ill—Heavy rain in afternoon. Showers with thunder & lightning all night.

[January] 5 [1862]

Still rainy feel disappointed in not being able to attend church to hear Bro Branham preach it is too wet. Thomas went. Lou & I have been at home all day.

[January] 28 [1862]

Sowed peas collard beets.

[January] 30 [1862]

Attended Miss Z. Glasss Wedding. A very pleasant party.

Feb 10 [1862]

Aunt Rhoda has been with me three weeks feel very low spirited to night every thing seems gloomy. The South has met with several defeats lately. We have had a long spell of rainy weather but five pleasant days since the new year came in. Been to Sandtown called upon the bride Mrs. Gay bought some goods at store. Commenced hauling out manure & bedding up burnt field for cotton. Putting the manure in the bed. I think it too early & that the strength of the manure will be gone before the cotton matures but Thomas thinks otherwise. We have nothing comparatively on the farm as yet.

[February] 11th [1862]

The Dillards & Harwells visited me to day.

[February] 14th [1862]

Lou is making a bed quilt but says she is never going to cut up peices of cloth again for such work that only poor white folks make bed quilts that the rich buy blankets! Martha is spooling some of Webb thread. Such work. I never intend to buy any more of Webbs thread!

[February] 22 [1862]

Jefferson Davis The first President of the Southern Confederacy inaugurated to day! Sallie & Henry rode down this evening. Had pound cake. Planted Irish potatoes.

[February] 28 [1862]

Finished breaking up all of the old house & lower swamp that is dry enough. The little boys cutting briars & cleaning off ditches. Lewis making Plough Stock. Says they should last eight years. Our sheep are not doing very well several have died & we have thirteen lambs. Have lost three litters of pigs died in their bed. The sows had cholera last year. We have had a great deal of rain this winter so that we have been unable to do much work upon the farm only such as could be done where it was dry. The boys have been cutting in pine thicket &c. It has been a fast day appointed by Pres Davis in view of our defeats & the gloomy state of the country. Went to Church or prayermeeting with Mrs. Perry up to our church—

March 1st [1862]

The peach trees have not bloomed yet although we have had a mild rainy winter. Every thing is backward. Been bedding out potatoes. They have kept well. Still hauling manure.

[March] 2d [1862]

Been to church this the first Sabbath of March. It is a cloudy cool day. We have all had colds. Bro Evans administered the sacrament.

Recieved letter from Augusta with sale of cotton 8 bales sold for 8 cents expenses 22 dollars.

It thunders & lightnens [sic] to night & will rain probably tomorrow.

[March] 3d [1862]

A rainy morning. Looks sad for farmers. We have as yet very little done on the farm towards a crop. Lou is making gingham dress for herself.

[March] 14 [1862]

Set out one square of plants. Trees blooming.

[March] 26 [1862]

We can have but a few days ploughing done at a time it is so rainy & wet. When we shall get into the swamp is uncertain. Everybody says we must plant little or no cotton. I hardly know what to do about it. O that we could read the future & know when this wicked war would end this month several disasters have befallen our arms in the fall of Henry, Donalson & Nashville[43] but still we hope for the best.

April 1st [1862]

Yesterday & to day have been very pleasant & spring like. We are planting corn. Lou Sada & myself have been spending day at Mr. Graves had a pleasant visit.

[April] 2d [1862]

Hunting turkeys nest all morning. Mrs. Fretwell & Henry came just before dinner in afternoon we rode over to Mr. Rakestraws a heavy rain come up & we got wet.

[April] 3d [1862]

My company left this morning still wet & rainy have finished packing our cotton. Made 49 bags & left over enough for another one but had no rope.

[April] 7 [1862]

Set two turkey hens 17 eggs apeice.

[April] 8 [1862]

Dyeing & sizing thread. Rain again this evening. Will stop work.

[April] 9 [1862]

As no ditching could be done Lewis has gone to whitewashing my rooms how I hate housecleaning.

[April] 10 [1862]

Commenced planting cotton 5 ploughs.

[April] 12 [1862]

Finished. Sallie Annesley came down to night to go to Oxford to Quarterly meeting tomorrow—

[April] 13 [1862]

Hard rain all day.

[April] 14 [1862]

Still raining. When we shall be able to go into the swamps I cannot tell. Wheat looks well.

May 1st [1862]

April has been a very rainy month & one of a great deal of excitement several battles having been fought. We have lost some very important points but have gained at Shiloh in Mississippi. Wiley has spent several days with us the last week & Mrs. Annesley his sister. The rumor is that New Orleans has fallen. If so it will be a great loss to the Confederacy.[44] Upon evil days are we surely fallen. The poor must suffer for everything is so high. Salt 4 pounds to the dollar the same of sugar. Mollasses $1.25 a gallon & many things cannot be had. I got a bolt of long cloth for Lou & paid fifty cents a yard for it.

Been warping a peice of cloth to day. It rained all the morning & the boys went to the pine thicket. Unfortunately Bob stumbled as he was getting out of the way of a tree & broke his leg by the top of the sapling falling upon it. It is broken below the knee in two places so says Dr. Perry who has set it. I feel very sorry. Bob is a good boy—[45]

[May] 2d [1862]

News came this morning. Bob Wright was brought from Yorktown a corpse. Another soldier fallen by sickness not the sword. We are still planting corn. Get very little chance to do anything in swamp.

May 3d 1862

It has been our two days meeting but was not able to go. Been washing wool not willing to leave boy with broken leg but this afternoon been to the funeral of Mr. Wright buried with military honours. Sadai was very much frightened at the firing of the guns. Old Uncle Allen Turner staid all night with us. Poor Sadai does not like Uncle Allen very well for last Sabbath at church after the preacher had got through Mr. Turner gave out the hymn & after singing instead of saying prayer as usual he told them to sit down while he took a text & preached another sermon. Sadai turned & knelt as usual & did not discover her mistake but when she did she was so mortified she burst into tears & I had to send her out. She thinks everybody laughed at her.

[May] 6th [1862]

Been ploughing up pine thicket & planting corn where I had cotton. It is so unlikely that I shall have a market for cotton it is best to put it in corn. I dislike doing it however. Have had setting out of potatoes three times.

[May] 8 [1862]

Ploughed with sweeps the lot feild this evening the cotton looks badly. The wheat has a mold or rust upon the blade caused by the rains which will injure it very much I think. I had Dutch hitched to go strawberrying with Sada but concluded they were not ripe enough so Lou & I rode up to Mrs. Perrys. When we returned thought I would ride down & look at the wheat. Calling Sada who I saw down the road to ride she got up behind the buggy standing. I popped the whip at the horse. He jumped & she fell backward on the ground & could not at first get up. I was very much alarmed & springing from the buggy ran to her fearing that her back was broken & my child ruined for life but Thanks to the Good One her bones were sound

& she was stunned only. She moaned & cried a good deal & looked very pale but soon got over it.

What shall I render unto Thee O my Father for all Thy mercies & benefits?

[May] 9th [1862]

My neighbor's sons the Glasss started for camp this morning. It was a sorrowful parting. Dr. Perry called to see Lou who is quite unwell.

June 3d 1862

The last day of May & the first of June was a most bloody battle near Richmond on the Chickahominy fought hundreds were killed on both sides. The Federals retreated. Since then nothing has been done. Chatanooga & Charleston are both seriously threatened. What the End will be the All Wise One only knows. The Conscription[46] has robbed almost every household in coming from the Factory yesterday where I had been to make purchases it was sad to see the homesteads left with only the sad & lonely wife & mother to look after its interests & yet if their temporal necessities could be supplied it would not be so sad but to think of the hundreds & thousands that cannot obtain that which is absolutely needful. And it is not the poor alone. I have hundreds of dollars in my pocket book & yet I cannot buy a yard of calico to make my Sadai a sunbonnet it cannot be had. For weeks she has been wearing a bunch of rags for her bonnet is nothing else. Yesterday however Aunt Polly Davis gave me a peice of a dress of hers which I shall gladly make up to day. Salt is from forty to fifty cents a pound sugar the same coffee a dollar & not to be had. Whole shoes, flannels &c., spices, & a great many other things are among the things money cannot buy in this Confederacy! How little did we as a Nation appreciate the blessings of Peace.

We are cutting wheat to day the crop with all our other misfortunes has proved a failure. The mold or rust took it early in the season consequent upon a warm & rainy winter & the yeild through all this country will be scarcely nothing at all. With a good Season I should net 275 or 300 bushels but now not more than forty five. We are still planting corn & it is to be hoped that Providence will smile upon our effort & that we shall make plenty of that grain which is both bread & meat to us—

[June] 14 [1862]

Threshing out Wheat. Grain is so small it runs through the Thresher. We have plenty of vegetables.

[June] 17th [1862]

Lou who has been at the Factory[47] for a week or more has returned she looks feeble & is no better than when she left home I think. I sold 12 bags of cotton to F. Davis & Co. for which I got 1½ cts. per pound.

[June] 27th [1862]

A battle has commenced near Richmond which will probably decide the fate of that city & how many on both sides will see their last of earth.

[June] 28th [1862]

Quarterly meeting commenced this morning at our church. I sent for Aunt Rhoda to come & go with me as she has no way for going & she enjoys meeting so much. Mr. Knowls preached Mr. Yarbrough exhorted he is suffering from cancer on the face.

[June] 29 [1862]

Mr. Yarbrough could not preach much to my disappointment. A telegram from his sons who are at Richmond says the Battle is still raging. The victory is on the side of the Confederates through great loss of life & limb. The blessing of God is on our arms & may His Spirit incline all Hearts to Peace—

July 1st [1862]

If I had sowed my cotton I could have got 15 cents for it at the gate one week from that week & 18 three weeks after.

July 4th [1862]

Many a time have I seen this day ushered in by the ringing of bells & the booming of cannon. Manifestations of a peoples joy in their liberty their independence their freedom from tyranny. But how changed is all now. Warring one with the other. Mourning & lamentation in every household. It is a very cold day for the week past fires morning & evening have been very pleasant. Miss Johnson & Gresham came down to see Lou. So did Mrs. Perry & Clarridan Dr. Perry & wife. She has had chills every day this week. I am preparing to leave home with her next week for the Chalybate Springs.[48] We have had corn to buy.

[July] 8th [1862]

Left home with Lou. Consulted Dr. Powell of Atlanta in regard to her health. Met Wiley T. who prefered to go with us. On the cars were many wounded soldiers returning to their homes. Sada was sorry for them & carried them some pears to eat—Stopped at Atlanta House all night. A very warm & sleepless night I passed.

[July] 9th [1862]

Took the cars at six for Barnesville.[49] Thence Hack to the Chalybate. A tiresome & fatiguing ride of 22 miles. It was after much trouble we obtained a room or cabin.

July 15th 1862

Wiley & myself left the Springs this evening at ½ 4 leaving Lou at Mr. Cheneys. The Hack was out of order & every few moments the gentlemen would have to get out & lift the coach into its place the coupling pin being broken. We had to get out & walk some of the hills after dark. Wiley took the lines & drove. Got into Thomaston after ten. Wearied enough to go to bed without supper.

[July] 16th [1862]

Took the cars to Barnesville. Parted with Wiley from there. I went to Sister Leaks found her very feeble just recovering from sickness her youngest son James came home sick from the Army the day before he was in the [battle] of Tuesday July 1st under "Stonewall" Jackson. Mrs. Leak reminds me very much of Mr. Burge.

[July] 21st [1862]

Left Mr. Rivers a son in law of Mrs. Leak for home. Elbert Leving come after me. Called at young Manson Glasss who is sick with Hemmorage of lungs. Got to Mr. Dick Fretwells where I staid all night.

[July] 22d [1862]

Arrived safely home this morning home what sweeter word to the wearied traveller is there than that. Sada is not well found all well & glad to see me crop looks well but it is needing rain badly.

[July] 23rd [1862]

A very hot day. Sada quite unwell fatigue of journey & eating too much honey I reckon. Read letter from Wiley. Wants me to help him get a substitute for the War.

[July] 31st [1862]

Mrs. Cook & Mrs. Alfred Shaw from Madison came to day & with them a heavy shower of rain which is greatly needed.

August 5 [1862]

My friends from M left. I took them to "Circle." Spinning wool two women.

[August] 9 [1862]

Making Cider. One of Mrs. Leaks sons sick from Richmond came to day. Dr. William Leak—

[August] 14th [1862]

Commenced shearing sheep. Punished John [50] for stealing.

August 16th [1862]

Went up to see Capt Annesley & wife this evening. Mr. Leak still with us. Rcvd letter from Lou. Says she is still improving.

Sept 29th [1862]

I am forty five years old to day! Little did I imagine when twenty four that I should live so many years & that I should be a widow for the second time & situated as I am. But Thanks unto God who has kept preserved & been with me all my life long & now that I am going down the shady side of life I trust He will still be with & sustain me whether in prosperity or adversity.

Yesterday Nephew Thomas Sada & I went to Uncle Len Fretwells in Walton Co. Got there just as sundown. Aunt Polly had been boiling syrup from the Sorgho. It was very nice. This morning drove into Monroe done some shopping & then home.

This month the 17th & 18 has been fought the bloodiest battles of the war.[51] My heart sickens when I think of it & the affliction it has brought upon thousands & thousands of our countrymen. Even our own county has been greatly afflicted in the death of Coleman Brown, Lamar, Simes & others.

Oct 9h [1862]

Lou came home from the Springs & La Grange to day. She looks very much better. Eliza came with her after an absence of four years nearly! Tom went over to the depot for them in the carriage & they got home about midnight.

Dec 28h [1862]

Sunday Rev G W Yarbrough preached Manson P Glass' funeral to day at Sandtown. He died ten days ago since when his youngest child had died & been buried. Died Christmas day. They are greatly distressed—We have all been down to meeting to day. There was quite a crowd out. Had a fine turkey for dinner it is the last one Tom will carve for me for a long time I fear. G W Yarbrough spent night with us. Right merry with the girls.

[December] 29 [1862]

Thomas has left me to day for Mr. Graves plantation. right sorry to have him go. He thinks I can get along very well by myself.

March 1st 1863

This is the first day that I have been without company since Oct 9th first Eliza then Aunt Rhoda Julie Adams then Mrs. Davis & three children & servant. We have not got the pine field in yet & but very little land broken up for corn. The manure is not hauled out nor cotton land bedded. This backwardness is owing to the season which has been very unpleasant. Bedding out yams. Done no work in garden scarcely.

[March] 13 [1863]

Commenced planting corn the old pine field next to Mr. Glasss. Went to meeting no one there or the preacher was not owing to the waters being so high. My garden looks badly the rabbits have eat down all of my peas.

April 13th [1863]

At last they have got the pine field back of the old house ready to plant it has been on hand nearly two years. They commenced planting cotton there to day. Had 207 pounds of sugar brought home on Saturday, the price one dollar a pound. Lou is poorly coughs a great deal. Miss House is weaving a piece of cloth for me.

[April] 22d [1863]

Part of the ploughs got through the pine field & went to breaking up the lower swamp. The other hands are replanting corn.

[April] 25 [1863]

Got through planting cotton. We broke the second time & then bedded & the planters followed directly it has taken us two weeks. Finished the lower swamp—& are breaking up potato patch.

[April] 27th [1863]

Putting out potato slips. A dog came into the house last night & took a whole Ham out of the dish & eat it nearly up. I had him killed this morning. Prince my dog was found dead yesterday near Mrs. Perrys. A fine rain this morning. Commenced on the boys pants.

May 21st [1863]

Lou is so poorly I have sent to Rebecca [52] to come to see her! She came & brought her little girls. I was so glad to have her come again. Sally Anesley came down also with Sarah & Rachel who had been up there strawberrying. It is quite warm now. Crops are very backward.

June 26th 1863

Lou is 19 years old to day the first birthday she has lain in bed all day. She has a great deal to live for & I sincerely pray that health may be given her to enjoy it. We have had rain nearly every day this month the swamps are nearly ruined with water & the grass is nearly as high as the corn. We are ready to commence laying bye. Cut wheat the 11th but not dry yet— Aunt Rhoda came today—

[June] 27 [1863]

Rebecca & Eliza came. Lou is very poorly lying in bed all of the time nearly. Dr. Cody [53] has ordered Cod liver Oil.

[June] 28th [1863]

A rainy unpleasant morning but towards noon it cleared away. Rebecca left this morning. E staid. Mr. Anderson Rakestraw & sister Mary rode down & spent a couple of hours. Mrs. Laura Perry & others in Lou's room annoyed her considerably by talking. Just as I was sitting down to supper Sally Ansly & Henry Graves came in to spend the night. He feels very much troubled about Lou.

[June] 29th [1863]

Lou is no better but feels troubled about her spiritual condition. O that she might believe in Jesus & be saved. She will probably never recover her health. Her constitution has contained the seeds of consumption ever since she left Macon College in the spring of sixty one. She was to have been married last Oct. The war came. The one dear to her was among the first to leave. She bore it well & for many months letters came regularly but as is often the case they ceased for awhile then came again torturing her with uncertainty & forcing into destructive action those seeds which had it not been for that love that passion, might have lain dormant for years. How rejoiced how happy she was in anticipation of seeing him last April how cruelly disappointed.

[June] 30 [1863]
Mrs. Fannie Dickens, a neice of Mr. Burges from Miss. & two servants arrived to day refugees from home by this cruel war—
I do not think Lou any better she does not sit up any of the time now.

July 4th 1863
Sally Ansley came down to day bringing Sadai who has been up to Mrs. Graves this week. She will spend some time. Lou has been quite ill & I feared that she was going to die speedily.

[July] 5th [1863]
Rev A Turner called & talked very plainly with her & prayed for her. She feels her situation very sensibly. We have none of us been to meeting to day—

[July] 6th [1863]
I sent for Uncle Billy Parks to come & see Lou he came & spent the morning he thinks her a true penitent. It has been a rainy day. Uncle Turner dined with us & bro Parks—

[July] 7th [1863]
Wiley T Burge came from Charleston this evening brought some peaches & watermelons for Lou—

[July] 9th [1863]

Fletcher Davis & wife spent day with us. Mrs. Pitts & Robinson [54] called. We have house full of company all of the time.

[July] 12th [1863]

Colonel Dickens & Fanny Ogleby from Miss arrived. Henry Graves Sally A Mrs. House & daughter Wiley & some others here. Lou is very patient & talks to those she loves a good deal—

[July] 13th [1863]

Colonel D & Fanny left. Wiley left yesterday.

[July] 16 & 17th [1863]

Got out wheat. Made 233 bushels.

August 7th [1863]

Colonel Dickens came after Fannie & they have left to day. I shall miss her. She is a sweet woman.

[August] 8 [1863]

Eliza Sada & Rachel have gone to Rebeccas. Will be at home on Monday. Lou & I are all alone—

Sept 11th [1863]

I have been very sick with Cholera Morbus today vomiting all night. Eliza has gone to her sisters. Miss Libby [55] is with me. Jack Harwell & wife called this evening. Lou seems to be taking the disease.

[September] 13th [1863]

Lou has the bloody dysentery very badly. I sent for Dr. Cody yesterday. He says she cannot live long & he can do nothing for her. Mrs. Graves & Glass & Perry all here this evening. Sent for Dr. Cheney.

Dolly Sumner Lunt Burge (1817–1891) in a satin mourning dress, shortly after the death of Thomas Burge (1806–1858). She holds his daguerreotype.

Dolly Burge, probably about 1864. Her dress is simple, with a long shoulder line, indicative of the 1850s and early 1860s. Her cap, probably made of lace and ribbon, signifies maturity and marriage or widowhood.

Dolly Burge Parks, about 1885. Her dress, with its shorter shoulder lengths and velvet ribbon trim, probably dates to the mid- to late-1880s.

William Webb Lunt
(1788–1863), Dolly's
father, about 1855. He
wears a double-
breasted frock coat and
holds a cane, probably
made of bamboo.

Priscilla Purrington
Lunt (1795–1863),
Dolly's stepmother,
about 1855. She wears
soft leather gloves
and a pleated skirt,
probably over several
petticoats.

Thomas Burge and his daughter, Sadai (1855–1892), about 1858. Probably, this was taken as a keepsake when Thomas was quite ill. He wears a gentleman's suit and, possibly, a Phi Beta Kappa key. In typical fashion, Sadai is dressed like a lady in an off-the-shoulder dress.

Sadai Burge and her slave nurse, Rachel (1846–1872), about 1858. Rachel wears a well-made cotton dress with a printed belt and a head wrap and apron, marking her as a house servant. Sadai wears an ornamental hat and a cape, known as a tippet. She holds a small reticule, or purse.

Louisiana Burge (1844–1863), about 1860. Her dress is simple and her expression belies her determined personality.

Sadai Burge Gray, about 1875, probably upon her engagement or marriage. She wears a snood (an open-weave hairnet) behind her head covering, which signifies marriage.

Reverend John Davis Gray (1852–1887), Sadai's husband, probably upon his engagement or marriage in 1875. He wears a casual, youthful collar and tie.

Sadai Burge Gray, about 1880. She wears a tailored adaptation of a gentleman's coat. Her uncovered hair signifies youth.

Reverend William J. Parks
(1799–1873), about 1870. He
appears relaxed and informal, with
an open vest, disheveled coat, and
no tie.

Reverend William J. Parks's home in Oxford, now the President's Home at
Oxford and the residence of the dean of Oxford College.

Lydia Glass Burge
(c. 1823–after 1920), about
1890. She wears a man's coat
and shirt collar.

Lydia Glass Burge, about 1910. She wears a shawl with some ornament, a gathered
mob cap, a well-worn work apron, and possibly slippers. Lydia supposedly lived to
be over one hundred years old.

George and Sidney Gunn (1854–after 1920), Lydia's son-in-law and daughter, about 1920. This photograph reveals the Gunns' ambiguous place as African American caretakers of a southern tenant farm and former plantation. They sit upright and confidently, albeit on the porch stoop. George wears a formal coat with his work pants and shoes. Sidney wears a simple work dress and a clean, pressed apron. The broom beside her reminds viewers of her domestic responsibilities, and a white woman looks down on them from a chair on the porch.

The Burge home, about 1913, where Dolly lived from 1850 to 1867 and 1875 until near the time of her death.

The Burge home, about 1916. The boy in knickers probably is Merritt Dutton Morehouse (1905–1991), Sadai's grandson. In 1918, Sadai's daughter, Dorothy Gray Bolton, moved this house across the street to land she owned.

In 1920, Ida Gray Morehouse (Sadai's daughter) and her architect husband, Merritt Josiah Morehouse, replaced the original house with this large home modeled after a James River Plantation. At this writing this is the site of Burge Plantation, a private club and entertainment facility owned and operated by Sadai's great-grandson, Alexander "Sandy" Gray Morehouse, and his wife, Betsy.

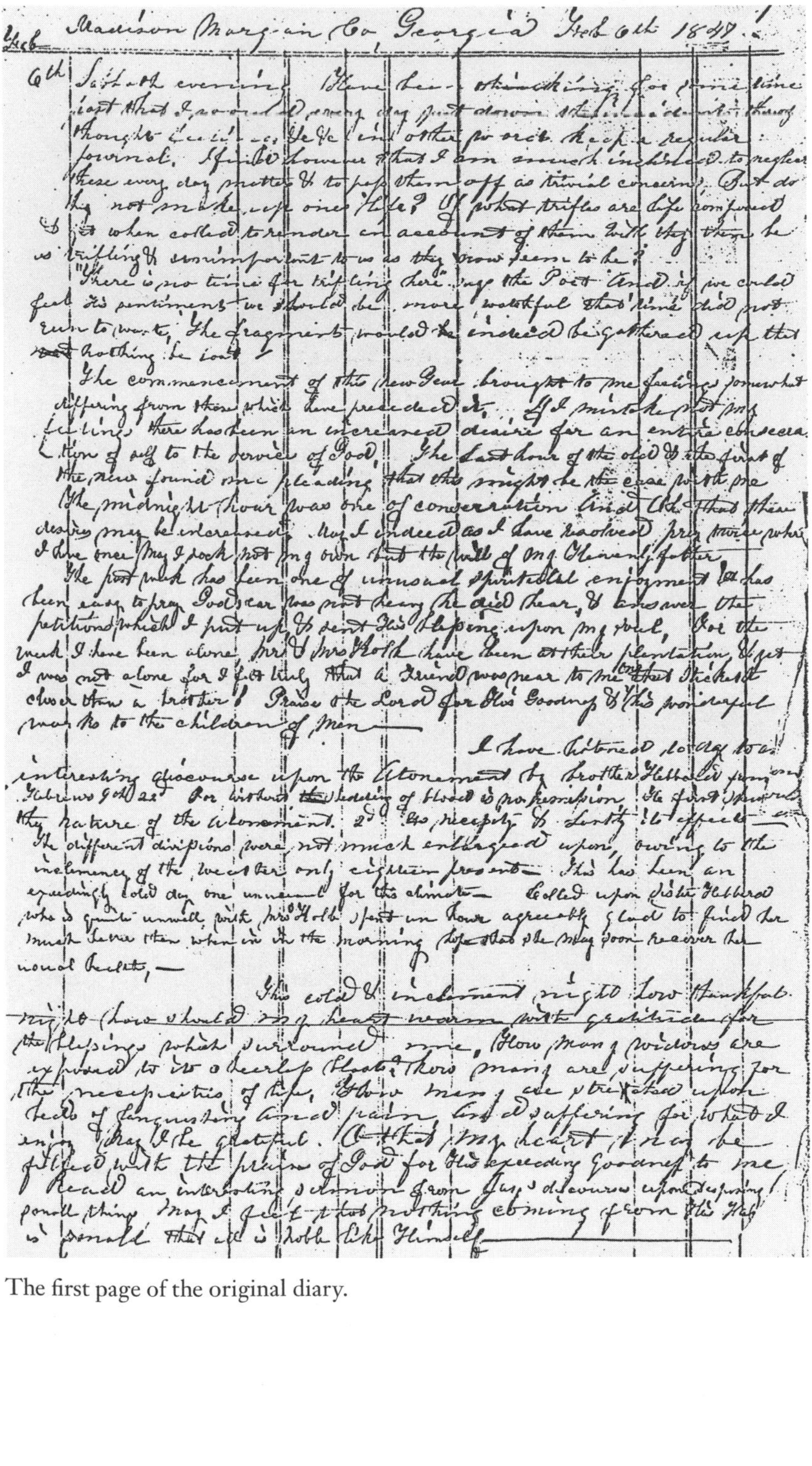

Feb Madison Morgan Co Georgia Feb 6th 1848.

6th Sabbath evening I have been thinking for some time past that I would every day put down such incidents & thoughts [illegible] &c &c in other words keep a regular journal. I find however that I am much inclined to neglect these every day matters & to pass them off as trivial concerns, But do they not make up ones life? Of what trifles are life composed & yet when called to render an account of them will they then be as trifling & unimportant to us as they now seem to be?

"There is no time for trifling here" says the Poet And if we could feel his sentiments we should be more watchful that time did not run to waste, The fragments would be indeed be gathered up that nothing be lost.

The commencement of the New Year brought to me feelings somewhat differing from those which have preceded it. If I mistake not my feelings there has been an increased desire for an entire consecration of self to the service of God. The last hour of the old & the first of the new found me pleading that this might be the case with me The midnight hour was one of consecration And Oh that these desires may be increased. May I indeed as I have resolved pray twice where I have once May I seek not my own but the will of my Heavenly father

The past week has been one of unusual spiritual enjoyment It has been easy to pray God's ear was not heavy He did hear, & answer the petitions which I put up, & sent His blessing upon my soul, For the week I have been alone Mr & Mrs Kolb have been at their plantation, & yet I was not alone for I felt truly that a Friend was near to me one that sticketh closer than a brother! Praise the Lord for His Goodness & His wonderful works to the children of men

I have listened to day to an interesting discourse upon the Atonement by brother Hubbard from Hebrews 9th 22d For without the shedding of blood is no remission. He first showed the nature of the Atonement. 2d Its necessity & lastly its effects — the different divisions were not much enlarged upon, owing to the inclemency of the weather only eighteen present — This has been an exceedingly cold day one unusual for this climate — Called upon sister Hubbard who is quite unwell, with Mrs Kolb spent an hour agreeably glad to find her much better than when in in the morning hope that she may soon recover her usual health, —

This cold & inclement night how thankful night how should my heart warm with gratitude for the blessings which surround me, How many widows are exposed to its cheerless blasts, how many are suffering for the necessities of life, How many are stretched upon beds of languishing and pain, & suffering for what I enjoy May I be grateful. O that my heart may be filled with the praise of God for His exceeding Goodness to me

Read an interesting sermon from Jay's discourse upon despising small things May I feel that nothing coming from the Holy is small that all is noble like Himself

The first page of the original diary.

Oct 1st 1863

We had a very heavy wind & rain last night. Have been sitting up with Lou. I went into the other rooms & put down the windows & fastened blinds.

[October] 2d [1863]

Miss Libby Dutton has been with us all the week. Lou is so very sick do not like to be alone with her—She sat up part of the night. I have not been in bed all night without getting up since the first of June. The poor child will not need attention much longer—

[October] 3d [1863]

I was up with Lou most of the night & moved her early this morning into the bed in which I usually slept. She was very faint & sick. Her days are nearly over. She has suffered all day more than usual with sick stomach. Wiley T came this morning brought oranges & lemons. Her mouth & throat are extremely sore. She swallows nothing but a little milk & water. O what a sick time she had this morning before I moved her into the other bed. Deathly sick & could throw so little from her stomach—a dark green matter her bowels have never been well, but worse for a few days as opiates do not check them. Rebecca came tonight. Will sit up part of the night—

[October] 4th [1863]

The last Sunday of Lou's life was spent in suffering & pain but I trust ready for the exchange. Slept most of the day. Towards night she became a little delirious. Thought something was after her & calling upon me to save her. Sent for Miss Matilda to sit up. She wanted water constantly through the night had a great deal of fever. I got up at two o clock & sat with her & waited upon her. She seemed to be easier after day.

[October] 5th [1863]

Mrs. Lee left in the evening. I sent for Mrs. Jack Harwell. Aunt Rhoda came. Another restless night. Was up nearly all night. Her constant cry was for Water.

[October] 6th Tuesday Morning [1863]

Lou grows weaker & weaker her bowels are constantly running off. At ten o clock I saw that she could live but a short time. She panted for breath. Miss Libby & Miss Susa Strong came down. She was calm & not suffering much. I feared she would die without saying anything of her hopes & I asked her of them. She said she was going home & could put her hands quietly into Death as she could into mine for His Rod & His staff they comforted her.

Directly after dinner I thought her time was come but she revived & hearing some one cry says "Stop." She said she wanted none that loved her to cry for her. Upon asking her for messages for friends she says tell them I shall watch for them up yonder & wait for others in Heaven. Directly after supper she coughed & strangled & struggled for breath. O it was hard distressing. She had asked me at four o clock if I thought she could live untill six. O she said it will be so long. She often said Father if it be possible let this cup pass from me. Nevertheless not my will but thine be done. Though I walk through the valley & shadow of Death I will fear no evil for His rod & staff they comfort me. Her sufferings in dying were severe no place for rest. The pillows could not be placed to ease her.

Towards the last she begged us to pray for her release. Ma are you praying? Sister are you praying? Miss Libby read the 14th of John after which I tried to pray. Had she not asked me I could not have done it. But all along I had granted all of her requests & should I fail now—After prayer they sang Jesus lover of my Soul. Before they got through singing she asked to be turned over & died without further struggle. I rejoiced that her soul was delivered that her sufferings were over that she had gone home to God. Gone where her father & mother waited for her gone to praise God forever. I bless His Holy Name for giving her space & time to repent. Her funeral was preached by Rev W J Parks after which we laid her beside her father in the graveyard to rest forever.

Nov 5th [1863]

Yesterday I went to Major Lees with Eliza & Sadai. The first time I have visited Rebecca, had a pleasant visit. Came home just at dark found Rev Richard Harwell & sister here. He has taken his sisters away from their home in Walker County as it is the seat of war now. The lines of battle were formed right by their house & cannon planted in their yard.

[November] 6 [1863]

I sent Cousin Dick to the depot & kept the girls with me. A pleasant day. Aunt Rhoda came over & staid the day. I warped a piece of cloth & before getting done Mrs. Glass & Shug came.

Picking cotton over to the old place the new pine field.

[November] 7th [1863]

On this day morning I started to Sandtown to see Dr. Perry who is very sick took Sadai with me. When we got opposite Mr. Glasss turnip patch a Negro boy threw a basket of leaves over the fence which frightened the mare. I was driving & she commenced running. The dogs took after us & she became more frightened. I held her. Sadai said "Ma my bonnet is off— Never mind Sadai said I the horse is running away hold on." I guided her safely around the corner but the velocity with which we turned threw the buggy over & we both were thrown out. We both jumped up. I thought neither of us was hurt. Sadai says Ma see our buggy" which had been turned loose from the horse.

It seems to me I never felt so grateful to God as then that our lives & limbs were spared. Mrs. Glass & family were soon there & I began to feel my bruises & with difficulty walked to the house. They soon had the carriage ready to send me home & when I got here I had to be sat in a chair & brought to the house. I sent for Dr. Cheney. He after examination said no limbs were broken. I was confined to my bed nearly a week the next to my chair after which I began to get about.

[November] 30 [1863]

Killed 21 hogs very cold. Very busy with my sewing have got behind. Martha was laid up two months in the spring. Hannah since Sept. & then so much company.

Dec 17th [1863]

Finished picking cotton.

[December] 19 [1863]

Went to town to get order from court for the division of the negroes of the estate. Very cold. Eliza & Susan Harwell went with me had to go by Dolneys bridge. Paid tax 548 dollars.

[December] 20 [1863]

Went to Mr. Sam Meeks funeral. Mules would not cross pole bridge took them out & pushed carriage over. Got home & found George Parks wife here feel troubled & uneasy about the division. Oh what a break does death make when it takes the head of a family.

Dec 22d [1863]

The court appointed Mr. Glass, Sims, Perry, Jones Beeland, James Robinson, & Weston Pitts, as distributors & they came this morning & after valuing the negroes at 75 thousand dollars Confederate money proceeded to divide according to the will—I am very well satisfied with the division & hope others will be. Thus has the delegated power which Mr. Burge gave me passed out of my hands. I have tried to do as he would have had me do as I think he would have done. O my husband let thy spirit still guard & watch over us that remain. I hope yet to meet thee to meet in Haven [*sic*]. I have as thou badest me put my trust in God & I hope all things will yet work out right.[56]

Dec 25th [1863]

Christmas morning unlike many of its predecessors was not ushered in with shouts & crackers & fun but all seemed sad. No stockings were filled by Santa Claus. The servants dislike to leave their homes for those they know nothing of. Self Eliza & Sada had an invitation to dine at Mr. Graves. Eliza would not go. Just before starting had a note from Major Lee which troubled me exceedingly about Lou's servants. Met at Mr. Graves Rev W J Parks Mrs. L. Q. Lamar[57] Miss Johnson & the family pleasant visit. Dear Brother Graves is very feeble. Will he be with us at another Christmas? I fear not—

Miss Johnson came home with me—

[December] 28 [1863]

Took Miss Johnson up to Mr. Graves found Wiley T Burge there. As we were on our way to Major Lees, we could not take him in. Went on & found Rebecca very poorly. Everything seems pleasant & agreeable. Took out Lous servants & hired those that were to be hired out.

[December] 29 [1863]

Started home this morning had a settlement with Eliza in regard to her expenses. Went by Mr. Graves & got Wiley found all well at home—The Harwells & Mr. Ward are still here. Mr. Glass is very sick I learn & a grandchild of Mrs. Perrys shot himself badly yesterday. Wiley went back. James Harwell & wife called in evening. Rained hard all day & last night.

CHAPTER FOUR

In Sherman's Path

January 1st 1864

A new year is ushered in but peace comes not with it. A bloody war is still decimating our nation & thousands of hearts are to day bleeding over the loss of loved ones. Scarcely a family in the land but has given some of its members to their country. Terrible terrible indeed is war. O that its ravages may soon be stopped. Will another year find us amid carnage & bloodshed. Shall we be a nation? Or shall we be annihilated? The prices of everything are very high corn 7 dollars a bushel calico 10 dollar a yard salt 60 dollars a hundred cotton from 60 to 80 cents a pound everything in like ratio. It has cleared off very cold. Went to see Judge Glass. Was too sick to see company. Went from there to Mrs. Perry to see her grandchild. Found him better came home met Mr. Thompson who wants me to send him &

family to the Circle in the morning. Hate to do it but must do as I would be done by. Sent to mill to day. Boy came home & could get no grinding done. No flour nor meal in the house.

[January] 2d [1864]

Sent to Mr. Stanton. All the other mills are washed away. Got both wheat & corn ground—Coldest day I have ever known in Georgia I think.

[January] 3d [1864]

Sabbath the first in sixty four. I am at home by myself. Rebecca Harwell Eliza & Sadai have gone to church to Carmel after which they go to Jack Harwells to dine. I want this year to serve God & be a better woman than I have ever been. His Mercies are abundant towards me & mine. May I praise & love Him all the days of my life.

Feb 10th [1864]

Little did I think while writing the above that away in Maine my native state friends & relatives were laying in the grave my father & stepmother. By a letter received through "flag of truce" I learn they both died the last day of the old year. Of what disease I know not. Oh this cruel war that has deprived me of being with them & ministering to their wants. I have felt very solemn all day. The generation between me & the grave has passed away. I step into my parents place & will soon follow them to the grave. And my Sadai will stand in my place. Thus one generation cometh & passeth away & another followeth.

[February] 13 [1864]

Ploughing old house swamp.

Feb 15 [1864]

Took Sadai down to Sandtown & entered her as a scholar into Mr. Mixons school.[1] Mr. Ward is attending to my business. We are fencing, it has been a very severe winter. Some of the hands are breaking up for peas. Hannah is very sick.

[February] 21st [1864]

I was summoned early this Sabbath morning to go to Hannah who was dying. I sat by her several hours. She is ready & willing to go. She bade us all farewell & dropped asleep in Jesus at a few minutes after ten o clock. Thus one after another of our family depart for the Kingdom. Mr. Burge had the greatest confidence in Hannahs piety & I trust they have met ere this in the Spirit land.[2]

[February] 22d [1864]

About two o clock this evening we buried Hannah by the side of her father & son William who died seven years ago. Trimmed up orchard. Fanny Kennon & boy came to buy a horse.

[February] 25th [1864]

Went out to Rebeccas with Rebecca Harwell. Had a pleasant visit.

[February] 26th [1864]

When we returned from our visit found Henry Harwell their brother here he is going to Dalton hoping to get his mother from out of the enemies [sic] lines.

Ploughing in the lower swamp—fire got out burnt some fencing.

[February] 28 [1864]

Clinton Lee[3] came to day to go to school to Sandtown with Saydee.

March 7th [1864]

Commenced planting corn the pine field & the old house place. Very cold yet it is time to commence.

[March] 14th [1864]

Finished planting those fields. Have been to town to day & sold three bales of cotton to fund money for my taxes. This year got 75 cents per pound.

[March] 15 [1864]

Sent off cotton & three hundred pounds of meat 5 pounds of wool five bushels of oats for my thithes [*sic*].

March 19th 1864

Been down to lower swamp on old Dutch to see what they are doing there. Rebuilding burnt fence the swamp needs more ditching. It would make an excellent meadow if only had seed to seed it down.

[March] 20 [1864]

Intended taking the children to church or to Sabbath school this morning but it was showery so I did not. Rebecca Harwell & Ward have gone to Mr. Parks. I find upon referring back to ten years ago to day that there is a great change in our family & circumstances. That day we spent at Widow Perrys mother Carrie & self while father & Mr. Burge went to the Circle. There they received a telegram that Orrington was on his way to Georgia & would be in Covington that night. Now father mother Mr. Burge & Lou are in another world our family divided & scattered. What changes a few years make & O what changes this war has made.

[March] 22 [1864]

A very hard rain yesterday. This morning it thundered & lightened. Afterwards it hailed & then snowed until the ground was covered. It looked very singular to see the trees all in bloom & icicles hanging from them. I fear that we shall have no fruit this year.

[March] 23d [1864]

A very cold morning ice aplenty but a very gloomy one for farmers.

[March] 25 [1864]

I took Clinton Lee & Saydee & went up to Major Lees.

April 3d [1864]

I have no plants in the garden. My potatoes have not sprouted & everything looks like January instead of April. We have no corn up though it has been planted a month.

[April] 10 [1864]

Mr. Mixon & family down with smallpox. School dismissed.

May 5th [1864]

Mr. Ward from Walker County a refugee who has been attending to my business & Miss Rebecca Harwell a second cousin of my husbands also a refugee were married here this evening. Dr. Cheney performing the ceremony. I sent for Saydee to come from School. She was very much surprised & overjoyed to be at a wedding. Nobody present but her cousin Amanda & her sister. All but Saydee dressed in homespun.

June 15th 1864

Commenced cutting wheat. Showery weather. Went up to Mr. Graves in my carriage to call upon Mrs. Paine from Miss. Mrs. Perry & Ezzard went with me. Miss Susan fixing to go to Alabama.

[June] 24 [1864]

Finished cutting wheat made three hundred & some odd bushels. Gave the servants a supper which they enjoyed hugely.

July 9 & 10 [1864]

Quarterly meeting at Mt Pleasant. Very pleasant exercises not many out. Feel very little of the life & power of religion everything apparently succumbs to the war.

[July] 20 [1865]

Went to Mr. Graves again to see Sally Ansley & her husband poor fellow he was wounded at the battle of Missionary ridge & has never recovered the use of his limb. LQC Lamar & wife with their family & Mrs. Paine were also there. So Henry poor fellow he looks sad.

[July] 22d [1864]

A never to be forgotten day. We have heard the loud booming of the cannon all day nearly. I intended to have gone to the burial of Thomas Harwell a son of James whose death I witnessed yesterday & a sad one it was. He was perfectly delirious. His last words being Whoa Whoa. Mr. Ward & Rebecca went over to the old ladies to see him buried. They had but just gone when Rev A Turner wife & daughter drove up with their waggons desiring to rest awhile. They went into the L & laid down I following them wishing to enjoy their company. Eliza was just leaving for Major Lees Elbert driving her. I saw the servants running to the palings & I walked to the door when such such a stampede I never witnessed before. Here came Eliza back the road full of carriages wagons men on horseback all riding at full speed. Judge Floyd stopped saying Mrs. Burge the Yankees are coming they have got my family & here is all I have upon earth. "Hide your mules & carriages & whatever valuables you have. Sadai says Oh Ma what shall we do. Never mind Sadai they won't hurt you & you must help me hide my things. I went to the smoke house & divided out the meat to the servants & bid them hide it. Julia took a jar of lard & buried it. In the meantime Sadai was taking down & picking up our clothes which she was giving to the servants to hide in their cabins. Silk dresses challis muslins & merinos linens & hoseiry [sic] all found their way into the chests of the women & under their beds. China Silver was all laid away under ground & Sadai bid Mary to hide a bit of soap under some bricks that Ma might have a little left. Then she came to me with part of a loaf of bread asking if she had not better put it in her pocket that we might have something to eat that night. And verily we had cause to fear that we might be homeless for on every side we could see smoke arising from burning buildings & bridges—Major Annesley Wife & Sister with their two little ones & servants came from Mr. Graves here thinking to get on to Eatonton[4] but he was so wearied that he stopped with me that night. I was so glad to have them. I shall sleep none to night. The woods are full of refugees—[5]

[July] 23 [1864]

This morning I have been getting off Mr. Annesley & family Eliza Mr. & Mrs. Ward to Eatonton. Major Annesley had a bed in the little wagon Mid driving him. He was wounded in the hip at Missionary Ridge & has not recovered. I am left all alone in my home with Sadai & have had a lonesome day of it. Have seen nothing of the Raiders though they burnt the buildings around the Depot at the "Circle" this morning. I have sat in the porch all of the day nearly & hailed everyone that passed for news. Just as the sun set here came Major Ansley family & Eliza. They heard of the enemy all about there & concluded they were as safe here as any where. Rebecca & Mr. Ward went to James Harwells. Just before bedtime John our boy came from Covington with word that the Yankees had left. Wheelers men were in Covington & going in pursuit. Well we slept sweetly & felt safe—

[July] 24 Sunday [1864]

No church. Our preachers horse stolen by the Yankees. Sally & I went up to Mr. Graves to see how they all fared found they had not been molested nor lost neither negroes or mules. Mr. Hinton[6] lost several & fifteen head of horses. We on our return got badly frightened by Old Dutchs kicking & hearing that the enemy was at Sandtown—Found everything safe when we got home. This raid is headed by Guerrard[7] & is for the purpose of destroying our railroads. They cruelly shot a George Daniel & a Mr. Jones of Covington: destroyed a great deal of private property & took many citizens prisoners.

[July] 25, 26, & 27 [1864]

The Major & family still with me. We have got over our fright & have settled down quietly & occasionally bringing to light the things we need. Sally will leave for Mr. Graves in the morning. Sent Rev W H Potter to Madison. Eliza went to her sisters.

[July] 28th [1864]

I rose early & had the boys to plough the turnip patch their mules were all in there & we were just rising from breakfast when Ben Glass rode up with the cry The Yankees are coming Mrs. Burge "hide your mules." How we were startled & hurried the Major to his room. Report says there is forty thousand in Covington & vicinity. Infantry Cavalry & Artillery.

A negro comes in occasionally & tells us what they are doing in the upper settlement. They have been within a mile of us stealing mules & horses yet they have not come here. As night comes on we think it best for Major Anesly to leave fearing that he may fall into their hands. With the advice of Mr. Graves we all coincide. I send him & family tonight to Madison.

[July] 29 [1864]

Last night was a sleepless one. At two o clock I had the carriage at the door. Miss Mary[8] took me out & showed me where she had buried the silver then she her brother & Sally took the carriage for Madison leaving me all alone again. I feel very much alarmed about them fearing they will be molested.

All day I have walked about. Mrs. Graves & Libby came down to see if Sally had left. The Yankees left Covington for Macon headed by Stoneman to release prisoners held there. They robbed every house on their road of provisions sometimes taking every peice of meat blankets & wearing apparel silver & arms of every description. They would take silk dresses & put them under their saddles & things for which they had no use. Is this the way to make us love them & their union? Let the poor people answer whom they have deprived of every mouthful of meat & of their stock to make any. Our mills too they have burned destroying an immense amount of property.

[July] 30th [1864]

Wheelers cavalry are again in pursuit. There are not more than three thousand Yankees. Eb is sick. Dr. Cheney with him.

[July] 31s [1864]

I slept scarcely none last night. We heard the enemy were below Sandtown destroying everything & that wheeler[9] was in pursuit. I was looking for them all night. I could hear their cannon. Sadai had the toothache. Mr. Rakestraw came in to dinner & wanted me to send him to Rutledge. I am so very lonely no one passing.

August 1st 1864.

I have walked about all day scarcely doing anything. Indeed work of all kind is laid aside. Servants & all scarcely know what to be about. This evening learn by several of Wheelers men who passed that the Federals were met & fought before getting into Macon & that our Cavalry with Militia captured their leader Stoneman Who Surrendered with most of his command. They say Wheeler might have got them all had he been at his post but that was three hours after the white flag was shown before the General could be found. They had two prisoners with them. Miss Shug Glass came over to spend the night with me. Our men tell us that five hundred of Stonemans men got away & that they are endeavoring to make their way back to their Army. Laid down to night without any fear that I should be disturbed by the raiders.

[August] 2nd [1864]

Just as I got out of bed this morning Aunt Julia called me to look down the road & see the soldiers. I peeped through the blinds & there they were sure enough the "Yankees" the 'blue coats.' I was not dressed the servant women came running in. Mistress they are coming. they are coming they are riding into the lot. There are two coming up the steps. I bid Rachel fasten my room door & go to the front door & ask them what they wanted. They did not wait for that but wanted to know "What the door was fastened for." She told them the White folks were not up. Well they said "they wanted breakfast & that quick too."

Shug & Sadai as well as myself were greatly alarmed as soon as I could get on my clothing I hastened to the kitchen to hurry up breakfast. Six of them were already in there talking with my women. They asked about our soldiers & passing themselves off as Wheelers men said "Have you seen any of our men go by." Several of Wheelers men passed last evening. Who are you? said I. "We are a portion of Wheelers men" said one. "You look like Yankees said I. "Yes" said one stepping up to me "We are Yankees did you ever see one before? Not for a long time & none such as you I replied.

"Well now tell us how many of Wheelers men passed." I told them & asked how many of them I had to get breakfast for; they said "twenty six." They were in a great hurry & were so frightened that I became reassured.

Breakfast was got speedily that morning. A picket was placed before my front gate but one of my servants run to Jo Perrys & told him that they were at my house he informed some of the Calvary [*sic*] that were camped some two miles from here & soon after they left here. Which they did taking off three of my best mules they were captured.

None of my servants went with them for which I feel very thankful. Miss Fannie Perry & Mrs. Ezzard came down this evening. Oh how thankful I feel that they have done me no more injury. They were Ill & Kentucky men but of German origin. To night Capt Smith of an Alabama regiment with a squad of twenty men are camped opposite in the field. They have all supped with me & I shall breakfast them. We have spent a pleasant evening with music & talk they have a prisoner along. I can't help feeling sorry for him.

[August] 5 [1864]

I sent for Mr. Ward & Rebecca to come back. The Yankees robbed him of his watch pencil & shirt & seared the house where he was with Rebeccas trunk &c. &c.

[August] 7th [1864]

Wiley my stepson arrived to day he is one of Wheelers men they are constantly passing.

[August] 9 [1864]

I sent for Mr. Glass to go to town with me to day to get an order for my mules which were recaptured from the enemy. We met as many as two thousand soldiers waggons &c. It was a fearful ride upon my return home I learned that my mules were at a camp by Little River & that they would leave there that night. I immediately made ready & with Mr. Ward started for camp. It was seven miles from home & when I got there it was so dark I could not recognize my mules. Went back a little way & staid at Mr. Montgomerys. What a night it was of bustle & confusion thousands of soldierry all camped about.

[August] 10th [1864]

Went down to camp this morning & got two of my mules boys Mose & Sanford[10] mounted them & rode off proud enough. We hear the cannonading every day of Atlanta.[11]

[August] 23d [1864]

Sadai has the fever.

[August] 31st [1864]

Atlanta has fallen. We could hear the blowing up of the magizines [*sic*] which shook my house.

Sept 29 1864

I am forty seven years old to day. How ought I to praise my God that I have lived so long have seen so many returns of this day. While So many loved ones are sleeping the sleep that knows no waking. It has been a year of trial. Providence has watched over me & blessed me & I trust will still keep me amid these troublesome times. I thank God that I am not turned out of my house & refugeeing as so many are. I have a camp at my creek of forty negroes belonging to Mr. Morris of Marietta. George Yarbrough left us this morning. I spent yesterday with Mr. Graves. Sally is there again. Dut is at home. Mr. G is very feeble.[12] Bought or bargained for some oxen.

[September] 30 [1864]

Mrs. Lee & Eliza came down this evening. She wants the loan of my mules to take them to Alabama. I cannot let them go.

Oct 1st [1864]

I sent for Floyd & Shug Glass to dine with me to day as Eliza was here. Mrs. Perry & Clarissa came down in the evening. Refugees are still passing.

[October] 2d [1864]

Rebecca & Eliza returned this morning. I went to church & heard a good sermon by Bro Gray.[13]

[October] 8th [1864]

Was Quarterly at Sandstone. Thomas came last evening. Was truly glad to see him.

[October] 9th [1864]

Bro Branham & Knowls spent night with us. Bro Branham preached For ye have need of patience that after ye have done the will of God ye might receive the promise. After which was the Sacrament. I fear that I often take of it unworthily. Oh that I may live nearer to Him & feel the blessed assurance in my heart that I am His child. The brethren with Thomas Rebecca & Mr. Ward sung several fine hymns before retiring.

[October] 10 [1864]

Went in the carriage with Thomas & Sadai to Mr. Graves. Did not intend to spend the day but it was so pleasant up there both Henry & Dut & Major Anesly that I could not refuse. Mr. Graves cannot live long he is very feeble. Rode home by Wilsons place to see Mr. Smart who bought eight bags of cotton of me.

[October] 11 [1864]

Mr. Cooper came over & paid me for the cotton eight bags brought me four thousand two hundred & forty dollars (4240)

Oct 14 1864

I bought a yoke of oxen of Mr. Graves which were not broken. I had lost one of mine from eating peas while they were gathering corn. It died to day & I think the other one will die. It is a great loss to me. Will probably cost me eight hundred or a thousand dollars. Boys getting in their syrup corn. Have not got in our corn yet.

[October] 16d [1864]

Went to Harris Spring church. Called to see Mr. Graves very low.

[October] 19 [1864]

Thought I would ride up to Sister Parkers this evening. Started but was told the Yankees were coming this way so turned about & came back. A Miss White staid here all night had been hiding meat & salt from the Yankees.

[October] 21s [1864]

I made myself ready this morning to go to Madison. Got as far as Mr. Graves & found them anxious for me to remain there as he was dying. I went into the room & Oh how changed. Deaths signet was there. The last hour had come. Dear Mrs. Graves sat by him holding his hand others gathered around. Occasionally he would raise his hands in supplication & say "Take Oh take me blessed Saviour. Just as the Sun went down his prayer was answered & his Saviour that he had so long loved & served took him to himself. Henry & Dut were both in Savannah in the defense of their country—I assisted in shrouding as much as was suitable for me & saw him laid safely away in the parlour looking so calm & peaceful—The rest he so long desired he had obtained at last. Staid all night slept with Miss Johnson.

[October] 22d [1865]

Came home about noon. Cut & made Sada a dress with the help of Mrs. Ward. Very cool. Paid Rev W J. Parks the remainder for my carriage.

Been getting in corn all the week. Shall not make as much as last year. But if I am allowed to keep it I shall have enough for my own family. The servants have a candy pulling to night & are enjoying themselves right merrily dancing & frolicking. How much happier than their mistress—

23 October 1864

Uncle Wm J Parks preached by Mr. Graves request his funeral sermon—His text was Acts 11, 24 For he was a good man & full of faith & the

Holy Ghost & what was said of Barnabas might with truth be said of Bro Graves. He made it a very practical discourse as he always does. Dr. Means made some very eloquent remarks in the conclusion of the services. President Thomas, our circuit preacher Mr. Knowls were also present.

We shall so miss him & his prayers our little church is almost gone— Mrs. Baker Parker Anesly Mr. Burge & now Mr. Graves in the short space of six years have all left us for the church triumphant. May we that are left meet them there.

[October] 25 [1864]

Mr. & Mrs. Anesly spent day with me had pleasant visit from them.

[October] 26 [1864]

Went in my carriage to the Circle accompanied by Miss Floyd Glass & Sadai from there took cars for Madison. Just as I was getting out of carriage the mules took fright from the whistle blowing behind them & started off. Providentially nothing was hurt only bruised myself some. Maj Brown [14] was very kind & polite. Got to M about 10 o clock called on Mrs. Shaw from there went to Mrs. Cooks found them well & glad to see me had a good long chat with her of old times & of the present gloomy ones. Saw Maj Ivey [15] & got money for the beeves.

[October] 27 [1864]

Returned home to day. Very rainy & unpleasant morning. Sent to Charleston from Madison per express two thousand (2000) dollars to be invested for Sadai in Bonds 500 million loan. Mrs. Cook came home with me. Saw plenty of our Cavalry on the road. The rain ceased about the time we got to the "Circle" found Eb with the carriage waiting for us.

[October] 30 [1864]

Sent Mrs. Cook to the Circle this morning. Went to bed after she left as I got up at three o clock to get her off. No church to day. Three soldiers took breakfast with us. Yesterday they took three barrels of my corn.

900 pounds of fodder & nine bushels of wheat that was at the mill. Oh what a wretched thing is war truely [*sic*] no man can call anything his own!

Nov 8th 1864.

To day will probably decide the fate of this confederacy if Lincoln is reelected I think our fate is a hard one, but, we are in the hands of a merciful God & if He sees that we are in the wrong I trust that He will show it unto us. I have never felt that Slavery was altogether right for it is abused by many & I have often heard Mr. Burge say that if he could see that it was sinful for him to own slaves, if he felt that it was wrong, he would take them where he could free them he would not sin for his right hand. The purest & holiest men have owned them & I can see nothing in the Scriptures which forbids it. I have never bought nor sold & have tried to make life easy & pleasant to those that have been bequeathed me by the dead. I have never ceased to work, but many a Northern housekeeper has a much easier time than a Southern matron with her hundred negroes.

[November] 11th [1864]

Finished hauling in my corn have made about 1200 bushels have 900 put up but how uncertain whether I keep it. Commenced digging potatoes. Cool & pleasant.

[November] 12th [1864]

Warped & put in dresses for the loom. Oh this blockade gives us work to do for all hands.

[November] 13 [1864]

Been to Sandtown to church & heard bro Gray from the words Rejoice always & in everything give thanks. His best sermon for the year. Mrs. Glass rode as far as her house with me. Says they had a letter from Mr. Austin her brother who says the Federals have taken every thing from them save a pot plate & knife that bed & wearing clothing are all gone save what they had on that they regret that they had not refugeed for they had as well perished away from home as there.

[November] 14 [1864]

Mrs. Perry & Ezzard came down this morning to see my cloth in the loom liked it much. Evening Dr. Hendrick & lady called. Am digging potatoes have a fine turn out.

[November] 15 [1864]

Went up to Covington to day to pay Confederate tax. Did not find commissioners. Called at Mrs. Ushers.[16] She is in fine spirits thinks refugees had better all come home. That there is no danger from raiders. That the Federal army is evacuating Atlanta & returning north. Mid drove me with Beck & the buggy. Got home about 3 o clock feel wearied. How very different is Covington from what it used to be & how little did they who tore down the old flag & raised the red white & blue realize the results that have ensued.

Nov 16th 1864

As I could not obtain in Covington what I went for in the way of dye stuffs & I concluded this morning in accordance with Mrs. Wards wish to go to the "Circle." We took old Dutch & started had a pleasant ride as it was a delightful day but how dreary looks the town where formerly was bustle & business. Now naked chimneys & bare walls for the depot & its surroundings were all burned by last summers raiders. Engaged to sell some Bacon & Potatoes. Obtained my dye stuffs. Paid seven dollars a pound for coffee five dollars an ounce for Indigo twenty dollars I think for a quire of paper five dollars for ten cents worth of flax thread six dollars for pins & &c. forty dollars for a bunch of factory thread! On our way home met bro Evans accompanied by John Hinton who inquired if we had heard that the Yankees were coming! Said a large force was at Stockbridge & that a dispatch was received in Covington to that effect & that the Home Guard were all called out. That it was said that they were on their way to Savannah. We rode home chatting about it & finally settled it in our minds that it could not be so probably a foraging party. Some hour or so saw a Mr. Smith returning who had been refugeeing his stock with them all with him. I went out & told him the report, but he did not believe it. Just before night walked up to Jo Perrys to know if they had heard anything of the report. He was just starting off to join the company being one of them.[17]

[November] 17th [1864]

Saw men going up from below to town did not believe the report. Have been uneasy all day. At night some of those neighbors called who went to town. Said it was a large force but could not tell what or where they were going. They moved very slow. What shall I do? Where go—

[November] 18th [1864]

Slept very little last night. Went out doors several times. Could see large fires like burning buildings. Am I not in the Hands of a merciful God Who has promised to take care of the widow & the orphan—Sent off two of my mules in the night. Mr. Ward & Frank took them away & hid them. In the morning took a barrel of salt which cost me two hundred dollars into one of the black womens gardens put a paper over it & then on the top of that leached ashes fixed it on a board as a leach tub daubing it with ashes. Had some few pieces of meat taken from my smoke house Henry & James Around assisting & carried to the old place & hid under some fodder. bid them hide waggon & gear & then go on to ploughing told them to hide all of their things. Went to packing up my & Sadais clothes fear that we shall be homeless. The boys came back & wished to hide their mules. Said the Yankees camped at Mr. Gibsons the night before & were taking all the stock in the country. Seeing them so eager I told them to do as they pleased. They took them off & Elbert took his forty fattening hogs to the old place swamp & turned them in. We have done nothing all day that is my people have not. I made a pair of pants for Jack. Sent Nute up to Mrs. Perrys of an errand. When he came back said two Yankees met & begged him to go with them. Asked if we had stock & came to Mrs. Laura Perrys. I sat for an hour expecting them but they went back. O how I trust I am safe. Think the army have gone down the railroad to Augusta & will not pass here. Mr. Ward is very much alarmed he is my overseer his wifes father was a cousin of Mr. Burge. Their home was in Walker County are refugees & have been living with me during the year.

[November] 19th [1864]

Slept in my clothes last night as I heard the Yankees went to neighbour Montgomerys thursday night at one o clock & searched his house drank his wine took his money &c. &c. As we were not disturbed I after breakfast with Sadai walked up to Mr. Jo Perrys my nearest neighbours where the Yankees were yesterday to learn something of their movements. Saw Mrs. Laura in the road surrounded by her children seeming to be looking for some one. Said she was looking for her husband that old Mrs. Perry had just sent her word that the Yankees went to James Perrys the night before plundered his house drove off all his stock &c. & that she must drive hers into the old fields. Before we were done talking up came Jo Jim & George Guise from their hiding place. Jim was very much excited. Accidentally I turned & looked behind me & saw some "blue coats" coming down the hill by old Mrs. Perrys. Said I "I believe there *are some* now." Jim immediately raised his gun swearing that he would kill them anyhow. No don't said I & ran home as fast as I could with Sadai. I could hear them holla Halt, Halt, & their guns in quick succession. O God the time of trial has come. Give me firmness & remember thy promise to the Widow & Orphan "upon which Thou hast caused thy Servant to hope!"

A man passed on his way to Covington. I halloed to him asking him if he did not know the Yankees were coming. No! are they? Yes said I, they are not three hundred yards from here. Sure enough," said he, Well, I'll not go. I don't want them to get my horse & although in hearing of their guns he would stop & look for them. Blissful ignorance! Not knowing not hearing he has not suffered the suspense the fear that I have for the past forty eight hours—

I walked to the gate, there they came, filing up. I hastened back to my frightened servants & told them they had better hide & then went back to the gate to claim protection & a guard—

But like Demons they rush in. My yards are full. To my smoke house, my Dairy, Pantry, kitchen & cellar like famished wolves they come, breaking locks & whatever is in their way. The thousand pounds of meat in my smoke house is gone in a twinkling my flour my meal, my lard, butter, eggs, pickles of various kinds, both in vinegar & brine. Wine, jars, & jugs, are all gone. My eighteen fat turkeys, my hens, chickens & fowls. My young pigs are shot down in my yard, & hunted as if they were the rebels themselves. Utterly powerless I came to appeal to the guard. I cannot help you Madam it is the orders & as I stood there from my lot I saw driven first Old Dutch my dear old Buggyhorse who has carried my dear dead husband so many miles, & who would so quietly wait at the block for him to mount & dismount, & then had carried him to his grave, performing the same sad office to dear Lou & who had been my faithful servant so many years. Then old Mary, my brood mare. Who for years has been too old & stiff for work. With her three year old colt my two year old mule & her last little baby colt—there they go—There go my sheep & worse than all My boys, my poor boys, are forced to get the mules.

But alas little did I think while trying to save my house from plunder & fire—that they were forcing at the point of the bayonet my boys from home. One (Newton) jumped into the bed in his cabin & declared himself sick another crawled under the floor a lame boy he was but they pulled him out & placed him on a horse & drove him off. Mid, poor Mid, the last I saw of him, a man had him going round the garden looking as I thought for my sheep as he was my shepherd. Jack came crying to me the big tears coursing down his cheeks saying they were making him go.[18]

I said stay in my room but a man followed in cursing him & threatening to shoot him if he did not go. Poor Jack had to yeild. James Arnold in trying to escape from a back window was captured & marched off. Henry too was taken. I know not how or when but probably when he & Bob went after the mules.[19] I had not believed they would force from their homes the poor doomed negroes, but such has been the fact here cursing them & saying that Jeff Davis was going to put them in his army but they should not fight for him but for them. No indeed! No! they are not friends to the slave. We have never made the poor cowardly negro fight & it is strange, passing strange, that the all powerful Yankee Nation with the whole world to back them. Their ports open, their armies filled with soldiers from all nations. Should at last take the poor negro to help them out, against this "little Confederacy" which was to be brought back into the Union in sixty days time. My poor boys my poor boys, what unknown trials are before you. How you have clung to your mistress & assisted her in every way you knew how. You have never known want of any kind. Never have I corrected them.

A word was sufficient it was only to tell them what I wanted & they obeyed! Their parents are with me & how sadly they lament the loss of their boys.[20] Their cabins are rifled of every valuable, the soldiers swearing that their Sunday clothes were the white peoples & that they never had time to get such things as they had. Poor Franks chest was broken open, his money & tobacco taken, he has always been a money making & saving boy. Not infrequently had his crop brought him five hundred dollars & more. All of his clothes & Rachels clothes that dear Lou gave her before her death & which she has packed away were stolen from her.[21] Ovens skillets, coffee mills of which we had three, coffee pots, not one have I left. Sifters all gone. Seeing that the soldiers could not be restrained the guard ordered me to have their things that remained brought into my house which I did & they all, poor things, huddled together into my room fearing every moment that the house would be burned.

A Mr. Webber from Illinois & a Captain came into my house of whom I claimed protection from the vandals that were forcing themselves into my rooms. He said he knew my brother Orrington of Chicago. At that name I could not restrain my feelings but bursting into tears implored him to see my brother & let him know my destitution. I saw nothing before me but starvation. He promised to do this & comforted me with the assurance that my dwelling house would not be burned though my out buildings might. Poor little Sadai went crying to him as a friend & told him they had her doll Nancy he begged her to come to see him & he would give her a fine waxen one. He felt for me & I give him & several others the character of gentlemen. I don't believe they would have molested women & children had they had their own way. He seemed surprised that I had not laid away in my house flour & other provisions. I did not suppose I could secure them there more than where I usually kept them for in last summers raid houses were thoroughly searched. In parting with him I parted as with a friend. Sherman with a greater portion of his army passed my house all day. All day as its sad moments rolled on were they passing, not only in front of my house, but they came up behind tore down my garden palings, made a road through my back yard & lot field, driving their Stock & riding through, tearing down my fences & desolating my home. Wantonly doing it when there was no necessity for it. Such a day if I live to the age of Methuselah may God spare me from ever seeing again—Such were some of the scenes of this sad day & as night drew its sable curtains around us, the heavens from every point were lit up with flames from burning buildings! Dinnerless & supperless as we were it was nothing in comparison to the fear of being driven out homeless & houseless to the dreary woods. Nothing to eat I could give my guard no supper & he left us. I appealed to another asking him if he had wife mother or sister, & how he should feel were they in my situation. A Col from Vermont left me two men but they were Dutch & I could not understand one word they said. My Heavenly Father alone saved me from the destructive fire. My carriage house had in it eight bales of cotton with my carriage buggy & harness. On top of the cotton was some corded cotton rolls a hundred pounds or more. These were thrown out of the blanket in which they were taken & a large twist of the rolls set on fire & thrown into the boat of my carriage which was close up to the cotton bales. Thanks to my God the cotton only burned over & then went out! Shall I ever forget the deliverance?

This was after night the greater part of the army had passed. It came up very windy & cold. My room was full nearly with the bedding of & with the negroes. They were afraid to go out for my women could not step outside of the door without an insult from them. They lay down on the floor. Sadai got down & under the same cover with Sally while I sat up all night watching every moment for the flames to burst out from some of my buildings. The two guards came into my room & laid themselves by my fire for the night. I could not close my eyes but kept walking to & fro watching the fires in the distance & dreading the approaching day which I feared as they had not all passed would be a continuation of horrors.

[November] 20 [1864]

This is the blessed Sabbath the day upon which He who came to bring Peace & good will upon Earth rose from His tomb & ascended to intercede for us poor fallen creatures. But how unlike this day to any that has preceded it to me in my once quiet home. I had watched all night & the dawn found me watching for the moving of the Soldiers that were encamped about us. Oh how I dreaded those that were to pass as I suppose they would straggle and complete the ruin that the others had commenced. As I had been repeatedly told that they would burn everything as they passed. Some of my women had gathered up a chicken that they had shot yesterday & they cooked it with some yams for our breakfast. The guard complaining that we gave them no supper. They gave us some coffee which I had to make in a tea kettle as every coffee pot is taken off. The rear guard was commanded by Colonel Carlow, who changed our guard leaving us one while they were passing. They marched directly on none scarcely breaking ranks. A bucket of water was called for & they drank without coming in. About ten o clock they had all passed save one who came in & wanted coffee made which was done & he too went on. A few minutes elapsed & two couriers riding rapidly passed back again they came & this ended the passing of Shermans army by my place leaving me poorer by thirty thousand dollars than I was yesterday morning. And a much stronger rebel. After the excitement was a little over I went up to Mrs. Lauras to sympathise with her for I had no doubt but her husband was hung. She thought so & we could see no way for his escape. We all took a good cry together. While there I saw smoke looming up in the direction of home & thought surely the fiends have done their work ere they left. I ran as fast as I could but soon saw it was below, a ginhouse belonging to Col Pitts.[22] My boys have not come I fear they cannot get away. Two of my cows came up this morning but were driven off again by the Soldiers.

I feel so thankful that I have not been burned out that I have tried to spend the remainder of the day as the Sabbath ought to be spent. Eat dinner out of the oven in Julias house some stew, no bread. She is boiling some corn. My poor servants feel so bad at losing what they have worked for. Meat hog meat that they love better than anything else is all gone.

[November] 21st [1864]

We had the table laid this morning but no bread or butter or milk. What a prospect for delicasies!! My house is a perfect fright I had brought in Saturday night some thirty bushels of potatoes & poured down in the hall or passage ten or fifteen bushels of wheat & that poured down on the carpet in the hall. Then the few gallons of syrup saved was daubed all about.

A backbone of a hog that I had killed on Friday & which the Yankees did not take when they cleaned out my smoke house I found & hid under my bed & this is all the meat I have.

Maj Lee came down this evening having heard that I was burned out to proffer me a home. Mr. Dorsett was with him. The army lost some of their beeves in passing. I sent to day & had some driven into my lot & then sent to Judge Glass to come over & get some. Had two killed. Some of Wheelers men came in & I asked them to shoot them which they did. About ten o clock this morning Mr. Joe Perry called. I was so glad to see him that I could scarcely forbear embracing him. I could not keep from crying for I was so sure that the Yankees had shot him & I felt so much for his poor wife. The soldiers told me repeatedly Saturday that they had hung him & his brother James & George Guise. They had a narrow escape however & only escaped by knowing the country so much better than they did. They laid out until this morning. How rejoiced I am for his family. All of his negroes are gone but one man that had a wife here. They are very strong Secesh.[23] When the Army first came along they proffered to guard her house but she told them she was guarded by a Higher Power & did not thank them to do it. She says that she could think of nothing else all day when the army was passing but the devil & his Hosts. She had however to call for a guard before night or they would have taken everything out of her house.

[November] 22d [1864]

After breakfast this morning I went over to my graveyard to see what had befallen that & if it had been molested. To my joy I found it had not been disturbed. As I stood by my dead I felt to rejoice that they were at rest. Never have I felt so perfectly reconciled to the death of my husband as I do to day while looking upon the destruction of his lifelong labour. How it would have grieved him. How troubled him to see such destruction. Yes theirs is the lot to be envied. At rest[,] rest from care, rest from Heart aches from trouble. Found one of my large hogs killed just outside of the grave- yard. Walked down to the swamp looking for the wagon & gear which Henry hid before he was taken off. Found some of my sheep. Came home very much wearied having walked over four miles. Mr. & Mrs. Roqemore called. Maj Lee came down again after some cattle & while he was here the alarm was given that more Yankees were coming. I was terribly alarmed & commenced or rather packed my trunk with clothing feeling afraid that we should be burned out now. Maj Lee swore that he would shoot & that frightened me so much he was intoxicated enough to make him ambitious. He rode off in the direction it was said they were coming. Soon after returned saying it was a false alarm that it was some of our own men—Oh dear are we to be always living in fear & dread. Oh the horrors the horrors of war—

[November] 26th [1864]

A very cold morning. Elbert has to go to mill this morning & I shall go with him fearing that my mule may be taken from him as there are so many straggling soldiers about.

Well mounted in the little wagon I went carrying wheat not only for myself but for my neighbours. Never did I think I would have to go to mill. Such are the changes of life. History tells us of some illustrious examples who have done likewise. Got home just as night. Mr. Kennedy stopped all night with us. Has been refugeeing & on his way home. Every one we meet gives us painful accounts of the desolation caused by the enemy. Each one has to tell his & her own experience. & fellow suffering makes us all equal & all to feel interested in one & another.

Dec 21st 1864

Went up to Mrs. Graves this morning with Saidee. Rode in the wagon as Elbert was going to mill. Called to see Mrs. Peck before walking down to Mrs. Graves. Very cold I was when I got there. Found Misses Libbie & Hattie so glad to see me they were so lonely as Mrs. Graves has gone to her plantation. We had so much to talk about, that night found it unsaid, & I tarried with them all night & till after dinner to day, the 22d.

[December] 22 [1864]

Tuesday the 19th of this month I attended Floyd Glasss wedding. She was married in the morning to Lieut Doroughty. Expected to have been the week after the Yankees were here but her groom was not able to get here. Some of the Yankees found out that she was to have been married some way & annoyed her considerably by telling her that they had taken him prisoner that he had just got off the train at the Circle & they took him & some said shot him. They found Mrs. Glasss china, & glassware that she had buried in a box & broke it all up & then sent her word that she would set no more fine tables. They also got Mrs. Perrys silver.

Came home from Mrs. Graves this evening found all well at home. Rebecca & Mr. Ward kept house for me.

[December] 23d [1864]

Just before night Mrs. Robert Rakestraw & Miss Mary drove up to spend the night with me. They have started down into Jasper having heard that there were several buggies left at Mr. Whitfields by the Yankees. Nothing new it is confidently believed that Savannah has been evacuated. I hear nothing from my boys. Poor fellows how I miss them.

[December] 24th [1864]

This has usually been a very busy day with me preparing for Christmas. Not only for my own tables but for gifts for my servants. Now how changed no cakes, pies or confectionary, can I have. We are all Sad. No loud jovial laugh from our boys is heard. Christmas Eve that has even been celebrated here with mirth & gayety. That has witnessed the passing of crackers & the hanging up of stockings is one now of sadness & gloom. I have nothing to put even in Sadais stocking which hangs so invitingly for Santa Claus. How disappointed she will be in the morning though I have explained it all to her why he could not come. Poor children! Why must the innocent suffer with the guilty?

[December] 25th [1864]

Sadai jumped out of bed very early this morning to feel in her stocking. She could not believe but she would find something in it. She crept back into bed pulled the covers over her face & I soon heard her sobbing. The little negroes all came in "Christmas gift mistress Christmas gift mistress." I pulled the cover over my face & was soon mingling my tears with Sadais.

This is the Sabbath day. Though it is a gloomy foggy morning I went to church to Shoal Creek to hear preaching. Frank drove me in the buggy. But few out. Elder Johnny Montgomery preached. Returned home & eat my frugal dinner & have been reading ever since. Oh My Heavenly Parent give me patience & grace to bear the troubles & misfortunes that surround me. Sanctify them to my good & may I love the world less & long for my Heavenly home more & more—

[December] 26th [1864]

Went over to James Harwells to see if I could get some fowls & some pigs to raise something to eat. Spent a pleasant day with them. Promised to do all they could for me.

[December] 29 [1864]

Went to town very cold. Maj Lee will not turn over to me the negroes belonging to my dear Lou & I went to consult Judge Luckey in regard to it. He says there is no reason why it should not be done as there are no outstanding debts. A mans enemies are those of his own household & how bitter they can be. I have truly found them so. Dear Lou you wanted me to have them & I would be so glad to keep them for your sake.

[December] 31st [1864]

New years night. It has been very cloudy & cold & to night is exceedingly so. & how gloomy to me—I have read & prayed, prayed, for comfort for aid & protection, but O how dark are my prospects. Have watched the old year out, & the New Year in, but if this year is to be as full of trials & losses as the past what will become of me.

One year ago to night my dear father was dying, my stepmother a few hours before breathed her last! What scenes were enacting in that distant home & I here so totally unconscious of it. It is my hearts desire to meet them in the Heavenly Mansions where I trust they are at rest!

Will the Lord have mercy on me & spare me another year! May I enjoy more of His presence more love more joy than I ever have—

CHAPTER FIVE

A New Union

January 1st 1865 Newton County

    This new years day is the Sabbath the day of the Lord. May I spend it aright Oh Lord. May I trust in Thee, & find Thee as an anchor to my soul sure & steadfast—

[January] 3d [1865]

    Miss Amanda & Lizzy Petrie came over to spend day. Clinton Lee came down with a note from his father respecting the servants. I let Kit go with him & yet I do not feel exactly right about it. I do not believe I ought to have done it.[1]

[January] Sunday 8th [1865]

A cold day. Mr. Ward went yesterday to see if he could get a home at Mr. Dilliards. I sent for him this morning. A Mr. Park had come from Madison to see him respecting returning home to Walker County.

[January] 9th [1865]

Early this morning I loaned my mule & buggy for Mr. Ward to go to Ransom Harwells. Soon after one of the servants came in & told me that I could get some more of my hogs by going down to Mrs. Lloyds that she knew where they were & would tell me. I sent up & borrowed Mr. Perrys horse, put my saddle on, but my riding skirt I found the Yankees had stolen. Started off in company with Eb & his cart. Saw them but they were not mine & came back in as hard a rain as I ever wish to see. Wet & cold. Oh me how desolate & gloomy I feel. I have ridden ten miles on horseback & am wearied. Changed my clothes & sat down on the carpet before the fire with my head resting on a chair & was soon fast asleep.

Woke warmed & refreshed & thankful to my Maker for my shelter from the storm & for the abundance of wood to make fires with. How many are suffering from exposure to the elements to night while I am now sheltered & warm.

[January] 10 [1865]

Last night it thundered & lightened & the rain poured down in torrents all night. everything is deluged water courses all up, bridges gone & I fear great damage done—

Rebecca & Ward both left for Harwells. How glad I am to be once more alone with none but my own family about me.

[January] 16th [1865]

I have commenced Sadai in her books again & to stimulate her have let come in 5 of the neighbours children, to study & say lessons in the morning. Nothing encouraging from the army. Commenced breaking up land for corn three ploughs. Am trying a mule belonging to Mr. Graham.

[January] 27 [1865]

Sent mule home & started for Walton up to Uncle Len Fretwells to see if I cannot buy one. Very cold. Sent Sadai to Judge Glasss to stay until my return. Eb drove me in buggy.

[January] 28 [1865]

Returned from Walton this evening bought a young mare between five & six years old gave fifteen hundred dollars for her. Think I shall be pleased with my bargain.

Found Uncle Len much changed he is evidently drawing near the time "When the keepers of the house shall tremble" seventy years old he told me. How many that have started on lifes race since he did have fallen by the way. He & his wife have lived together over fifty years.

[January] 29 [1865]

Sunday again, no church. I am at home reading. Sadai teaching the little negroes to read. I killed my two hogs last Tuesday the 24 but have not been able to salt them down upon account of the extreme cold weather—The past week has been colder than any I ever knew in Georgia. It was many years ago a saying here that we might expect cold weather if many came from the North to spend the winter South & we surely never had so many before & we never had such weather.

[January] 30 [1865]

As the moon has changed Julia has gone to making soap again. She is a strong believer in the moon & never undertakes to boil her soap on the wane of the moon. It won't thicken Mistress see if it does. She sez too we must commence gardening this moon.

I have felt a strong desire to day that my captured boys might come home. Oh how thankful should I feel to see them once more at home.

Feb 2d 1865

Went to pay my state tax but did not meet the collector. Am very sorry about it.

[February] 5th [1865]

Mrs. Graves sent me word that we would have preaching to day but as the day is unpleasant rainy & windy shall not go. I want to hear a good sermon again.

April 9 [1865]

Went to Sandtown & Lous servants were divided between Sadai & self.[2] Mrs. Ward & infant came.

April 29 [1865]

Boys ploughing in the old house field corn. We are needing rain. Just finished housecleaning. Sent Eb down to Madison last Monday with letters for Mrs. Cook to take North with her for my brothers & sisters. Everything looks pleasant again. The state of our country is very gloomy. General Lee has surrendered his army to the victorious Grant. Well if it will only hasten the conclusion of this war I am satisfied. There has been something very strange in this whole affair, to me, & I can, attribute to nothing but the hand of Providence Working out some problem which has not yet been revealed to us poor erring mortals. At the commencement of the struggle the minds of men their wills their self control seemed to be all taken from them in a passionate antagonism to the coming in president (Abraham Lincoln[)]. Our leaders to whom the people looked for wisdom were led by them into this perhaps the greatest error of the age. We will not have this man to rule over us was their cry. For years it has been stirring in the hearts of Southern politicians. The North was enriched & built up by Southern labour & wealth. Mens pockets were always appealed to & appealed to so constantly that an antagonism was excited which had become impossible to allay. They did not believe the North would fight. Said Robert Toombes "I will drink every drop of blood they will shed." Ah blinded men. Rivers deep & strong has been shed & where are we now? A ruined subjugated people & What will be our future? is the question which now rests heavily upon the hearts of all—This has been a month never to be forgotten. Events of a lifetime have transpired within its limits. Two armies have surrendered. The President of the U. States has been assassinated Richmond evacuated

& Davis the President of the Confederacy put to grief to flight—The old flag has been raised again upon Sumpter & an armistice accepted.

May 1st 1865

Commenced washing the wool the Yankees left me. Sally & Rachel. Two soldiers called dined with me. Said they were from Texas or at least Ingle-hart was the other from Arkansas named Goodrich. They were very bitter. Went to church to Sandtown yesterday & dined with Mrs. Pitts enjoyed my dinner very much.

[May] 7 Sunday eve [1865]

Had company every day last week. Soldiers returning paroled returning to their homes. Last night a Mr. & Mrs. Adams refugees from Albert who have been spending the time in Eatonton called to stay all night. I felt like I could not take them in. I had purposely kept in back part of the house all the evening with my blinds down & doors locked to keep from being troubled by Soldiers & had just gone into my room with a light when some one knocked at the door & wanted shelter for himself & family. I could not turn away women & children so I took them in found them very pleasant people they had government wagons along & he had them guarded all night. I fear there was something in them which had been surrendered & belonged to the US but he assured me that with the exception of the mules & wagon, all belonged to himself. He said that he left Jeff Davis at Washington in this state on Thursday morning last. His enemies are in close pursuit of him offering a hundred thousand reward to his captors. After those people left this morning I prepared for church. On the way I met Susan Harwell who left me last July to visit relatives in Alabama. I went on to church sending Sadai back with her, before getting there I overtook Mr. Riker the impressing officer for this district he told me the US troops were on behind & it would not be safe for me to leave my mule at the church & go in. I was sadly troubled wanted very much to go in yet fearing to do so. I however concluded to venture & got Mrs. Graves boy to take my buggy round into the woods with Kit & hide them. Meeting with so many obstacles I was late sermon had commenced. I took a seat near the door but did not enjoy the services at all for I was all the time looking & listening for the Yankees.

When services was over I had some difficulty in finding my boy buggy & mule. Got home at last unmolested but wearied & full of care.

May 8th 1865

Miss Susan met Miss Amanda last night & this morning she is going over there to spend the day. Mrs. Pitts came up for her wool spent several hours. Mr. James Harwell called & rented some land of me for the Mitchum boys.[3] I have some thought of going to Macon & trying to obtain some stock of the Yankees. Rain a very little—

[May] 9th [1865]

Have concluded it will not be best to go to Macon. I fear to leave home as the US troops are all about in the neighbourhood—There are several hundred camped at Mt Pleasant. They are taking meat corn &c. but giving receipts for them.

[May] 14 [1865]

Miss Hattie rode down this evening. Says they were not badly troubled by the soldiers that Dut has got home & that Henry is in Carolina. I expected to have staid all alone last night as Susan & Sadai had gone down to see Rebecca but Shug Glass came over & soon after Mr. Knowles our circuit preacher came to spend the night with me so I had plenty of company. I like Mr. Knowls. We agree upon a good many contested topics. He loves the old flag as well as myself & would be glad to see it floating where it ever has—Rebecca came home with the girls.

[May] 17th [1865]

I hear to day that our negroes are all freed by the US government. This is more than I anticipated yet I trust it will be a gradual thing & not done all at once but the Disposer of All knows best & will do right—

[May] 21s [1865]

I had a long conversation with my man Elbert to day about freedom & told him I was perfectly willing but wanted direction. He says the Yankees told Maj Lees servants they were all free but they had better remain where they were until it was settled as it would be in a months time.

[May] 25 [1865]

This morning bro Knowles came for some corn soon after Jessie Camp & Mr. Dorset from Covington bringing me a letter from Dr. Comings with some photographs. How my heart rejoiced to once more see a long letter from him. I have been excited all day about it & it seems to me that I have seen father & mother so life like are their pictures.

Dr. Cheney came in the evening to see me & we had a long talk about carrying out the advice of Dr. Comings in regard to our servants. We hear so many conflicting rumors we know not what to do but are willing to carry out the orders when we know them.

[May] 28 [1865]

Went to Mt. Pleasant to church heard sermon from Pres Thomas dined & spent evening with Mrs. Graves. We had a long talk upon our duties &c.

[May] 29 [1865]

Dr. Williams from the "Circle" came this morning to trade me a horse. He tells me the people below are freeing their servants & allowing those to stay with them that will go on with their work & obey as usual. What I shall do with mine is a question that troubles day & night it is my last thought at night & the first in the morning. I told them several days ago they were free to do as they liked. But it is my duty to make some provision for them. I thank God that they are freed & yet what can I do without them? They are old & young not profitable to hire. What provision shall I make for them?

Dec 24th 1865

It has been many a month since I wrote in this journal & many things of interest have occurred. But above all thanks be to God for His goodness in preserving my life & so much of property for me. My freedmen have been with me & have worked for one sixth of my crop. I have had frequent letters from my kindred though I have seen none of them.

The refugees Mr. & Mrs. Ward & Susan left me the middle of July for their home in Walker. I had a week of sickness after they left suffering from an attack of Cholera Morbus. Aunt Rhoda staid with me. The second Sabbath in July a meeting commenced in Sandtown which resulted in the conversion of many with many additions to the church. We just took our two horse road wagons & took along with us all that would go. I never expect to see just such another time.

For the last six weeks I have had Mr. John Cash here ginning & putting up my cotton for market. I have not got it off yet though I have got an advance of seven hundred dollars on it.

The first of September visited Gainesville. Took Eliza & Sadai with me.

This is a very rainy unpleasant day & how many poor freedmen are suffering from it. I know there must be thousands exposed to the pitiless rain. Oh that everybody would do right & there would not be so much suffering in the world! Sadai & I are all alone in the house. We have been reading talking & thus spent the hours until she went to bed that I might play Santa Claus. Her stocking hangs invitingly in the corner. Happy child & childhood that can so easily be made happy.

[December] 25 [1865]

Sadai woke very early & crept out of bed to her stocking. Seeing it well filled she soon had a light & eight little negroes sitting around her gazing upon the treasures in her stocking & everything opened that could be divided was shared with them. Then their presents that she had collected the night before & laid upon the table were distributed amongst them. 'Tis the last Christmas we shall probably be together Freedmen! Now they will I trust have their own homes & be joyful under their own vine & figtrees with none to molest or make afraid.

The holidays are always sad to me & as one friend after another departs to the better land I always at such seasons call them to mind & live over again the times we have been together. We have been by ourselves all day.

[December] 26 [1865]

Disagreeable day. Mr. Cash who has been living with me for the few weeks past has returned. Made Sarah a balmoral⁴ which she found attached to her stocking.

[December] 27 [1865]

Dr. Cheney called & left his daughter to play with Sadai while he went below. Returned & dined with me. Paid my account 18 dollars for fees this year. Rachel my waiting maid has a candy pulling tonight. I reckon 75 or a hundred negroes are there. I feel very lonely no white person here but Sadai & little Lula Cheney whom we persuaded the Dr. to leave until tomorrow evening. I feel too very uneasy fearing that something sad must occur with so many freedmen about me. I have sat up until after midnight. How happy how joyful are they spending the time dancing juba singing playing &c. &c.

[December] 28 [1865]

Well the night passed away & with it all my fears.

Jan 1st 1866

I live to see the opening of another year thank God & may I through its coming days & weeks & months be led by my Fathers hand. In all that I do say & feel may the Almighty Power be recognized & felt. May I trust & love Him with all my heart & if spared to see the close of the year may I feel that His mercies & blessings have been multiplied & innumerable. This is a rainy day. Hired boy Peter formerly belonging to Wm. Montgomery. Frank married Lydia⁵ yesterday. I gave them a supper last night. Sadai came home from Mr. Glasss quite provoked that I did not send for her yesterday but it rained incessantly & indeed she had to come to day in the rain.

[January] 6 [1866]

Went up to church. Heard a very few remarks from Bro Evans. Went to Mrs. Graves. Found them all well. She is very despondent about her affairs.

[January] 7th [1866]

Went again to day with Sadai. Came home to dinner.

[January] 8 [1866]

Very cold but went out this evening to Mr. Elliots to buy a mule did not trade called for Aunt Rhoda to come home with me but she thought it too cold to venture out.

[January] 10 [1866]

Aunt Rhoda came to make her annual visit. Mrs. Sue Harwell brought her over as she was on her way home from the wedding of Matt Elliot.

[January] 22d [1866]

This has been a day of company one after another has called upon business principally. Mr. Levit came with some mules. I bought two for which I paid 350 dollars.

[January] 23d [1866]

Went to Sandtown to pay for mules. Called on Mr. Boland about contracts & the case of an old woman who is here & can give no account of herself but who is an object of charity. What can be done with these helpless ones? Surely their former owners should be made to take care of them & not allow them to wander about & perish. Got home to dinner. Breaking up stubble land. All are at work. Renters busy. Received a letter from bro William yesterday.

Newton Co January 24th [1866]

Attended to my domestic concerns this morning & this evening went out to Dr. Cheneys to buy meat for Eb. Aunt Rhoda stopped at Mrs. Jo Perrys. I sat later than I ought & as I started Sadai begged Lula to come home with her. She had to be made ready so that it was nearly sundown when I left. Deep mutterings of thunder told of coming rain & I hastened on but my harness breaking I was detained some time on the road. It was dark & raining hard when I got home. The storm seemed to increase in violence accompanied by vivid lightning & hail but little did I think of its destructiveness a few just three miles hence. There was a terrible tornado bearing away in its resistless might the shattered fragments of four dwellings with out buildings, furniture clothing splintered timbers uprooted trees & human bodies all whirling amid the darkened circles of a wrathful tornado. I have read of tornadoes but never have I seen anything like this. As one gazes upon its track its appalling ruin its mutilated dead, its bruised & mangled victims, he is lost in astonishment that one living thing should have escaped its fury. As I wandered over the ruins I felt more than ever the importance of frail humanity before Jehovah's breath. How sad the hearts of Colonel Pitts & family & of Mrs. Baily. There lay their dead James & Margaret married but three short months now cold in death upon the same bed. Lovely in their lives & in death not divided. Better thus than one should grieve & mourn for the other. There are two others dead in the village & a dozen maimed & bruised. I came home & sent a messenger to Oxford for Eld Branham to come down to preach their funerals as he had married them so recently. The boy returned late the preacher was not at home.[6]

[January] 26 [1866]

Mrs. Perry Aunt Rhoda Sada & Lula went with me in my carriage to the funeral. The little town of Newton was alive with people but O the desolation of a part of the place. As the arrangements to bury could not be ready until late we visited the sick looked over the ruins & came home to adore the Goodness that had spared us. Oh God let the lesson sink deep into all hearts so that if Thou callest in the wind or storm or in the silence of the night Wherever or whenever may we be ready to meet Thee—

[January] 27 [1865]

Our circuit preaching at Mt Pleasant to day & tomorrow. I went in my buggy & suffered much from cold dined with Mrs. Graves. Came home early. Peter had returned from town. Ol & Maz[7] still hauling wood.

[January] 28 [1865]

So cold did not go out to church this morning. have read & wrote & done divers other things. It does not seem right to stay at home all day.

[January] 29 [1865]

Found ground covered half an inch with snow this morning so not much will be done to day. Aunt Rhoda has my warm corner. Went to Sandtown this evening. Maz drove me in buggy with the new mule the grey. Had contracts signed & approved that is made with servants done at Gays store.[8] Went up to Mrs. Gays & engaged board for Sadai & Lou Cheney. Shall start them to school next Monday. This is very dull for farmers.

Feb 1st [1866]

Attended a sale at the residence of the late Alexander Pharr. I never went to an Administrators sale before how sad thus to see everything broken up & sold off but then not so bad for them as for thousands for they have plenty. I went with Eb to buy him or Frank meat but it sold for thirty cents & over so I did not buy. Had a very nice dinner there. Mrs. Pharr & Miss Jane were both pleased to see me. Paid for some iron that George bought.

[February] 3d [1866]

Finished breaking up pine field next to Mrs. Glasss. Ploughing my garden planting out potatoes beets &c. &c. Aunt Rhoda took Julia & went to Sandtown to church. She will stay until after tomorrows preaching feel quite tired with my days work.

[February] 4 [1866]

Went to Sandtown heard a good sermon from bro Evans. Returned home to dinner. Dr. Cheney brought Lou down to go with Sadai to school tomorrow.

[February] 5 [1866]

Took the two girls to Sandtown & entered them as pupils. Shall miss Sadai so much. Bought myself a pair of shoes Sadai calico for bonnet.

[February] 6 [1866]

Mrs. Glass sent for me to take her to town to day but could not. She got up her mules & came by to take me but I had gone to carry Aunt Rhoda home. Spent the day at Mrs. Patricks. Brought Amanda home with me.

[February] 7th [1866]

James Harwell & wife visited me to day he went over my swamp & told Peter what to do. Came up heavy rain this evening & they could not get home.

[February] 8th [1866]

This is one of the coldest days I ever knew in Geo thermometer hanging in entry is only nineteen above zero everything frozen in my room. Mr. & Mrs. Harwell started for home but it is very cold—

March 12 [1866]

Commenced hauling corn to Circle a gloomy unpleasant morning & I've got to go & attend to it all myself. Got to go to Mrs. Parkers & get Tim to go to Circle for me.

[March] 13 [1866]

Been wandering about feeling badly all the morning. Started again to Circle after an early dinner as passes were not sent yesterday. Feel uneasy about it. Met wagons all safe.

[March] 15 [1866]

Been to town. Sold there six bales got 30 cents. Offered it for the whole lot but don't know what to do about accepting. If it was not for that advance. Here let me record what I hope I may never do again get an advance on my cotton. I done it for a friend. I have done it to my great injury. Had it not been for turning it over to Bruce & Co. it I think would have been sold long ago. I don't know though. I was keeping it for higher prices though I could have sold long ago for forty cents. I did not know what to do & thought I was acting for the best. Poor ignorant creature that I am. Called to see Judge Floyd not at home & this worries & troubles me no little this Stanton case. O that I could give it all up to my Heavenly Father & feel at peace & rest.

[March] 20 [1866]

Summoned to court this morning. Peter drove me in buggy. Dined at Judge Floyds. Was obliged to go into Court House in evening to see the notes. Compared them with other writing & made my affadavit that I believed Mr. Burge never gave them. O this case how it troubles me. How often I have taken it to the Throne of Grace & striven to leave it there but back it comes with all its weight of care & disquiet. It rained so hard that I did not come home but spent night with Mrs. Floyd. It seemed like old times for I boarded there years ago but alas how changed I am & not me alone but Times hand has been over us all.

Newton Co March 21st 1866

Had a very restless night & feel consequently badly this morning. Still raining. While at breakfast Uncle Billy Parks came in to talk over the case as he is one of the witnesses Stanton having gone to him & taken up a note which Mr. Burge gave him for Emory College passing himself off as administrator but when requested to give a receipt to that effect replied that he was acting as my agent I wishing him to do it &c. &c.

Came home weary & careworn found Sadai suffering with toothache so we both had a sleepless night again. Poor child she was very patient getting up & down to the fire & suffering so much & still sorry to keep me awake.

[March] 22d [1866]

Well it has cleared away & I had promised to take Sadai to the dentist but Mrs. Callahan & daughter came to spend day & I had them to entertain when it was so great an effort for me to keep off my bed. Sally took Sadai to Sandtown in the evening & Dr. Wilson extracted her tooth she bearing it like a soldier. My case comes off tomorrow.

[March] 23d [1866]

Very rainy. Quite a storm. Mr. Glass called & I sent him in my carriage as it had to go to the shop & he is on my business. Well another day will pass before I know the result. I will go hard to work & thus keep off my fears. Elder Purington came to spend night. While taking supper Mr. Glass returned & told me I had gained my suit. Thank the Lord! Praise His Name! I felt so joyful I could not keep still so glad to know that there is some justice in the land yet some law that my charge is sustained. Shall I ever doubt His goodness & care for the widows again.

[March] 24 [1866]

Slept but little for joy & thankfulness last night. Company this morning yet I have a great deal to do for tomorrow is Sunday & I expect Mr. Branham & Miss Johnson to spend night with me & shall have others tomorrow.

[March] 25 [1866]

Listened to a most excellent sermon from Mr. Branham on the death of Mr. Bailey & wife. We do all fade as a leaf was his text.

the last time I heard it preached from it was Mr. Lewis funeral my dear early companion my precious husband now in the better world for the last twenty three years. How many sad reminiscences it called up! Mr. Graves & Calb & Miss Johnson dined with me.

[March] 26th [1866]

Mr. Glass came over this morning & I loaned him one hundred & fifty dollars he has often accomodated Mr. Burge. Evening took supper at his house. Met Mrs. Webb Gay Robinson & the two Mollies. Nice time & nice supper. Agreed to spend next day at Mrs. Webbs.

[March] 27 [1866]

Settled at stores some things that boys had got there & spent day as anticipated. Did not enjoy myself much.

April 9 [1866]

As cotton keeps declining concluded to go to Augusta Wednesday & sell mine. Went up for Miss Hattie to make me a dress. She came down & we are both busy.

[April] 11 [1866]

Left home this morning with Sadai. Took cars at Circle. Mary Hinton accompanied me in my carriage from her house & Oscar & Henry in buggy. At the Circle in good time & on board. Found Mr. Anesly at depot waiting for us & all at his house glad to see us. Very tired. Miss Libbie & I occupied the same bed & room.

[April] 12 [1866]

Went shopping bought carpet bonnet & divers other things. Returned Saturday the fourteenth had a delightful visit. It has really made home seem sad & lonely. No body here to meet or greet me. Don't feel just right about not selling my cotton & buying so many things.

[April] 15 [1866]

Went to Sandtown & heard Professor Smith preach. Dined at Cousin Margarets.

April 16 [1866]

Upon examining my cotton seeds which my folks were planting found them very unsound & yet they have gone on planting while I was away knowing that they were of no account. Well I will have to wait a few weeks for to see whether they come or not. It is almost always the way if I have a few joyous light hearted days dark ones are sure to follow.

[April] 18 [1866]

Papered my dining room. Made me sick.

April 20th 1866

Sadai's music teacher Miss Mollie Evans had a rehearsal of her pupils at Sandtown this evening. Maz drove me down & I returned the same night. Sadai did very well considering she has been taking lessons but six weeks. Recieved small box from Sister by Willie Anderson just came in time for Sadai to wear some of the pretties it held.

[April] 25 [1866]

Mrs. Pitts Glass & Mr. Glass dined with me to day. Very windy & paper cracking & coming off from dining room. Had my first chicken pie.

[April] 26 [1866]

Commenced ploughing up my cotton & replanting. No stand scarcely anywhere the heavy rains lake the earth & the seed is of no account from their having laid so long in the lint. I ought to have my ploughs in swamp but so it is feel very much discouraged wish I had rented out all my land but hope for the best. Oh that I could more fully rely upon the promises of my Heavenly Father.

May 1st [1866]

Still replanting cotton in big field next to Mr. Glass. No stand scarcely & yet they say it is coming up they are hoeing & replanting.

For a week it has rained. Water in pools over our fields—

June 5th [1866]

These are very gloomy days for planters. We have such floods of rain. Cotton just up & the grass covering it. O that I had rented all out last fall & not attempted farming. My swamp cannot be ploughed or gotten in on account of rain.

[June] 11th [1866]

Commenced cutting wheat eight cradles had two running on Saturday. Crop thin. Sport killed to day for the harvesters. Shall finish to night.

[June] 14 [1866]

Finished planting swamp corn. We have had a bad time with our swamp this year owing to the heavy & long continued rains. Just as it would do to work another rain would come upon it & keep us back. The weeds Oliver says are as high as his head. It is exceedingly hard work on my mules.

[June] 15 [1866]

Rode over this evening where boys were at work. They are getting along very well. What cotton is there looks very well. Hope it will come out & do well. When I came home & found Sadai had gone to Dr. Cheneys with Cora Perry & Lou Cheney. Am not at all pleased about it.

[June] 16th [1866]

Wandering about lonely & sad. How many such hours do I spend by myself—

[June] 17 Sunday [1866]

A cloudy rainy morning had the mules kept up hoping to go to church but it did not break off soon enough. Oh I am so lonely & no one here but myself. Have read & read & now writing. The weather has changed considerably since yesterday. God is good in not sending the hail upon my fields. Oh that I felt His fatherly goodness & care more. My heart is so cold & hard.

[June] 27th [1866]

Went to Covington carried Miss Fannie Perry. Went over to Rebeccas & from there to the female college to attend the exercises Was much more interested than I expected to be. A poem recited by Miss Barber an old friend was very good but she did not speak loud enough to be heard. It really seems like old times to be out in such a crowd with its surroundings.

Dined at Maj Lees & returned home.

July 1st [1866]

Went up this morning to Oxford to hear Bishop Pierce preach commencement sermon. Very good. Went to Oxford as stated. Dined at Mrs. Briggs Perrys in Covington as I carried over her daughters to Oxford. Was obliged much to my regret to return there.

Rebecca & her two little ones came home with me to spend several days. The weather is very warm & dry crops are suffering from it.

[July] 4th [1866]

Several ladies from Sandtown dined with me to day invited to meet Rebecca. Wiley came just as we were going out to the table. It is nearly three years since I saw him & how many distressing events & scenes I have passed through since then he left early in the evening. Sadai went with him to Mrs. Graves.

[July] 5th [1866]

Sadai & Miss Libbie came down in the buggy which took Wiley up there.

[July] 6th [1866]

Rev W Evans & Miss Ella, his daughter came & dined with us & Miss Minnie Glass⁹ so I have had another party.

[July] 10 [1866]

We spent with Mrs. Pitts. They had quite another storm there yesterday several trees were blown down & my crop looks bad. Grass is tall as cotton.

We have a very hard rain as we were coming home. I spoilt a new calico colours running together but I gladly took the rain for it will do a great good—

[July] 13 [1866]

Rebecca left this morning. Have cleaned up & been this evening over to swamp & about my crop. Are ploughing swamp corn for the first time. It is small but a late season will bring it all right I hope.

[July] 15 [1866]

Last evening Mark Harwell came & is here to day. I did not go to church. Kept Katy out of pasture for that purpose as I concluded not to go opened gate for her to feed about & she took to her heels & ran off.

[July] 16 [1866]

Found Katy after hunting all day.

22d July Newton County 1866

Went to Mt Pleasant to church taking Miss Hattie Dutton who came home with me from Mr. Montgomerys examination where I went on Friday after a ride to the Circle for some money. Stopped at Mrs. Graves for Miss Hattie to dress. When we got to church found Dr. Thomas & Rev W J Parks who preached to us. After meeting was over Dr. Thomas handed me a letter which I put in my pocket carelessly thinking it from Mr. Knowles. What was my surprise when at Mrs. Graves I took it out & found it to be from "Uncle Billy" stating his intention of visiting me on the ensuing Tuesday in view of a matrimonial connection. O how I wished he had never written it. I showed it to Mrs. Graves & we had a long talk about it. Well I will carry it all to God.

[July] 25 [1866]

Mr. Parks came as expected. I could not tell him that I would take his name. Many obstacles are in the way. I don't know what to do.

Sept 1866

On the thirteenth of September at one o clock pm I was married to the Rev W J Parks by Rev James Thomas (President of Emory College.) About thirty guests were present including my neighbors & friends from Oxford. We had a nice dinner & the company appeared to enjoy themselves very much. Rebecca Lee made me quite unhappy for a while. Sadai looks strange & embarrassed but dear child I feel that it is for her good & happiness as well as my own. I know she will love him & be happier than ever.[10]

The next evening after our marriage we went to Oxford his home where he gave a nice supper to his neighbors & myself. Pres Thomas Dr. Thomas Prof Stone Rev W Bencher Mr. Harrison[11] the Dr. & their respective ladies were present. On Saturday we dined at President Thomas on Sunday at Mr. Harrisons on Monday we returned home to our farm. We shall remain for the present.

Sept 29th 1866

To day completes my forty ninth birthday. forty nine years is a long time to live. When in my teens the thought of living till twenty five seemed to be an age. Here I am now in my fiftieth year.

In the first place let me record my thanks to My Heavenly Father that He has preserved my life my health & above all that He has given me one of His servants to love & cherish me. Yes, I trust God has led me to love him whom I now call my husband & to so love him that the remainder of life shall be devoted to his happiness & comfort. After Thee O God may I serve & honour Him! May I never be an hindrance to him but a helpmeet. With prayers sympathy & the labours of my hands if need be may I be enabled to comfort him—Make me worthy O My Father of the love he bears me & hear his prayers in my behalf that I may be a holy & pious woman. This day help me to renew my covenant with Thee to give my life into Thy hands for another year. May it be a year of great blessing & comfort.

We have been to church to Sandtown to day there is a revival in the church there & many are seeking their Saviour. My husband Rev W J Parks preached from Luke 9th 37 to 45. How strange it seems for me to listen to such loving lips. How my sympathies go out for him while labouring in the pulpit. What an anxiety I have that his labours may be blessed & owned of God to the awakening & comfort of souls.

My little Sadai is seeking the forgiveness of her sins a humble penitent I trust. May the Good Lord reveal Himself in such a manner to her that she may never doubt. How blessed I am on this my birthday! Sadai has made me a present. My husband a book of his own writing precious gift. James Harwell came home & dined with us. Jake Cash spent night—

Tomorrow my husband preaches again which is the Sabbath.

Newton County Dec 31st 1866

The closing evening of this year finds me in health & in the enjoyment of many blessings. As I look back upon its past hours & days I find many things to regret while again I have much to rejoice & be glad.

January 17th [1867]

Attended Miss Libbie Duttons marriage with Judge Pace[12] at Mrs. Graves had a very pleasant time but exceedingly cold came home after midnight. Left Sister Carrie there to go with Mrs. Strong. Found Mrs. Harrison up waiting for us having a good fire. Miss Libbie has been unwell for several days & got up out of her bed to dress for the ceremony. They had a very fine supper.

[January] 22d [1867]

I walked over to Mrs. Dukes this evening whose husband is a renter on our place. While on my beach met a messenger who told me Eliza & Rebecca had come. I hastened home & found poor Eliza upon my bed looking O so much as Lou did just before her death so wearied so worn &

emaciated I could scarcely see a resemblance to her former self. Rebecca has at last brought her home glad to find a place for her.[13]

[January] 23 [1867]

Rebecca left this morning leaving Eliza who had passed a restless nervous night. I find her this morning with a short breath hacking cough & very much prostrated. She got up about eleven put on her dressing gown & was brought into my room. She sat & eat dinner by the fireside. About two o clock feeling tired she said she would like to lie down on my bed. She told me of the unkind treatment she had received at Maj Lees & expressed so much joy that she was away. Poor child would that I had known it sooner. At about eight that evening she had a most suffocating spell. She wished to go to bed. I had been sitting in the L with Mr. Parks who had gone in there to smoke when she sent for me. I came in & laid her on her low bed. We had prayers after she had become quieted & Mr. Parks talked with her on her prospects for another world. She said she was prepared for a change & had felt willing to die after he left her she called me & said tell Uncle Billy not to pray for me as a Christian but as a sinner.

At ten o clock I laid down at her request. My bed was opposite hers. I watched her for I could not sleep. Apparently she was sleeping but her breathing was so much like her fathers that I knew she could not last long. About eleven I got up went to her & felt her pulse it was scarcely perceptible. She said do go to bed. I cannot sleep if there is any one up. After lying down I told Mr. Parks I wished he would make an excuse to get up & feel her pulse he done so & remarked to her that she was very ill. He told me he could perceive scarcely any pulsation. I got up & gave her a stimulant which she could scarcely swallow. She begged me to help her & seemed alarmed at seeing us so & kept begging for "Uncle Billy" to feel her pulse. After crying to me for help I told her we could not help her that her Heavenly Parent could to look to Him. She quieted herself immediately & in less than ten minutes without a struggle breathed her last. The family had been called up. We sent for Mrs. Glass & left her in her last long sleep.

In the early morning we sent messengers for her sister to have the Major get her coffin & to attend the funeral the 25 being the next day.

[January] 25 [1867]

Henry & Dutton Graves sat up with the corpse last night. Mrs. Lee arrived with her two children. It was very cold but pleasant. This morning it is cold & cloudy looks like rain. Friends many of them arrived & after arranging her for her burying she was laid in her coffin prayers singing & a few remarks by Mr. Parks. During the services a heavy rain accompanied with thunder & lightning came up. Oh it was a dreadful time to see one so young laid away with scarcely a tear bedewing her corpse. I thought of her bright promising childhood her affectionate disposition her love for me when small. Then of all the past few years with all the changes that had come over her. I tried to bury it all with her in the grave & to question my own heart of its faults & misdoings. We could none of us go to the grave at least none of the women & so she was laid away beside her father & sister with the raindrops alone bedewing her grave—

Sept 29th 1867

This Sunday morning ushers in a return of my birthday. I am fifty years old at four o clock this evening half a century just to think of it how many have died since I was born how many loved ones I have laid in the grave. How many tears I have shed over desolated hopes & crushed expectations. How have I lived to be this old? How little good have I done how unlike one professing to follow Christ. The Past O the Past how its memories come thronging home to me this day. How varied has been my life. How much of happiness of the most exquisite kind has been mine & how much sorrow have I drunk its bitterest dregs. 29 years agone I was near & making preparations for my first bridal. My youthful love my Samuel—It was to take place just one week hence the 7th of Oct 1838. How short lived was my happiness. Years nearly seven after of widowed. Then again a home & loved one & eight years of happiness with Mr. Burge & I laid him in his grave & returned to a desolate a lonely home. Nearly eight years of widowhood in which I saw many grievous trials & bore weighty cares, many of which are recorded in these pages. Then God again blessed me with one of His own Servants giving me again a husband to watch over & love me. I have now lived with him over a year & I find that our tastes are congenial our hopes & feelings the same.

Truly he is one that I can & do love with all of my heart. He is tender & loving affectionate & devoted a kind & tender parent to my fatherless little one & a husband to myself. Oh that I was more like him & served my God as he does doing daily His service.

We have to day with us Dr. James Thomas & lady with their little one from Oxford they spent last night with us. My husband & he have gone to Sandtown to hold a meeting. Sallie Harrison being sick I could not go so Mrs. Thomas remained with me. Mrs. Graves Oscar Graves Miss Hattie Mr. & E Baker dined & spent evening with us. Bro & Sister Thomas went over to Judge Glasss to spend night. I have had rather a wearisome day & now I am to take little Henry to sleep with us. I fear me that I shall get but little rest tonight.

I grow older but I fear not better not more holy as I should as years pass on. May I live nearer my Saviour this year than ever realizing that my time is short.

Oxford Jan. 1st 1868

Here I take a new page a new home & a new year. Would that I could as easily turn over a new page of lifes destiny & have naught to record upon it but purity of heart & life thankfulness to the Giver of all blessings & the record of days spent in doing good. Alas, alas, these pages show broken resolutions vows badly kept, & promises forgotten. But let me tell you journal somewhat of the past few months for I see it has been some time since I wrote of myself—

The past year has been one of pleasantness & peace. I have visited Atlanta & Augusta, been up the country for a month visiting Mr. Parks children & friends then again to Atlanta to the Annual Conference where we stopped with Mrs. Solman & enjoyed ourselves very much. Upon our farm we have had exceedingly favourable seasons. Most of the land has been rented. Mr. Parks has tested about twenty acres upon which he has made a most excellent crop. The boys have not done as well as they expected not making as much cotton but their corn has turned out well & I hope they have made plenty for themselves & us. For the coming year we have rented all of our land & come up here to Mr. Park's house & home. Our main reason for thus doing was the sending of Sadai to school. We were too far from schools for her to go from home & I felt that she was too young to board. I did not know how attached I was to my old home until I was near leaving. It has been a quiet peaceful one for many years eighteen next January. This is a beautiful place every convenience that heart could wish or desire. I have never had so nice a one of my own before room for everything & I hope that I shall have strength to keep it nice with everything in its place.[14]

Nine o clock pm. My dear husband & I are sitting here in our nice family room with the stand between us he reading the Sentinel[15] often commenting upon what he has read. Sadai gone to bed in the next room with a friend of hers (Cora Perry) who has been spending the holidays with her. It has been very warm & pleasant thermometer above sixty until within the last forty eight hours it has rained sleated & snowed. Snow is now on the ground in patches & it is quite cold. I think I shall try to write oftener than I do. When I am happy & satisfied dear Journal I know that I forget & slight you—

Oxford Sept 29 1868

I am well & happy to night just fifty one years old. How swiftly & pleasantly have passed the days weeks & months of this year. I have had many cares but the comforts have overbalanced them all. I have had boarders all of the year now have thirteen. I rather like taking them when everything is quiet & I can obtain provisions for the table but of to night I write. I felt that I had nothing to write about. My husband begged me to write something so I merely say we are quite as happy as last year. Every day that I live with him I love him better & better. If he was kind & affectionate the first year his kindness & affection have only increased with time as it passes. We are sitting here to night he shaving the little girl has gone to bed. He has read The Sentinel & sealed & directed it to Mr. Carr of Macon & is now making ready for bed.

Above my wife has been writing I know not what as I have not read it yet! Judge she has been writing something appropriate for her *birth day*. She says she is fifty one years old this day. I am in my sixty ninth year. The verry [sic] year my dear wife was born in the state of Maine I was teaching a school in Georgia. About fifteen hundred miles then separated us. How strange the ways of providence! From my heart this night I thank God that he so ordered it as for us to become acquainted and that she consented more than two years ago to become my *wife*. How happily we have lived together. I took her as a gift from God and am now more and more fully confirmed in my opinion that God in mercy to me in my old age opened up the way for our union. I hope while life lasts our union will be as in the past both a happy and profitable one. Oxford Sept 29 '68 W J Parks.

Oxford Dec. 31st 1868

Another year has followed in the footsteps of the past & still I live & enjoy the bounties of a merciful Providence. My health & that of my family has been excellent all of the year. Mr. Parks has lost a sister aged about eighty four[16] how old that seems to me now but when twenty five fifty was a long time to look ahead to.

This holiday week was ushered in by an exceeding cold Christmas. We dined at Brother Branhams with other neighbors & friends. On Saturday Professor Clark wife & daughter came back from Augusta accompanied by Professor Hopkins.[17] Sallie & her children are with us as is Rev John Harris who married Mary Parks. They have five very energetic & enterprising children.[18]

To day it has been raining all day so it was yesterday. Sallie has had a chill. My dear good husband is sitting on the other side of the stand reading Partons Life of Aaron Burr.[19] We are sitting in one of the sitting rooms with comforts all about. All have retired but us & we are now ready to bid good bye to the old year of Sixty eight trusting & hoping to be spared through the days & months of its successor.

Oxford Dec 31st 1869

This evening closes another year of our stay upon earth. How swiftly they pass one after another. We have been exceedingly blessed in our health & family the past year. Mr. Parks has gained in health & flesh & is now looking as well as I ever saw him. He is the same tender kind & loving husband that he has ever been & truly I am blessed as his wife.

Sadai is a sweet precious child now just entered upon her fourteenth year. I trust she is one of Christs own children loved & accepted of Him. Her own precious father gave her to God in faith with much prayer & comforted himself with the promises of God that He would accept & care for her—May she prove to all that she now promises to be kind loving & unselfish.

The past week we have had Rev H H Parks & family[20] with us on their way to their pastorate work in Augusta. They have tarried a week with us. Christmas was a rainy day but Santa Claus made his usual visit to the children & a merry time they all had. I found a five dollar gold piece under my plate enclosed in a pocketbook just large enough to hold it.

Mr. Parks & I are alone to night. We have been over to town & settled a little outstanding affair with Cody which I have never intended paying but to avoid trouble I did so. Sadai has gone to Mrs. Graves to a Christmas tree so we are alone this last night of 1869.

The past year has been one of care. I have had most of the time a large family of boarders young men to whom I have become much attached. They indeed seem like my own children. All but two have been happy in the love of God & have rejoiced in a sin pardoning Saviour. Very happy times have they all had. We have had great reason to rejoice for the great work of revival here in Oxford. This fall many were reclaimed & scores converted—

Our crops have suffered greatly from drought. The second week in May we had a heavy rain after which none fell to do any good until some time in August. Made twenty one bales of cotton very little wheat & corn.

Jan 1st 1870

A new year. We have spent the day at Mrs. Graves going down after Sadai. Came home in the rain. This is Saturday night & raining very hard. I wish every one had as warm & comfortable a room as I have to night.

[January] 2d [1870]

A bitter cold morning it ceased raining early in the night & the wind blows & the ground is frozen with the water frozen all about. Occasionally we see a little snow spitting about. We have sat by the fire all day reading writing & talking these are happy days so happy journal that I sadly neglect you.

Sept 13d [1870]

The anniversary of my marriage with my dear husband but what a day it has been. Here let me record it. We went out to the Camp Meeting yesterday did not return until this morning. Mr. Parks preached from the words "Trust in the Lord & do good deeds." It was a sermon to the point. A feeling one. I trust good was done this was last evening. It was so late we did not return home & he was not feeling as well as usual. Complained a great deal of his shoulder hurting him. We had a nice ride home though raining I enjoyed it much. Got here about eleven had fire made & got Mr. Parks some warm tea & he laid down before the fire to heat his aching shoulder & rest his weary limbs. I had no good anniversary dinner. Neither did I have a present for him as I would like to have done. About three he got up. Soon after he felt very sick. I rested his head upon my shoulder & I felt his whole system relax & give way. He was perfectly unconscious. I was greatly alarmed. Help came in after my calling & we laid him on the bed apparently dead! dead! Words cannot express my horror my alarm. I felt his heart. It beat & I had hope. He had only fainted he said. Truly the Lord has given him again to me to me [*sic*] on this the 13th day of Sept 1870. Bless his Holy Name!

Oxford Oct 3d 1870

This has been a trying day to me. My little one my baby my Sadai has left me for school for Macon. My heart has long been heavy & sad about it but to day it seems that it will break. I have slept but sparely for a week thinking thinking the long night through weeping when no eye could see. She has been sick the past week so have I. I almost hoped it might prevent her going but she has gone & how lonely the house. How I wished last night to take her in my arms & hug her to my heart as of old. I yearned to have her on my bosom. I wished her a babe again mine mine mine.

I would not have let her see me cry for I knew it would hurt & spoil her pleasure if she realized how I suffered.

She has been a good child obedient & loving. My selfish heart would have all her love. I don't love even for her to waste it on Emma Stone. She doesn't appreciate Sadais pure & generous love I think as it deserves to be appreciated & felt.

She goes from me pure & guileless goes into the world of strangers where now she must act for herself. She was exceedingly anxious to go to Macon. Nay it would have been grevious disappointment to her to have been kept from there. But I would have been so glad to have heard her say once "Mother I hate to leave you & home." I can't think but that she felt it if not I know she will. I give it all up hoping to still these longing heart throbs for her presence knowing she is to come back or hoping so improved & educated & prepared to adorn her situation in life & make my last years happy ones. Her father her dear dead father has been brought very forcibly to mind these few days. Just his last blessing was upon her "Bless the child." Bless the child & she will be blessed.

I am still keeping boarders. Mr. Parks is quite feeble. My own health as usual. We have had quite a rain for the few days past. I am alone this evening.

Oxford Dec 31st 1871

Finds me in the enjoyment of health & with many blessings surrounding me. I feel that I have reason to be thankful that the life of my husband has been spared for he has been very sick during the year. During the spring months he was mostly confined to his room & we all feared that he would never be about again but a merciful Providence has spared him. We have spent the year mostly at home. Carrie Thompson & her daughter have been with us. The first day of the present year a funeral a corpse went from our house. The dear, little daughter of Sallie Harrison Mr. Parks daughter came up from the farm to spend Christmas with us. Playful full of life & happiness she was called suddenly to her Heavenly Home. A brief hour of pain & all was over. The grief of father & mother was heart rending. Sadai did not come home. One month after Carrie's death I was again thrown from a buggy by a horse taking fright & was insensible for a few minutes it was a wonder that I was not killed instantly. My husband stood on the platform at the depot & saw it all. He says no one can tell his feelings. Thank God I was spared.

After his sickness he went up the country to Dr. Bede & after commencement I followed him with Sadai who returned from school rather jaded. She had a Readers place out of a class of fifty eight & has stood well in all of her classes. We returned before the opening of the term & in Oct she left us again for Macon. Mr. Parks children have all visited us this year. They love him & grieve at his failing health. A few weeks ago Dr. Harrison bought a new home & they have removed from the plantation to Monroe. Now none but negroes are there at the home place. This Christmas has been a sad one. My child is away & there are many trifling things to annoy. I wish I could arise above all such things & be contented & thankful as I ought. This is Sunday eve. My husband sits reading one of Abbots histories, Carrie the Bible.[21] Claude has gone to bed. I went to church by myself. Heard Mr. Stafford preach. Sadai spent Christmas in Augusta. Harwell came up here.

Oxford Nov 30th 1873

A number of years have elapsed since I penned a word in this journal & so many things have happened I know not how to record them. The failing health of my dear husband resulted in paralysis of his entire left side about the thirteenth of May 1872 for weeks we looked for his death. The children were summoned & friends thronged about him but he in a measure recovered not the use of his limbs but from prostration & for eighteen months it was my pleasure & privillage to wait upon him as no one but a wife can do. Day & night I sought to alleviate his pains & make him comfortable. A patient genial cheerful invalid he often thanked God that I had been given him & with health & strength to wait upon his declining years. I tried to make him comfortable & happy & to get everything possible to add to his comfort. During this long time by wheeling him in a little carriage we had bought for him he was enabled to go about the yard & town, to go to church when feeling able, & he even went to Decatur to the Orphans Home anniversary. By lifting him into the carriage we have been several times to the plantation & often to town.

Up to the last day of his life he was by our lifting him able to go out. On Wednesday the fifteenth of Oct he rode over to town with me in the Rockaway. The day before he went down to the college. On Thursday he seemed as well as usual but coughed a good deal. He went out & sharpened up all of our scissors I sitting on the steps by him & trying them while Daniel turned the grindstone. He eat his supper as usual & after supper Rev JP Duncan[22] called & sat an hour. He chatted cheerfully with him & after reciting a Psalm & having prayer he left. Mrs. Clark & Sister Carrie then came into our room & tarried until nine o clock. They left the room as he wanted to use a cup we had for him to relieve his bladder in & soon after he said if I would make him a hot stew he thought he could go to sleep.

I called Daniel in & after taking his stew prepared him for bed. We always moved him by lifting him on a sheet. As we laid him down a strange expression came over his face & a sort of quivering shudder. I was startled & in reply to my inquiry he said he felt sick & that I had better give him a Dovers powder[23] to make him sleep for he feared he was to have a restless night. I prepared it & called Daniel back to help me raise him up. I was not at all alarmed as I thought I had seen him so much worse but I sent for the Dr. Dr. Evans & called Mrs. Clark back. Sister was already in. We had sat him back into his chair. The doctor thought we had better give him an enema. We had put mustard on his chest so we laid him down again. He said to me I am suffocating. I raised him up in my arms & in a moment he was dead dead without one farewell word or kiss in parting. Gone to his God for Whom he had so long lived & served. Won the crown for which he had borne the Cross & labored in the Masters vineyard for upwards of fifty years.

From the time we first put him in bed till he breathed his last it was not more than ¾ of an hour so sudden & unexpected was the call but not unexpected to him for he had long said & felt that his life hung upon a thread which would snap in a moment as it were. He had always said that another stroke of paralysis would end his life & so it was no doubt attacking his heart & lungs. This was on Thursday night at quarter past ten on the 16th of Oct 1873. His children were all telegraphed to but none but Harwell got here. His funeral was preached on the following Sabbath by Dr. Means to a large congregation. He was carried to his grave by preachers & there his poor body rests in the graveyard in Oxford.

This is the anniversary of my dear husbands birthday of whom I have been writing. Had he lived he would have been seventy four. We have always kept it when together by a good dinner & little gifts to him. Twice I have been to conference with him & eat our dinner first with Mrs. Salmons & next at his sons Rev H H Parks. To day he is with his Saviour & I here by the lonely fireside a widow again thinking over all the past & wondering how I shall get along. May the God who has in the past been so merciful succor support & sustain me in this sad time.

Dec 25 [1873]

What a sad lonely Christmas this has been just such a one as I have never seen for my house is in disorder & every room but my own torn to pieces. My husband left me here at his Oxford home to stay in it if I chose two years but he neglected to say that I might have the use of his furniture so the *law* said it must be sold & consequently day before yesterday it was put up to the highest bidder. *How* my sad heart rebelled to see these home treasures go into stranger hands to hear the rude laughter & jest of the crowd of unsympathizing strangers. Many things I bought in order to keep them from unloved ones. Tis a hard law of this land I think selling at public outcry the home furniture from the widow of the owner. It is enough to lay the loved one in the grave to come home & hide ones self among the fireside relics & feel that they are all & almost parts of the lost & then & then [*sic*] to have them taken by rough hands from us is almost *too much*! Oh My Father help me to trust in Thee—

Sadai came home from Macon where she has been on a visit & to attend the meeting of the South Georgia Conference. I thank God for her in these my desolate hours. Santa Claus came with gifts to all.

Oxford Dec. 31 1874

This night finds me solitary & alone in my room a boarder in my own house. How strange & lonely everything is. Sadai is in Atlanta visiting at Dr. Crichtons. Oh how I miss her & how I miss the dear good husband that left me over a year ago for his home with Jesus but the days are passing swiftly on when I shall meet him there. Happy meeting blessed day. I have been very busy these holidays arranging my house for Dr. Haygood[24] putting away & fixing up my things so I have not lived over & dwelled upon the past as much as usual perhaps it is all for the best. The year has been one of health & blessing to me.

Oxford Jan 3d Sunday 1875

Sadai in Atlanta two letters from her this morning. Dr. Haygood in Nashville. Went to church this morning heard Dr. Means from Canbys prayer. Brother Florence concluded very feelingly. Have been reading. Commenced my Bible on New Years Day. Very rainy to night. May God keep & bless us.

Oxford Sept 28th 1875

I am alone in my chamber in the home where Mr. Parks brought me to here in Oxford so soon to pass out of my hands & of the family to be sold under his "will" to the highest bidder. I suppose it is for the best but oh how hard it is to give it up & go back to my country home again. I have been trying to wean myself all the year by renting it & boarding with the family of Dr. Haygood. To night I feel very lonely & sad. Sadai is in Covington at Mrs. Bettie Harriss. I could not send for her as I wanted to this evening so I sit here musing over the past & thinking how little I have done these fifty eight years I have lived & how soon in the course of nature it will all come to an end this long varied life of mine. I can't realize it all & yet it must be a few more years at least & this wearied frame will be laid to rest. How strange that we cling to life & its pleasures its joys & comforts though our eyes are dimmed & hair bleached with the snows of many winters. Why should we want to stay here when the friends & loved ones of our youth are passed away?

Sadai my child is all that I have to make me want to live.

Nov 2d 1875

To day may be counted as one of the sad days of my life. Last night Harwell P & John Harris came to attend the sale of the house. Dr. Haygood bought it for three thousand dollars worth at least five thousand and now that it is done I almost wish that I had bought it myself I so much hate to leave it. O my poor wearied heart when will it rest.

I shall begin to move back to my home tomorrow. Thank God Who put it into dear Mr. Burges heart to give me a home!

Newton Co Dec 12th 1875

Here I am at my old home. Alas how different from former times. Plantation all run down no stock no hands & nothing to make a beginning with.

We have made the house quite comfortable. The 12 of November Sisters two daughters came on from Brooklyn to spend the winter with us.[25] Mr. Abbot brought them down. Sadai my child is making her bridal robes for she has given herself to another. how shall I ever stand it how can I ever let her leave me for another home.[26]

Dec 17 [1875]

Yesterday is a never to be forgotten day. For weeks I had looked forward to it with a heart full of grief. I could not object. I had done so once & when their vows were again renewed should I oppose when her choice was one that no objection could be made to but that He was a servant of the Most High a consecrated preacher of His Word devoted to the service a member of the North Georgia Conference!

But what did all this imply for her? To me her mother it looked like taking upon herself trials & privations of which she had no conception giving up her home where she had always been surrounded by comforts & never known care or scarcely an ungratified wish leaving me. *How can I let her do it* was the unceasing cry of my poor bleeding heart for days & nights past. Yet I loved her too well to let her see my grief. What will not a mother do for a child. What will she not sacrifice. What not bear—It did seem to me the last night of her stay with me that I could not bear it that my efforts to keep it all back would kill me. It seemed that I wanted to go out into the forests & holler out my grief at losing her. I had prayed & wept wept & prayed over it. *But* here let me tell it all—As the day of the sixteenth of December 1875 dawned, her marriage day a strange quiet came over my rebellious feelings. My tears were dried & I thought while kneeling in prayer in the parlor how many times I had given her to God, even before her birth, I had promised Him if He would give me a living child I would train her for His service. Now He wanted her. I was for hours glad that such a husband such a guide & helper was to be hers. though I did not see her married a quiet joy filled my heart. I can express it no better than to compare my feelings to a rebellious child a disobedient one whose Parent has corrected & the child has submitted. Submitted at last given it all up & now lays it all quietly aside. Tears were all gone & my hearts desire was Make them holy useful & good. It was a hard struggle but it is over & may God accept us both!

The ceremony was performed by Rev Yarbrough. We wanted Dr. Haygood but he was at the South Georgia Conference. As we could not get him I would have been glad to have had Harwell Parks but Mr. Gray wanted his Presiding Elder & it made no particular difference. The party arrived from Covington about ten o clock. A few relatives only were invited. Mr. Gray had two young gentlemen Mr. Nolen & Mr. Henderson with him & Sadais dearest friend Miss Ida Evans & Mr. Fred Eve from Augusta. We had quite a nice lunch a table prettily spread cakes nice turkey well cooked & oysters very good. The last done up by dear good Fannie who has been such a comfort such a help in all these days of sewing & getting ready.

The party left about twelve o clock tarried some twenty minutes at the depot arrived in Atlanta at four o clock. Went to the Markham house.[27] Tarried till ten at night left then for Mr. Grays fathers near Forsyth at which place they arrived Sadai writes me about four o clock this morning.

Ida dear, precious Ida left us this morning. Fannie took her over to the "Circle." My home seems very lonesome. Still the "quiet" abides & I feel as though her dear fathers last earthly blessing abides upon her that He as well as her dear stepfather Mr. Parks, can, & do look down approvingly upon it all.

May all our prayers be heard & answered for her!

Dec 31st 1875

The last night of the old year is very sad & lonely to me here in my old country home. We had just got comfortably settled for the night when a voice called from the gate. I hastened out hoping to get the mail for I wanted so much to hear from Sadai but who should it be but Willie Foot on his way to Baldwin where the Conference had sent him. He put up his horse & said he did not want any supper as he had lunched from his saddle bags. We talked over old times & a much pleasanter evening passed than I thought possible for old memories will come trooping along at such times on such waymarks—

Newton County Jan 1st 1876

May this be a New Year to me a quiet, happy one. To day I have been some annoyed by a security note given by me to Mr. Stafford for Dave one of my tenants who failed to pay it. I cannot meet it & don't know what to do. I hope soon to get some money. If I don't I cannot tell what I shall do— [28]

Newton Co Sept 29th 1879

A long time has passed since I wrote in you old journal & to night I would take it up but that it is my birthday sixty two years since my Heavenly Father gave me the breath of life & what a failure I have made of it all—To day or this morning, found me at Sadais at Eatonton. I went down on Friday & came back to day with Miss Pennie Glass[29] Sadai's friend of early days. My child has two of the sweetest little girls. Ida the eldest is so good so amiable so interesting. I just long to keep her all of the time.

EPILOGUE

For another twelve years after her last diary entry, written on her sixty-second birthday in 1879, Dolly managed her farm and helped Sadai raise her children. She succumbed to illnesses associated with old age and died on October 26, 1891, at the age of seventy-four. Her body was buried next to her third husband, William J. Parks, in the Oxford Cemetery. Sadai inherited the Burge homesite, but scarcely a year later, at the age of thirty-six, she too died and was buried next to her mother. Sadly, since her husband had died in 1887, she left behind five orphaned children, the eldest of whom was fifteen. They lived temporarily with the nearby Graves family, who also managed the estate. Before long, two of the girls, Ida and Dorothy, moved to Evanston, Illinois, to live with Miss Cornelia Gray Lunt, the unmarried daughter of Dolly's brother Orrington. The other three, Fanny, Joseph, and Davis, went to live with Dolly's half brother Stephen Purrington Lunt and brother William Lunt in California.[1]

Miraculously, the house and property in Newton County were never sold out of the family but served as a tenant farm for many years under the able management of George and Sidney Gunn, an African American couple who had helped manage the plantation from about the time of William Parks's death. After Sadai's death, the Gunns moved into a wing of the house. Sidney's mother, Lydia, remained on the plantation with Sidney and George until all three died in the early 1920s. Lydia, a postwar Burge house servant and wife of former slave Frank Burge, is mentioned in Dolly's diary and some of the family correspondence. Two of Lydia's sons, Abe and Wiley, also worked on the farm during the 1910s. Most likely, they were all buried in the slave cemetery on the property.[2]

In 1906, Ida Gray Morehouse bought the shares of the Burge property belonging to the other siblings and either sold or gave a portion to her sister, Dorothy Gray Bolton. In 1918, Dorothy Bolton had the original house moved across the road to the portion of the land that belonged to her. In 1920 Ida Morehouse's husband, Merritt Josiah Morehouse, a Chicago architect, replaced the original house with a large home modeled after a James River Plantation. The two lived there from about 1935 until their deaths in the 1950s. In the 1970s, the Bolton family sold its holdings, including the original home, while the Morehouses' only son, Merritt Dutton Morehouse, inherited and retained ownership of the newer home and most of the land. Currently, his son, Alexander ("Sandy") Gray Morehouse and his wife, Betsy, own and operate Burge Plantation, a private club and entertainment facility on the nine-hundred-acre site.

Two other brief diaries by Burge women, Louisiana and Sadai, have been published as well. Louisiana kept hers from May 1861, when she had to leave Macon Female College because she was ill, until March 1862. It offers a brief glimpse of her personality, her concerns as a young woman, and her country's disunion. One of the more revealing entries conveys her resentment that she had been named salutatorian instead of valedictorian: "My bad health and bad behavior have prepared me for this some time since—I could expect nothing else. Flossie [the Valedictorian] is as much noted in College for her timidity and humbleness and meekness (some not her friends say that she is a *bootlick*) as I am for my independence, both of speech and action, always doing as I pleased. Teachers don't like such independence."[3]

Most of the diary, however, is an account of her own and her friends' preparations for war. She tells of companies forming, boys heading off to battle, and girlfriends weeping as they said good-bye. Throughout, Louisiana is a steadfast supporter of the southern cause, zealously proud of Georgia's secession and passionately convinced of a Confederate victory. Near the conclusion of her diary, she asserts, "It makes me laugh to hear what our contemptible enemies talk about annihilating us! The idea is simply ridiculous. . . . We cannot be conquered! Never, never." In 1952, Richard Harwell, a professor at Emory University, edited and published Louisiana's diary in the *Georgia Historical Quarterly*. The American Women's Diaries microfilm series published a copy of the original in 1983, along with Dolly's and Sadai's diaries.[4]

Eighteen-year-old Sadai kept a diary for three months in 1874 during a trip North with Dolly, but she was a far less devoted diarist than either her sister or mother. "If there is anything in this world that I have not a talent for it is writing journals. I am not fond of writing any way and above all other kinds of writing, that of writing journals is the worst, compositions always excepted," she complained in an August entry. "But Mother wants me to write this and my friends, so I try to keep up the appearance, anyway!" Despite her inclinations to the contrary, Sadai wrote in her journal fairly regularly from July through September 1874, while she and Dolly visited family and friends in Evanston, Illinois, Nyack, New York, and Brooklyn. She wrote about seeing Niagara Falls, bathing at Coney Island, reading novels, shopping, walking along Broadway, and attending various churches. The journal suggests Sadai was a carefree, content young woman who enjoyed her travels and her friends. Her daughters, Dorothy Gray Bolton and Ida Gray Morehouse, claim in the foreword to the published diary that Dolly had taken Sadai north in hopes of breaking up what might have been a girlish fancy for John Davis Gray. But Sadai says nothing of her beau and eventual husband in the journal. Of her mother, she says that Dolly wants her to learn to keep house and Sadai wants to be a good daughter to her.

Sadai's diary was transcribed and published by the family in 1950, approximately. Along with Dolly's and Louisiana's, a copy of the original is in the American Women's Diaries microfilm series. Taken together or separately, all three of these diaries offer valuable insights about life in the nineteenth-century South, white women's experiences during and after the Civil War, and the strength of familial ties that helped eventually to reunite a country.[5]

NOTES

Sources frequently cited have been identified by the following abbreviations:

BGC   Burge-Gray Collection, Special Collections Department, Robert M. Woodruff Library, Emory University

DAB   Dictionary of American Biography

DGB   Dictionary of Georgia Biography

GDAH   Georgia Department of Archives and History, Atlanta, Georgia

HNC   *History of Newton County*

IFP   In the Family's Possession

MDB   Genealogy provided by Mildred Diane Baynes, a descendent of the African American Burges

NAMP   National Archives Microfilm Publications

SBD   Servants' Births and Deaths (a list at the end of the diary)

Preface

1. Dolly Sumner Lunt, *A Woman's War-Time Journal*, edited by Julian Street (New York: Century Company, 1918; Macon, Ga.: 1927; Atlanta: Cherokee

Publishing Company, 1994); "The Diary of Dolly Lunt Burge," edited by James I. Robertson Jr., *Georgia Historical Quarterly* 44–46 (June 1960–March 1962); *The Diary of Dolly Lunt Burge*, edited by James I. Robertson Jr. (Athens: University of Georgia Press, 1962); *The Diary of Dolly Lunt Burge*, American Women's Diaries (Southern Women) (New Canaan, Conn.: Readex Film Products, 1988).

Introduction

1. *Diary*, February 2, 1847. Throughout the introduction I provide quotations from my transcription of the original, published here.

2. Orrington Lunt (1815–1897); William H. Lunt (b. 1819); and Sarah Ann Lunt Comings (1821–1881). In later years, Orrington married Cornelia Gray (1819–1909) and moved to Chicago, where he helped found Evanston, Illinois, and Northwestern University. William remained in Maine longer as a merchant and later a member of the state legislature. He eventually moved to Iowa and then to San Francisco. Sarah married Isaac Comings, a physician, and lived in Georgia for a time before ultimately settling in Brooklyn, New York. BGC, finding aid; "Orrington Lunt: The Discoverer of Evanston" (Souvenir Supplement, *The Evanston Press* 3, no. 4, January 23, 1892), IFP; *In Memoriam — Orrington Lunt*, IFP; Cornelia Gray Lunt, *Sketches of Childhood and Girlhood: Chicago, 1847–1864* (Evanston, Ill.: Printed privately, 1925), 22–23, IFP.

3. Cornelia Gray Lunt explained that while Dolly's mother had been refined and elegant, her stepmother was "sharp-tongued," domineering, and a source of much misery for her young stepchildren. If this is true, perhaps it helps explain Dolly's later permanence in Georgia. *Sketches*, 22–23. Cornelia's papers are in the Northwestern University Archives, Evanston, Illinois.

4. Samuel Lewis to Dolly Lunt, November 26, 1835, and March 26, 1837, BGC. The phrases "I love you" and "bosom friend" were doubly underlined in the original.

5. Samuel Lewis to Dolly Lunt, April 14, 1837, and June 5, 1837, BGC.

6. Samuel Lewis to Dolly Lunt, December 25, 1837, BGC. Little information remains to suggest Dolly's educational experiences as a student. One obituary indicates that she studied at the well-known Wilbraham Academy in Massachusetts. The entire diary's original editor, James Robertson, states that she studied in local schools and at Kent's Hill in Readfield, where she met Samuel. Obituary by Atticus G. Haygood, Oxford, Georgia, December 12, 1891, IFP; *The Diary of Dolly Lunt Burge*, ed. James I. Robertson (Athens: University of Georgia Press, 1962), viii.

7. Largely a reaction against traditional medicine, which relied heavily on purging and bleeding techniques, the Thomsonian system advocated the use of vegetable- and botanic-based remedies and steam baths. Opened in 1839, the Georgia Botanic Medical College in Forsyth was the second Thomsonian or botanic school in the United States, and the first in the South. The school moved to Macon in 1846 where Isaac Comings regularly taught. Gerald L. Cates, "Medical Schools in Ante-Bellum Georgia" (Master's thesis, University of Georgia, 1968), 116–29; "From the Memory Book of Sadie C. Langmuir, Evidently written about 1900." This unpublished memoir by the fourth child of Sarah Lunt and Isaac Comings describes her family's residence in Georgia at this time. One of her descendants has made a typed transcription for the family record. IFP.

8. Dolly L. Lewis to "My Dear Parents," probably Samuel's, November 1843, BGC. Teaching was one of the few vocations open to young women in antebellum America. Lee Chambers-Schiller, in *Liberty, a Better Husband: Single Women in America*, estimates that between 1825 and 1860, approximately one-fourth of all native-born New England women taught school for some part of their lives (New Haven: Yale University Press, 1984), 4, 32. Some southern historians, however, note that low pay, poor job security, and social disapproval among the elite made teaching an unfortunate last resort for southern women whose husbands could no longer support them. See, for example, Elizabeth Fox-Genovese, *Within the Plantation Household: Black and White Women of the Old South* (Chapel Hill: University of North Carolina Press, 1988), 46; Bertram Wyatt-Brown, *Southern Honor: Ethics and Behavior in the Old South* (New York: Oxford University Press, 1982), 229; Christie Anne Farnham, *The Education of the Southern Belle: Higher Education and Student Socialization in the Antebellum South* (New York: New York University Press, 1994), 97–98; and Steven Stowe, *Intimacy and Power in the Old South: Ritual in the Lives of the Planters* (Baltimore: Johns Hopkins University Press, 1987), 135. For a differing view, see George Rable, *Civil Wars: Women and the Crisis of Southern Nationalism* (Chicago: University of Illinois Press, 1989), 28–29.

9. Samuel Lewis to Dolly Lunt Lewis, May 18, 1843, and August 23, 1843; Dolly Lunt Lewis to "My dear Parents," November 1843, BGC.

10. Isaac Comings to Samuel Lewis, June 1, 1843; Samuel Lewis to Dolly Lunt Lewis, August 23, 1843, BGC.

11. Dolly L. Lewis to "My dear Parents," November 1843; poems in Samuel Lewis's diary in Covington, 1844 and July 13, 1844, BGC.

12. Isaac Comings to Dolly Lunt Lewis, January 19, 1844, and June 25, 1844, BGC.

13. Isaac and Sarah Comings to Dolly Lunt Lewis, September 10, 1847, BGC. The Comings moved back and forth between Georgia (mostly Macon) in the winters and the North in the summers. However, after the spring of 1859, the Comings left Georgia permanently because Isaac's outspoken opinions about sectionalism and slavery supposedly endangered his well-being. "From the Memory Book of Sadie C. Langmuir," IFP.

14. Letters to Dolly in Maine indicate she visited there in September 1846; Dolly to "Sister," Mary M. Lunt, January 30, 1847, BGC. For an example of another northern-born southern woman who quickly assimilated into the southern way of life, see Wilma King, ed., *A Northern Woman in the Plantation South: Letters of Tryphena Blanche Holder Fox, 1856–1876* (Columbia: University of South Carolina Press, 1993). See also W. Kirk Wood, ed., *A Northern Daughter and a Southern Wife: The Civil War Reminiscences and Letters of Katharine H. Cumming, 1860–1865* (Augusta: Richmond County Historical Society, 1976).

15. Dolly to "Sister" Mary M. Lunt, January 30, 1847, BGC. There were eleven private academies in neighboring Newton County in 1850, and by 1860, there were between eighteen and twenty-five schools of various sorts (*HNC*, 104–6). See Farnham, *Education*, for a comprehensive discussion of academies in the antebellum South. She suggests that during the early part of the century, northern women teachers were fairly integrated into southern culture, but that by the 1840s and with increased sectionalism, these teachers often felt alienated from southern society and quit the region (98).

16. Dolly lived initially with Mrs. Cook, a Connecticut-born merchant's wife. Later, she boarded with Wilds and Nancy Kolb, prosperous planters whose Madison home was across the street from the Methodist academy, where Dolly probably taught and which later became Madison Female College. U.S. Census Records, State of Georgia, 1850, Population Schedules, Morgan County, NAMP, 127; Newton County Superior Court Records, 1869–1875, GDAH, 33.

17. *Diary*, February 6, 1848.

18. Numerous studies illumine Dolly's religious experiences. See, for example, Donald Mathews, *Religion in the Old South* (Chicago: University of Chicago Press, 1977); Barbara Welter, "The Feminization of American Religion," in *In Dimity Convictions: The American Woman in the Nineteenth Century* (Athens: Ohio University Press, 1976); Susan Juster, "'In a Different Voice': Male and Female Narratives of Religious Conversion in Post-Revolutionary America," *American Quarterly* 41, no. 1 (March 1989): 51; Barbara Epstein, *The Politics of Domesticity: Women, Evangelism, and Temperance in Nineteenth-Century America* (Middletown, Conn.: Wes-

leyan University Press, 1981); Eugene D. Genovese and Elizabeth Fox-Genovese, "The Religious Ideals of Southern Slave Society," *Georgia Historical Quarterly* 70, no. 1 (spring 1986): 11; and Jean Friedman, *The Enclosed Garden: Women and Community in the Evangelical South, 1830–1900* (Chapel Hill: University of North Carolina Press, 1985).

19. *Diary*, February 26, 1848, and September 29, 1848.

20. See the list of family members and other principals for the names and life-spans of Thomas's children; *Diary*, December 29, 1849; Lee Chambers-Schiller, *Liberty*, 47–53; Catherine Clinton, *The Plantation Mistress: Woman's World in the Old South* (New York: Pantheon Books, 1982), 85; Steven Stowe, *Intimacy and Power*, 123–24. For more studies of nineteenth-century southern women and marriage, see Carol K. Bleser, ed., *In Joy and In Sorrow: Women, Family, and Marriage in the Victorian South, 1830–1900* (New York: Oxford University Press, 1991); Catherine Clinton and Nina Silber, eds., *Divided Houses: Gender and the Civil War* (New York: Oxford University Press, 1992); Bertram Wyatt-Brown, *Southern Honor*, 199–225, 250; Daniel Blake Smith, *Inside the Great House: Planter Family Life in Eighteenth-Century Chesapeake Society* (Ithaca: Cornell University Press, 1980), 126–74; and Jane Turner Censer, *North Carolina Planters and Their Children, 1800–1860* (Baton Rouge: Louisiana State University Press, 1984), 72–95.

21. *Diary*, December 29, 1849; Friedman, *Enclosed Garden*, 35–37; Carl Degler, *At Odds: Women and the Family in America from the Revolution to the Present* (New York: Oxford University Press, 1980), 9, 28; Lawrence Stone, *The Family, Sex and Marriage in England, 1500–1800* (New York: Harper & Row, 1977), 217–28; Rable, *Civil Wars*, 23; Linda Kerber, "Separate Spheres, Female Worlds, Woman's Place: The Rhetoric of Women's History," *Journal of American History* 75 (1988): 9–39; Elizabeth Fox-Genovese, "Family and Female Identity in the Antebellum South: Sarah Gayle and Her Family," in Bleser, ed., *In Joy and In Sorrow*, 18–20, and *Plantation Household*, 58–71, 78–80. Consider also Anne Scott, *The Southern Lady: From Pedestal to Politics, 1830–1930* (Chicago: University of Chicago Press, 1970), 34–44; Suzanne Lebsock, *Free Women of Petersburg: Status and Culture in a Southern Town, 1784–1860* (New York: W. W. Norton and Co., 1983), 17–18, 28; and James L. Leloudis, "Subversion of the Feminine Ideal: The *Southern Lady's Companion* and White Male Morality in the Antebellum South, 1847–1854" in *Women in New Worlds*, ed. Rosemary Skinner Keller, Louise L. Queen, and Hilah F. Thomas (Nashville, Tenn.: Abingdon Press, 1982), 2:60–75.

22. *Diary*, December 29, 1849 and January 2, 1850. Valued at $5,000 in 1850, the Burge plantation encompassed twenty-five slaves, 450 acres of improved land,

350 acres of unimproved land, cattle, swine, sheep, cotton, corn, and an assortment of vegetables for consumption. Newton County at that time had 13,296 people, one college, five academies and other schools, and thirty churches. Dolly was leaving neighboring Morgan County, which had 10,744 people, two female colleges, nine academies and other schools, and nineteen churches. U.S. Census Records, State of Georgia, 1850, Agricultural Schedules, Newton County, NAMP, 677–78; ibid., 1850, Slave Schedules, Newton County, NAMP, 71; SBD, a list at the back of the diary. *Seventh Census of the United States*, 1850. Vol. 1, Statistics of Georgia, 365–92. That Dolly's friends counseled her about her proposal was not uncommon, according to Steven Stowe, *Intimacy and Power*, 66–67.

23. *Diary*, January 23, 1850, January 27, 1850, and September 29, 1853.

24. Probably most of the work Dolly recorded was performed by the slaves, while she or Thomas supervised. In later years her daughter Sadai indicated that she had little experience keeping house and making bread; see Dorothy G. Bolton, *Little Sadai: Journal of Miss Sadai C. Burge, 1874* (Atlanta: Keelin Press, 1952), entry for September 1874, BGC. See also *The Diary of Sadai C. Burge*, American Women's Diaries (Southern Women) (New Canaan, Conn.: Readex Film Products, 1988) and the original in the BGC. Fox-Genovese notes the tendency among slaveholding women and men to document the work of their slaves as if they themselves had accomplished it, *Plantation Household*, 128–29. For discussions of southern plantation women's duties, see also Clinton, *Plantation Mistress*, 16–35; and Scott, *Southern Lady*, 27–44. For a striking regional comparison, see Nancy Grey Osterud, *Bonds of Community: The Lives of Farm Women in Nineteenth-Century New York* (Ithaca: Cornell University Press, 1991), 2.

25. For a thorough discussion of pregnancy and childbirth in the region and period, see Sally McMillen's *Motherhood in the Old South: Pregnancy, Childbirth, and Infant Rearing* (Baton Rouge: Louisiana State University Press, 1990), 31–33. See also Anne Scott, "Women's Perspective on the Patriarchy in the 1850s," *Journal of American History* 61 (June 1974): 52–64, and *Southern Lady*; Clinton, *Plantation Mistress*, 40; and Turner Censer, *North Carolina Planters*, 25–40.

In 1850, Thomas reported his farm was worth $5,000 and listed nothing for his personal estate. In 1860, Dolly reported the farm was worth $4,000 and her personal estate worth $25,700. In 1870, Dolly valued her real estate at $5,000 and personal estate reduced to $1,000. That year, Dolly's third husband, William J. Parks, appraised the farm at $5,950. U.S. Census Records, State of Georgia, 1850, Population Schedules, Morgan County, NAMP, 478; ibid., 1850, Agricultural Schedules, Newton County, NAMP, 677–78; ibid., 1860, Population Schedules,

Newton County, NAMP, 454; and ibid., 1870, Population Schedules, Newton County, NAMP, 78; Newton County, Court of Ordinary, Estate Records Vol. 14, 1869–1873, GDAH, 260.

26. Dolly L. Burge to Louisiana Burge, November 7, 1858, January 3, 1859, and December 27, 1860, BGC; Cornelia Gray Lunt, *Sketches*, 45–46. The Georgia Female College, also known as Macon Female College and today as Wesleyan College, was the first American college for women that had no affiliation with a men's institution and employed professors who had advanced degrees (Farnham, *Education*, 11, 1–7). On southern women's education, consider Fox-Genovese, *Plantation Household*, 212–13, 232; Mathews, *Religion in the Old South*, 111, 123–24; Anne M. Boylan, "Evangelical Womanhood in the Nineteenth Century: The Role of Women in Sunday Schools," *Feminist Studies* 4, no. 3 (October 1978): 62–80; Turner Censer, *North Carolina Planters*, 44–46, 57–59; and Rable, *Civil Wars*, 19–22.

27. Dolly probably received assistance from her slave Elbert, to whom Thomas had given directions about the plantation; her stepson Wiley who returned to the plantation after losing a clerking job in Marietta; her nephew Wiley who wrote her from Charleston with financial advice during the war; and a number of overseers whom she hired and fired as she saw fit. *Diary* January 2, 1859; Wiley Burge to Dolly L. Burge, March 6, 1864, October 2, 1864, and June [no day] 1865, BGC.

28. Wiley Burge to Dolly L. Burge, March 6, 1864, October 2, 1864, and June 1865, BGC; Will of Thomas Burge, Newton County Will Records Vol. 2, 1851–1871, GDAH, 117–18. As executor, Dolly needed to divide the slaves into two equal groups; one she would share with Sadai, and the other would be divided among Thomas's three youngest children, Wiley, Eliza, and Louisiana. Not only did he leave three of his children relatively small inheritances, he left Rebecca nothing except what he may have given her in his lifetime.

29. Although it is more likely that her stepson Wiley filed the suit, there is no way to determine conclusively that it was not Thomas's nephew, Wiley Burge. Either way, Dolly later maintained friendly correspondences with both of them. The former wrote her from his Confederate post and asked her to "send . . . a substitute if possible." The latter advised her occasionally about the plantation management. The original diary editor, James Robertson, concurs that Dolly failed to distinguish between the two Wileys. See *Diary*, ed. Robertson, 38. Wiley Burge to Dolly L. Burge, June 1863; Wiley Burge to Dolly L. Burge, March 6, 1864, October 2, 1864, and June 1865, BGC.

30. Despite the opposition, the court divided the slaves according to the will in

December 1863. The first lot went to Wiley, Eliza, and Louisiana Burge, and included Lewis, Martha, Winnie, Hester, Jane, Kit (perhaps Christopher), Corene (or Connie), Ann, Sally, Mary, Newton, Ned, John, and Oliver. The second lot went to Dolly and Sadai Burge and included Elbert, Julia, Willie, Uesley (or Ueole), Mid, Sam, Rachel, Lydia, Bob, James, Henry, Jackson, Frank, Hannah, Floyd, Millie, and Margarett. Both groups were valued at $34,900. Will of Thomas Burge, Newton County Will Records Vol. 2, 1851–1871, GDAH, 117–18; Dolly S. Burge v. Mathew A. Mitchell and Wiley Burge, Court of Ordinary, Newton County Minutes Records 1852–1863, GDAH, 241–42; Newton County Estate Records, Inventories and Appraisements, Annual Returns 1862–1864, December 22, 1863, 607–8.

31. William Lunt to Dolly L. Burge, February 12, 1859; Dolly L. Burge to Louisiana Burge, February 1860, BGC. See Lebsock for a discussion of guardianship, *Free Women*, 40–41. The Petition of Eliza G. Burge to the Court of Ordinary, Newton County Minutes Records 1863–64, GDAH, 6.

32. Dolly to Louisiana, January 1860, BGC; See Lebsock, *Free Women*, 36–39, 118–19; Clinton, *Plantation Mistress*, 76–77; Wyatt-Brown, *Southern Honor*, 240–42; and Rable, who sums it up succinctly: "a husband's death [often] brought his creditors down on the estate like vultures" (*Civil Wars*, 23–25). For another example of a successful southern widow planter who wrote about her experiences of plantation management, slaves, and religion, see John Hammond Moore, ed., *A Plantation Mistress on the Eve of the Civil War: The Diary of Keziah Goodwyn Hopkins Brevard, 1860–1861* (Columbia: University of South Carolina Press, 1993).

33. Cornelia Gray Lunt, *Sketches*, 47. On southern women's silences about sectionalism, see Scott, "Women's Perspective," 149; and Rable, *Civil Wars*, 42. On *Uncle Tom's Cabin*, consider Mathews, *Religion in the Old South*, 184; and Scott, "Women's Perspective," 59. Most historians today acknowledge that the majority of southern slaveholding women fully supported slavery and their silences about it indicate agreement. See, for example, Carol Bleser, "Southern Planter Wives and Slavery," in *The Meaning of South Carolina History: Essays in Honor of George C. Rogers, Jr.*, ed. David R. Chesnutt and Clyde N. Wilson (Columbia: University of South Carolina Press, 1991), 116; and the work of Elizabeth Fox-Genovese, such as *Plantation Household* and, with Eugene D. Genovese, "The Religious Ideals," 14.

34. *Diary*, May 13, 1850, December 28, 1852, and November 8, 1864. Dolly owned thirty-two slaves in 1860 and seventeen when Thomas's estate was divided in 1863. U.S. Census Records, State of Georgia, 1860, Slave Schedules, Newton County, NAMP, 42.

35. Louisiana to Dolly, October 4, 1862; Obituary of William Webb and Priscilla Purrington Lunt written by Orrington Lunt, BGC. As noted in the preface, the part of Dolly's diary that describes the war was edited and published separately before Robertson's 1960 and 1962 editions as *A Woman's War-Time Journal*, ed. Julian Street (New York: 1918; Macon, Ga.: 1927; Atlanta: Cherokee Publishing Company, 1994).

36. *Diary*, November 19, 1864. There is a significant historiography of southern women during the Civil War. See, for example, Catherine Clinton and Nina Silber, eds., *Divided Houses*; Rable, *Civil Wars*; Scott, *Southern Lady*, 80–102; Carol K. Bleser and Frederick Heath, "The Clays of Alabama: The Impact of the Civil War on a Southern Marriage," in *In Joy and In Sorrow: Women, Family, and Marriage in the Victorian South, 1830–1900*, ed. Carol K. Bleser (New York: Oxford University Press, 1991), 135–53; Victorian Bynum, *Unruly Women: The Politics of Social and Sexual Control in the Old South* (Chapel Hill: University of North Carolina Press, 1992); Marilyn Mayer Culpepper, *Trials and Triumphs: Women of the American Civil War* (East Lansing: Michigan State University Press, 1991); and Drew Gilpin Faust, "Altars of Sacrifice: Confederate Women and the Narratives of War," *The Journal of American History* 76 (March 1990): 1200–1228. Drew Gilpin Faust, *Mothers of Invention: Women of the Slaveholding South in the American Civil War* (Chapel Hill: University of North Carolina Press, 1996).

37. *Diary*, November 19, 1864. It is difficult to ascertain how Dolly's slaves responded to freedom and who among them remained on the plantation as tenant farmers or laborers. By 1870, Elbert and Julia, ages sixty-five and fifty-seven, and their son Christopher had moved to a nearby section of the county to live with freedman Henderson Glass, a twenty-four-year-old farmer, and probably his wife, Sophia, seventeen. James (b. 1838), Lewis (b. 1832), Ned (1846–1927), David (1848–1879), Lucy (b. 1838), and Hester (1854–1930) established families and households nearby in the county. Former slave Frank's wife, Lydia Glass-Burge, returned to the plantation, probably as a house servant for Dolly. Two of her sons, Abe and Wiley Glass, who had been taken by federal armies, returned to the Burge plantation after the war. Lydia's daughter, Sidney, helped to manage the plantation with her husband from about 1873 to about 1920. Theodore Davis, compiler, *The United States 1870 Census: Freedmen in Newton County, Georgia* (Oxford, Ga.: by the author, 1988), 33, 15, 56; Dolly to Sadai, undated, BGC; Julian Street, *American Adventures: A Second Trip "Abroad at Home"* (New York: Century Co., 1917), 399–401; MDB.

38. In 1860, William had a sizable estate valued at over $43,000, some farm land

and animals, and thirty-three slaves. He had served the Methodist church in various roles from the time he was admitted on trial into the South Carolina Conference in 1822, and he also helped to found Emory College and Macon Female College. W. J. Parks's Bible, IFP; U.S. Census Records, State of Georgia, 1860, Population Schedules, Newton County, NAMP, 434; ibid., 1870, Population Schedules, Newton County, NAMP, 78; ibid., 1860, Agricultural Schedules, Newton County, NAMP, 13–14; Alfred M. Pierce, *A History of Methodism in Georgia — February 5, 1736 – June 24, 1955* (Atlanta: North Georgia Conference Historical Society, 1956), 6, 7, 110.

39. Marriage contract, September 13, 1866, BGC. Despite this contract, probate records indicate that in 1870 William gave the court a security bond of $12,000 to annex the estate. That year he reported the property value as $5,950. There is no evidence that Dolly resisted this annexation or that it violated the marriage contract. Also that year, William reported that his real estate was worth $6,800 and his personal estate worth $10,000. And, as is mentioned above, Dolly retained real estate worth $5,000 and a personal estate worth $1,000. Newton County, Court of Ordinary, Estate Records Vol. 14, 1869–1873, GDAH, 260; U.S. Census Records, State of Georgia, 1870, Population Schedules, Morgan County, NAMP, 78. William J. Parks's home was the Emory College President's House on Wesley Street in Oxford.

40. William J. Parks to Dolly, December 25, 1867; *Diary*, December 25, 1873.

41. A February 1872 version of William Parks's will is in the Burge-Gray Collection. A slightly revised version, written in May 1872 and probated November 1873, is in the Newton County court records. Court of Ordinary, Will Records, 1870–1896, GDAH, 36–39.

42. Sadai graduated from Wesleyan Female College in 1873. Obituary of John Davis Gray written by the Church Conference, Methodist Episcopal Church, Covington, Ga., IFP; Dolly to Sadai, undated, BGC.

43. Dolly to Sadai, undated, BGC; Dolly's obituary appeared in the *Atlanta Journal*, October 29, 1891, 2, HNC, 595.

Family Members and Other Principals

The information in the following notes comes from Dolly's list of slaves at the end of her diary, entitled "Slaves Births and Deaths," and extensive genealogical research in probate, census, and manuscript records done by Mildred Diane Baynes, a great-great-granddaughter of Elbert and Julia Burge.

These notes provide biographical information on members of the African American families who are not mentioned directly in the diary text. Available biographical information for individuals who are mentioned in the diary is noted there.

1. Sold to Mr. Pace in 1856. He did not appear again in Newton County records.

2. Sold to Mr. Pace along with her brother Elbert in 1856. Sometime around 1866, she married Squire Mark and had one child, Sherman (c. 1867–c.1900).

3. Ned married Mary Dotson in 1868. Their children were Sarah, Tom Bell, Ned Jr., Julia, and Roger. He married his second wife, Catherine Ann Adams (c. 1850–c. 1922), in 1872. Their children were Willie, Elbert, Fannie, Margaret and Susan.

4. Married Thomas Brooks in 1868 and had at least one child, Baalam.

5. Married Sallie Adams in 1873 and Flora c.1878. He took the first name Burge in the 1870 federal census, and had at least six children: Mollie, Noble, Mattie, Luke, Emma, and Willie.

6. Married Robert Shepherd in 1877. They had eight children, including Willie, David, Clayton, Robert, Oscar, and Henrietta.

7. Sold to Mr. Perry in 1853.

8. Milly was a sister to Julia, Martha, and Hannah. She belonged to Love Zachariah Glass, and later to a Mr. Finley.

CHAPTER ONE. A Madison Teacher and Faithful Christian

1. It appears from the transition from her February entries to her March entries that Dolly miswrote the year during February. She actually began the diary in February 1848.

2. Dolly boarded with Wilds (1804–1861) and Nancy Clowers Kolb (1802–1869) in their Madison home, down the street from a Methodist female college where Dolly may have taught. The Kolbs maintained a large plantation, in addition to their town home. They had no children. U.S. Census Records, State of Georgia, 1850, Population Schedules, Morgan County, NAMP, 127; Newton County Superior Court Records, 1869–1875, GDAH, 33.

3. Winiphred Hebbard, wife of Mahitiah H. Hebbard, who died in 1861. John H. Hebbard, probably their son, served as agent for Mrs. Hebbard after her husband's death. Mahitiah, or M. H. as Dolly calls him, owned no real estate and only $400 when he died. He did, however, have three slaves in 1848. Morgan County Tax Digest for 1848, Morgan County Courthouse, Madison, Ga., 108.

4. Charles and Mary Silman Baldwin married on February 8, 1848, in Madison. Morgan County Marriage records, GDAH, 270.

5. Mrs. Sarah B. Cook, the Connecticut-born wife of a merchant tailor in Madison, was about thirty-one at this time. Reverend Homer Hendee was the headmaster of the school where Dolly taught. His wife was Frances King of Greene County, whom he married in June 1847. At this time, he owned no real estate or slaves. Mr. & Mrs. K. probably indicates the Kolbs.

6. Alfred and Susan Shaw were good friends of Dolly's in Madison. Susan was approximately forty-four at this time, and Alfred was about forty-two and ran a furniture store in Madison. In 1850, they had several children and two German mechanics living in their household. U.S. Census Records, State of Georgia, 1850, Population Schedules, Morgan County, NAMP, 140.

7. Dolly's friend Wilds Kolb of Madison had a brother, Valentine, who lived in Cobb County. Valentine's son, and Wilds's nephew, was also named Wilds and he apparently attended school near his uncle. Morgan County Superior Court Writ Records, 1869–1875, Morgan County Courthouse, Madison, Ga., 33.

8. Mrs. Sarah Floyd lived across the street from Dolly with her attorney husband, Stewart. He was approximately forty-three, she was eleven years his junior, and they had four children in 1850. U.S. Census Records, State of Georgia, 1850, Population Schedules, Morgan County, NAMP, 133.

9. There were several Saffold families in the Madison area at this time. Mr. Graves is most likely Iverson Lea (1799–1864), a prosperous planter in neighboring Newton County and longtime friend of Dolly. His second wife, Sara Ward Dutton Graves (b. 1814) had moved to Covington from New York to teach. In addition to having four of their own children, they raised Sallie Burge (1837–1886), the orphaned daughter of Hamilton Burge, Thomas's brother. *HNC*, 706–7; U.S. Census Records, State of Georgia, 1860, Population Schedules, Newton County, NAMP, 447.

10. Dolly probably meant the tenth.

11. Probably John W. Porter, a fifty-three-year-old farmer who lived in the area with his family. U.S. Census Records, State of Georgia, 1850, Population Schedules, Morgan County, NAMP, 107.

12. Rev. Charles M. Irwin pastored the Madison Baptist Church from January 1848 to 1856. *History of the Baptist Denomination in Georgia*, Compiled for the Christian Index (Atlanta: James P. Harrington & Co., 1881), 284–86.

13. Probably the wife of George H. Round, one of the three original officers

and second superintendent of Emory College. Henry Morton Bullock, *A History of Emory University* (Nashville: Parthenon Press, 1936), 36, 44, 62.

14. Perhaps Lucius L., a twenty-three-year-old teacher in Madison. Dolly occasionally mentions his wife, Julia, as well. U.S. Census Records, State of Georgia, 1850, Population Schedules, Morgan County, NAMP, 139.

15. Probably Mary F. Walton, second wife of Peter W. Walton, a wealthy planter in the area. U.S. Census Records, State of Georgia, 1850, Population Schedules, Morgan County, NAMP, 127.

16. *Neal's Saturday Gazette and Lady's Literary Museum*, published from Philadelphia between 1844 and 1848. *A Checklist of Pennsylvania Newspapers* (Harrisburg: Pennsylvania Historical Commission, 1944), 1:278.

17. Dolly entertained a couple of suitors named *Mr. B.* This probably was Leonard Bissell, a forty-three-year-old cotton dealer and native of Connecticut. She later visited with Thomas Burge (1806–1858), her second husband, sometime after his first wife died in August 1848. U.S. Census Records, State of Georgia, 1850, Population Schedules, Morgan County, NAMP, 103; Morgan County Tax Digest for 1848, Morgan County Courthouse, Madison, Ga., 102.

18. Jordan G. Howard was about twenty-nine at this time, a physician, and married to M. H., twenty-four. U.S. Census Records, State of Georgia, 1850, Population Schedules, Morgan County, NAMP, 120.

19. Probably Eliza F. Walker, wife of John B. Walker, planter and philanthropist. In 1850, he was forty-five, she thirty-five, and they had eight children. U.S. Census Records, State of Georgia, 1850, Population Schedules, Morgan County, NAMP, 115.

20. Orrington Lunt (1815–1897) was Dolly's second oldest brother. He married Cornelia A. Gray (1819–1909) in 1842 and moved to Chicago, where he became a successful businessman and helped to found Evanston, Illinois, and Northwestern University.

21. Probably Mary Homer Stearns Rivers (b. 1828), the eldest daughter of Silas Stearns and Mary Lunt Stearns, Dolly's aunt. Thomas Lunt, *A History of the Lunt Family in America* (Salem, Mass.: Salem Press Company, c. 1914; reprint, Decorah, Ia.: Anundsen Publishing Co., 1983), 126.

22. Rev. George W. Lane was a minister in the Georgia Methodist Conference, an early chair of the ancient languages department at Emory, and secretary of the board of trustees in 1836. Bullock, *History of Emory*, 36, 52.

23. John Quincy Adams, sixth president of the United States, died February 23, 1848.

24. Dolly's sister, Sarah (1821–1881), married Isaac Comings, a physician. The couple lived in Georgia when Dolly and her first husband moved South, but they lived alternately in the North and in Macon, Georgia, between about 1847 and 1859. They ultimately settled in New York. "From the Memory Book of Sadie C. Langmuir," IFP.

25. Martha Porter, nineteen in the 1850 census, was the daughter of John W. Porter. Virginia Jones was the daughter of Dr. E. E. Jones, who lived across the street from the Kolbs and Dolly. U.S. Census Records, State of Georgia, 1850, Population Schedules, Morgan County, NAMP, 107, 120.

26. Centurion's.

27. Probably a Presbyterian women's association.

28. Dolly's father, William (1788–1863) lived in Bowdoinham, Maine, with his second wife, Priscilla Purrington (1795–1863) and their children.

29. John Wingfield, fifty-nine in 1850, was a medical doctor and owner of a drugstore in Madison. It appears that his wife was named Mary M., aged fifty-seven in 1850. U.S. Census Records, State of Georgia, 1850, Population Schedules, Morgan County, NAMP, 103.

30. Rev. William J. Parks (1799–1873), or Uncle Billy as she sometimes called him, was a prominent Methodist minister in the area and longtime friend of Dolly's. He would be Dolly's third spouse, and she his, in 1866.

31. This could be Nancy Robinson, approximately twenty-two, married to John T., a farmer. They were residents of Newton County in 1850. Alternatively, this could be Martha Robson, about twenty-three, married to John Robson, an English-born merchant in the Madison area. Mrs. Burnet is probably Caroline Ray Burnett, wife of William Burnett, aged thirty in 1850. The original editor, James Robertson, suggests that the women were Nancy Robinson and Mary Burnet, two names I could not find in Morgan County at this time (12). Morgan County Tax Digest for 1848, Morgan County Courthouse, Madison, Ga., 114; Theodore Davis, compiler, *The Complete 1850 Federal Census of Newton County, Georgia* (Oxford, Ga.: Oxford Shrine Society, 1978), 59; U.S. Census Records, State of Georgia, 1850, Population Schedules, Morgan County, NAMP, 117.

32. Mary Thomas and Thomas P. Saffold were married in March 1847. He remarried Sarah E. Reid in 1854. Frances T. Ingmire, *Morgan County, Georgia Marriage Records, 1808–1865* (Madison, Ga.: privately printed, 1985), 41, Morgan County Courthouse, Madison, Ga.

33. Orrington Lewis was Dolly's son, born in 1843, who died in infancy.

34. Frances J. Baldwin was married to Thomas Baldwin. They were twenty-four

and thirty-four, respectively, in 1850. U.S. Census Records, State of Georgia, 1850, Population Schedules, Morgan County, NAMP, 118.

35. Probably Nathaniel Allen Jr., twenty-four, a Methodist minister. His father, also Nathaniel, aged sixty-five in 1848, was a prosperous farmer. A *colporteur* is one who sells religious literature. U.S. Census Records, State of Georgia, 1850, Population Schedules, Morgan County, NAMP, 117; ibid., 1860, Population Schedules, Morgan County, NAMP, 924.

36. Perhaps Elizabeth H. Harriss and John D. Harriss, a thirty-one-year-old Morgan County farmer in 1850. She was twenty-one in 1850, with three children. U.S. Census Records, State of Georgia, 1850, Population Schedules, Morgan County, NAMP, 118.

37. At this point, Susan had been Dolly's only child to survive infancy. She died at the age of three in 1844.

38. Augustus Baldwin Longstreet (1790–1870), attorney, state legislator, superior court judge, humorist, author, Methodist minister (in 1838), and president of Emory College from 1839 until 1848. After Emory, Longstreet served as president of other colleges, and later as a chaplain for the Georgia militia during the Civil War. *DGB*, 632–33.

39. Amy Vanlandingham lived in the lot behind the Kolbs. In 1850, she was sixty-six years old and the head of her household. Crawley's 1837 Survey in Madison (a map), Morgan County Courthouse, Madison, Ga.; U.S. Census Records, State of Georgia, 1850, Population Schedules, Morgan County, NAMP, 145.

40. Probably Katherine Swift, who was born in Ireland, lived in front of the Methodist Church, and was eighty years old in 1850. Crawley's 1837 Survey in Madison, Morgan County Courthouse, Madison, Ga.; U.S. Census Records, State of Georgia, 1850, Population Schedules, Morgan County, NAMP, 127.

41. The daughter of Mary F. and Peter W. Walton.

42. Merritt Warren, of Virginia. His daughter, Virginia, whom Dolly mentions occasionally, was seventeen in 1850 and appears to have attended Macon Female College. U.S. Census Records, State of Georgia, 1850, Population Schedules, Morgan County, NAMP, 144.

43. James Osgood Andrew (1794–1871) was a senior bishop of the Methodist Episcopal Church and at the center of the schism between the northern and southern wings of the church. In 1832, Andrew was elected bishop, it was thought because he was the only southern candidate who did not own slaves. In 1836, he moved to Newton County and became a trustee of the Methodist Manual Labor School, the forerunner of Emory College, for which he was a trustee as well. By

1844, he had acquired slaves through bequest, inheritance, and marriage, sparking heated debate within the national church. The southern caucus discouraged his resignation and subsequently separated from the northern church. *DGB*, 28–29.

44. There were several small, private schools in the area where Dolly may have taught. This could have been the Madison Female College, a Methodist school, but it did not officially open until 1849.

45. Cinthia Killian, wife of Daniel Killian, aged forty-nine in 1849. He was a contractor who built the Presbyterian Church in 1842, where Dolly occasionally attended services and which still stands today. U.S. Census Records, State of Georgia, 1860, Population Schedules, Morgan County, NAMP, 916.

46. The diary's original editor, James Robertson, indicates that John Robson and E. H. Cohen were partners in a successful mercantile business. I have found no reference to this business specifically, but John Robson had partners in dry goods stores, and one of them may have been Eleazer Hart Cohen. *Diary*, ed. Robertson, 21.

47. The diary's original editor, James Robertson, suggests that this was Thomas J. Burney. However, none of my investigations link him to a store. Town historians indicate that Thomas J. Burney was a well-known lawyer in Madison, and later mayor. In the 1850 federal census, Thomas J. Burney is listed as a forty-nine-year-old farmer, with a wife and several children. *Diary*, ed. Robertson, 21; U.S. Census Records, State of Georgia, 1850, Population Schedules, Morgan County, NAMP, 117.

48. Hugh Ogilby was a forty-eight-year-old physician in Madison in 1850. His wife, Sarah A., was twenty-nine, and they had three children. Dr. William W. B. Crawford married Mary M. Knight in December 1848. He too was a physician, aged thirty-eight in the 1860 census. U.S. Census Records, State of Georgia, 1850, Population Schedules, Morgan County, NAMP, 117; ibid., 1860, Population Schedules, Morgan County, NAMP, 922, 920; Ingmire, *Morgan County Marriage Records*, 12.

49. Priscilla Crocker Lunt (b. c. 1757) married Joseph Lunt (1753–1811). Thomas Lunt, *A History of the Lunt Family in America*, 66.

50. Caleb Key was a Methodist minister, about forty-five at this time, and the person who married Dolly and her second husband, Thomas Burge, in the Madison Methodist Church. He, his wife Elizabeth, and several children lived near the Saffolds and the Shaws in Madison. Their son Joseph became the first Emory College graduate elected Bishop of the Methodist Church. U.S. Census Records, State of Georgia, 1850, Population Schedules, Morgan County, NAMP, 140; *HNC*, 119.

51. Dolly mentions some of these women, such as Mrs. Shaw, Floyd, and Cook, throughout the diary and they have already been identified. Others are mentioned only here, and are not easily identified. Mrs. Allen is probably Emily, the wife of Nathaniel Allen, senior; Mrs. Burr is probably Harriett, aged thirty-four in 1849, the wife of a local dentist, William H. U.S. Census Records, State of Georgia, 1850, Population Schedules, Morgan County, NAMP, 117, 118; ibid., 1860, Population Schedules, Morgan County, NAMP, 924, 930.

52. Probably Amarintha Reese, wife of Augustus Reese, a lawyer who eventually became a prominent judge. Amarintha would have been twenty-eight in 1849. A slightly less likely candidate is Elizabeth A. Reese, a widow, who owned the lot next to Mrs. Katherine Swift, very near the Kolbs and Dolly, but she married Reuben Mann in 1841, so Dolly would likely refer to her as Mrs. Mann. U.S. Census Records, State of Georgia, 1850, Population Schedules, Morgan County, NAMP, 141; Crawley's 1837 Survey in Madison, Morgan County Courthouse, Madison, Ga.; Morgan County Marriage Records, 1821–1879, GDAH, 319.

53. Lancelot Johnston was a successful planter and inventor in the area. He was sixty years old in 1850, and his wife Margaret was fifty-six. U.S. Census Records, State of Georgia, 1850, Population Schedules, Morgan County, NAMP, 120.

54. Dolly probably meant March 9, or Saturday, March 11.

55. Dolly made two March 16 entries.

56. The Sons of Temperance and the Ladies of Madison were probably relatively short-lived local religious organizations.

57. Probably Richard M. Baker, a forty-year-old Presbyterian minister in 1850 living next to Thomas Saffold. U.S. Census Records, State of Georgia, 1850, Population Schedules, Morgan County, NAMP, 145.

58. Alexander Means (1801–1883) was a prominent Methodist minister and educator in Georgia. Licensed to preach in 1828, Means joined Bishop Andrew and Augustus Longstreet in conducting the first revival in Atlanta. Means was the first rector of the Methodist Manual Labor School, which became Emory College in 1836. He, Ignatious Few, and George Lane comprised the original faculty. Over the next twenty years, Means served as professor at the Medical College in Augusta, president of the Masonic Female College in Covington, fourth president of Emory College, and chair of chemistry at the Atlanta Medical College. *DGB*, 700–702.

59. Probably Mary Fannin, twenty-three, in the household of J. A. Fannin, twenty-seven, in 1850. U.S. Census Records, State of Georgia, 1850, Population Schedules, Morgan County, NAMP, 104.

60. The dashes that follow the entry, her quick letters to cousin Mary and

Mr. Graves, and the entries that follow suggest that Leonard Bissel, Thomas Burge, or both of them were escalating their pursuit of Dolly. She was engaged to Thomas by December 1849.

61. This entry suggests that Mr. Bissel was more interested in Dolly than she in him, a cause for some amusement to Mr. Kolb. Perhaps Dolly was most interested in Thomas Burge.

62. Again, Dolly remembers her child Susan.

63. Perhaps Dr. G. is Iverson L. Graves, but it is unclear why she refers to him as "Dr." Henry Lea Graves (1842–1892) was Iverson's eldest son, but he would have been only seven years old at this time *HNC*, 706–7.

64. The only Few living in Madison at this time was James F. Few. Alternatively, this could be Ignatious A. Few, one of the founders of Emory College and its president from 1836 to 1839. Morgan County Tax Digest for 1849, Morgan County Courthouse, Madison, Ga., 126.

65. This word is difficult to read in the original and define.

66. Probably Georgia's Stone Mountain, an enormous monolith with 683 exposed acres, about 15 miles east of Atlanta and 40 miles northwest of Madison. Today, the stone bears a carving that is 190 feet wide and 90 feet tall of Confederate President Jefferson Davis and Generals Robert E. Lee and Stonewall Jackson.

67. Dolly is referring to her first husband, Samuel Harding Brown Lewis (1816–1843), with whom she moved to Georgia in 1842. He died in September 1843.

CHAPTER TWO. A Happy Family Circle

1. During the 1850s and 1860s, Dolly often mentions Brother, Dr., and Mrs. Thomas. Most of the time, she probably means Dr. James R. T. Thomas (1812–1897), president of Emory from 1855 to 1867 and former professor at Wesleyan Female College. Bullock, *History of Emory*, 94–100.

2. Probably Nancy, fifty-four, and Virginia G., seventeen, living together in Newton County in 1850. Virginia is listed also in the Madison household of Lucius and Julia Wittich, with seventeen other school-age girls, all probably students at Lucius's school. U.S. Census Records, State of Georgia, 1850, Population Schedules, Newton County, NAMP, 511; 1850 Population Schedules, Morgan County, NAMP, 139.

3. Probably Rev. George W. Lane, a Methodist minister in the area, established a place for religious meetings.

4. Julia Clark-Glass-Burge (1813–c. 1878) and her three oldest children were

sold by Rebecca Clark to James Glass in 1836, and to Thomas Burge sometime after that. She and Elbert Leving-Glass-Burge had twelve children. This child was Ann, born February 8, 1850. MDB; SBD.

5. The Perrys were Dolly's closest neighbors. Clarissa Patterson Perry, the widow of Josiah Perry (1786–1846), managed a large plantation with her sons James (b. c. 1824) and Josiah Patterson (b. c. 1831), and Henry Branford (1830–1884). By 1860, Josiah had married Laura Ann Heard and had four children, all living next to Clarissa and Henry. *HNC*, 866–67; U.S. Census Records, State of Georgia, 1850, Population Schedules, Newton County, NAMP, 508; ibid., 1860, Population Schedules, Newton County, NAMP, 454.

6. There are several Glass families in Newton County at this time. Most likely, she refers to Minerva Glass, approximately thirty-six, wife of Manson Glass, who lived on a plantation very near the Burges. The diary's original editor, Robertson, suggests that she is referring to Mary and Zachariah Glass, approximately twenty-eight and thirty-two, on a smaller farm, further away in the southern part of the county. U.S. Census Records, State of Georgia, 1850, Population Schedules, Newton County, NAMP, 479, 457; ibid., 1860, Population Schedules, Newton County, NAMP, 454; *Diary*, ed. Robertson, 38.

7. Probably Joel Stansell, fifty-one-year-old Methodist minister in 1850. U.S. Census Records, State of Georgia, 1850, Population Schedules, Newton County, NAMP, 462.

8. Probably Robert Rakestraw, sixty-two, farmer and husband to Martha, sixty-one, and neighbor of the Burges. Presumably Robert's son, Robert M., thirty-one, lived nearby with wife, Louisa, twenty-nine, and three children. U.S. Census Records, State of Georgia, 1850, Population Schedules, Newton County, NAMP, 505, 478.

9. John M. B. Bonnell (1820–1871) was an adjunct professor of languages and mathematics at Emory College in 1848. In 1849, he was appointed librarian. He later served as president of Wesleyan Female College from 1859 to 1871. Bullock, *History of Emory*, 90, 115.

10. Born in 1819, Martha was one of the house slaves. She was married to Lewis, who was born in 1814, and they had several children. SBD.

11. Margaret (or Marguarrett) Louisiana Burge (1844–1863) was the fourth living child of Thomas and Mary Burge, and Dolly's stepdaughter.

12. Probably a local class for Bible instruction and Christian worship. At this time, it was illegal to teach slaves to read and write.

13. Probably Dolly's stepson, born in 1835.

14. Dolly records cryptically in incorrect French that she is not pregnant.

15. Most likely a different Floyd family from the ones who lived across the street from Dolly in Madison. This was probably John J. Floyd, an attorney in the Oxford-Covington town area. He was about forty in 1850, his wife Mary, thirty-one, with five children under fifteen years of age. He was one of the founding trustees of the Southern Female College in Covington, in 1851. U.S. Census Records, State of Georgia, 1850, Population Schedules, Newton County, NAMP, 441; *HNC*, 112.

16. This is probably Thomas's nephew. Dolly usually did not distinguish between his son and nephew.

17. This is present in grape juice and deposited in a crude form during fermentation on the sides of wine casks. It forms a hard crust, also called argol.

18. Dolly indicates—again, in cryptic, incorrect French—that she is pregnant.

19. Dolly spent a great deal of time with her neighbors, the Harwells. Jackson Harwell (1773–1852) married three times. His first wife Marthay (Patsy) Fretwell (1780–1808) was the sister of Nancy Fretwell Burge, Thomas's mother. Hence, Jackson was Thomas's uncle by marriage. In 1837, Jackson married his third wife, Rhoda Watts Patrick Harwell, a widow who was about forty-one years old. In 1850, the couple lived with Rebecca, his twenty-eight-year-old daughter, and Amanda, his and Rhoda's eleven-year-old child. Dolly frequently mentions "Aunt Rhoda." *HNC*, 725–26.

20. One of the Burge slaves, Hannah (1819–1864) was married to Franklin, born the same year as she. SBD.

21. The Pierce family, particularly father Lovick (1785–1879) and son George Foster (1811–1884)—both Methodist ministers affiliated with Emory—made frequent appearances in Dolly's diary. This is probably George Foster, who resided in Newton County in 1850, as president of Emory College. In 1838, he became the first president of Georgia Female College in Macon and then served as president of Emory from 1848 to 1854. He was elected Methodist bishop in 1854. His father, Lovick, was appointed agent of the Georgia Female College (later Wesleyan) in 1838, and then trustee of both Wesleyan and Emory Colleges. U.S. Census Records, State of Georgia, 1850, Population Schedules, Newton County, NAMP, 433; *DGB*, 795–98.

22. Dolly mentions the Rakestraws frequently. There were two Rakestraw families living close to one another in 1850. The older, headed by Robert, sixty-two in 1850, included wife Martha and two unmarried daughters. The younger, headed by Robert M., thirty-one in 1850, included wife Louisa and several young children.

U.S. Census Records, State of Georgia, 1850, Population Schedules, Newton County, NAMP, 505, 478; ibid., 1860, Population Schedules, Newton County, NAMP, 463.

23. Born in 1848, Sanford was a three-year-old slave, the son of Lewis and Martha. SBD.

24. Dr. Horace T. Shaw, age forty-eight in 1850, was married to Mary Ann, thirty. U.S. Census Records, State of Georgia, 1850, Population Schedules, Newton County, NAMP, 510.

25. Eliza Graves Burge (1846–1867) was the youngest child of Thomas Burge.

26. Probably William S. Montgomery, a planter and neighbor of Dolly's. In 1860, he was forty-three and his wife, Elizabeth, thirty-seven. U.S. Census Records, State of Georgia, 1860, Population Schedules, Newton County, NAMP, 451.

27. At this time, Isaac and Sarah Comings and their growing family lived alternately between Macon, Georgia, where he taught at a medical school, and the North.

28. Dolly's list of slave births and deaths includes no birth on this or any near date. It appears Dolly may have seen some mystical connection between the two events. SBD.

29. Dolly and Thomas founded Mt. Pleasant Church along with several friends and neighbors: Iverson Lea and Sarah W. Graves, John W. and Louisa Rogers Hinton, Isaac H. and Eliza Parker, Mrs. Adeline Strong, Mr. and Mrs. Horace H. Strong, Mr. and Mrs. Thomas Ansley Sr., Mr. and Mrs. Benjamin Ansley, William, Mary Ann, Matilda, Artimesia, and William Guice Jr., and Mr. and Mrs. C. C. Wright. Church records contradict Dolly's diary and date the founding to 1851. *HNC*, 321.

30. Rhody F. Callahan, a neighbor of Dolly's, was fifty-three in 1860. At that time, she headed her own household of seven young people between the ages of fourteen and twenty-seven. U.S. Census Records, State of Georgia, 1860, Population Schedules, Newton County, NAMP, 458.

31. According to Dolly's records, this was Winnie, Martha's tenth and youngest child. SBD.

32. Thomas's eldest daughter, Rebecca (b. 1830), was married first to Matthew A. Mitchell.

33. There were at least three Pitts families in Newton County in 1850. Davis, *1850 Federal Census of Newton County*, 54.

34. Dolly's father (1788–1863), stepmother Priscilla Purrington Lunt (1795–1863), and their third child Caroline E. (b. 1833).

35. One of the nearby sections of Newton County was Social Circle. It had a train depot.

36. There were at least five Parker families in Newton County in 1850. They were headed by a merchant, farmer, carriage maker, blacksmith, and chair maker. Davis, *1850 Federal Census of Newton County*, 51–52.

37. Dr. F. M. Cheney was a successful planter and physician who lived near the Burges. He developed a cough syrup, "Cheney's Expectorant," which was sold as late as 1937. *HNC*, 331.

38. Dolly's brother Orrington Lunt (1815–1897) came to visit as well.

39. Dolly mentions the Guice family frequently. It is difficult to determine Mrs. William Guice's first name, but Matilda, Mary Ann, Artimesia, and William Jr., probably all children of William, joined William Sr., in founding the Mt. Pleasant Church with Dolly and Thomas. All of these Guices lived at least until the 1860 census. *HNC*, 321; U.S. Census Records, State of Georgia, 1860, Population Schedules, Newton County, NAMP, 454.

40. John W. Talley was a prominent Methodist minister in the area and one of the founders of Wesleyan Female College. Samuel Luttrell Akers, *The First Hundred Years of Wesleyan College, 1836–1936* (Macon, Ga.: Beehive Press, 1976), 9.

41. Newton, born in April 1840, was the child of Martha and Lewis. He later married Julia Glass, circa 1866. Lydia, born on October 20, 1853, was the child of Hannah and Franklin. SBD.

42. Probably the wife of William P. Graham, one of the original trustees of Emory College. Bullock, *History of Emory*, 55.

43. There were several Roquemore families in Newton County in 1850 and 1860. Davis, *1850 Federal Census of Newton County*, 59–60; U.S. Census Records, State of Georgia, 1850, Population Schedules, Newton County, NAMP, 458; ibid., 1860, Population Schedules, Newton County, NAMP, 458.

44. Dolly probably remembered work accomplished on the thirteenth and noted it even though it was at least the fifteenth.

45. Probably Martha and Mary, then approximately thirty-five and twenty-six years old, the unmarried daughters of Robert M. and Martha Rakestraw. U.S. Census Records, State of Georgia, 1860, Population Schedules, Newton County, NAMP, 463.

46. Osborne L. Smith (1819–1878) was born in Green County, Georgia, and graduated from Emory College in 1842. In 1845, he became professor of Latin at Emory. He taught languages at Wesleyan College in 1850 and served as president of that institution from 1854 to 1859. During the Civil War, he served in both the

House and Senate of the Georgia legislature and later went into the ministry. He held the presidency of Emory College from 1871 to 1875. Bullock, *History of Emory*, 159.

47. Dolly is referring to one of two possible slaves: Lewis (b. 1814), the husband of Martha; or Lewis (1832–after 1880), the second child of Elbert and Julia. Around 1858, the latter married a woman named Eunice and had six children: Emma, James, Julia, Dock, Lucy, and Sarah. SBD, MDB.

48. Sarah Cornelia Burge, or Sadai, was Dolly's only child to live to adulthood. Dolly alternately spelled her name Sada, Sadai, and Saydee.

49. Born in April 1839, William was a seven-year-old slave. His parents were Hannah and Frank. SBD.

50. Thomas's uncle, his mother's brother Leonard.

51. Anna was very likely Ann Matilda Comings (b. 1840), the eldest daughter of Sarah and Isaac Comings.

52. W. T. Branham was a prominent Methodist minister in Georgia. In 1860, he was forty-six years old with a wife, Elizabeth, forty, and several children. U.S. Census Records, State of Georgia, 1860, Population Schedules, Newton County, NAMP, 434.

53. Probably Charles Strong, forty-nine in 1850. U.S. Census Records, State of Georgia, 1850, Population Schedules, Newton County, NAMP, 518.

CHAPTER THREE. A Widow Planter

1. Thomas Burge died on December 10, 1858. Elbert (1806–after 1880), Thomas's personal slave, and Elbert's mother, Lucy Glass-Harwell (c. 1781–after 1883), were owned by Zachariah Glass from 1826 until 1833 when Zachariah's death precipitated the liquidation of his estate. Lucy was sold to Richard Harwell and Elbert to Thomas Burge, who probably had been renting Elbert's labor since 1826. Thomas Burge purchased Elbert's wife Julia (1813–1878) and their three oldest children sometime after 1836. They had twelve children. SBD; MDB.

2. Probably Dolly's half sister, Caroline, from Maine. She was born in 1833 and Dolly refers to her alternately as Cally, Carrie, and Calla.

3. William D. Stanton (1820–1904), a carpenter, was the fifth child of Batt Short and Abigail Middlebrooks Stanton. In 1850, William was living with his older brother Henry T. Stanton, a farmer, and his family. William never married. He appears again in the diary when he filed suit against Dolly for payment of a debt allegedly incurred by Thomas Burge. *HNC*, 920; Davis, *1850 Federal Census of New-*

ton County, 66; Newton County Superior Court Minutes 1863–1868, GDAH, 165–66, 173, 195, 199, 257.

4. Probably Allen Turner. In 1860, Allen Turner was sixty-nine years old and a clergyman. He was married to Martha M., sixty-four, and had Martha A. W., thirty-six (perhaps a daughter), living in his household. Dolly refers to him alternately as "old Uncle Allen" and "Rev." U.S. Census Records, State of Georgia, 1860, Population Schedules, Newton County, NAMP, 419.

5. Probably Julia, her slave.

6. Probably William C. Davis, who helped to organize a local academy. He was seventy-three in 1850. *HNC*, 105; Davis, *1850 Federal Census of Newton County*, 16.

7. Dolly saw John Julius, who is listed as a forty-nine-year-old lawyer in 1860. She was seeking the legal guardianship of Eliza, her twelve-year-old step-daughter. U.S. Census Records, State of Georgia, 1850, Population Schedules, Newton County, NAMP, 441; ibid., 1850, Population Schedules, Newton County, NAMP, 406.

8. This entry indicates that Dolly allowed her slaves to grow a certain amount of cotton, for which they could keep the profits.

9. Mathew A. Mitchell, Eliza's brother-in-law and Rebecca's husband, was named Eliza's guardian. During this month, Mitchell sued Dolly on behalf of Eliza for a Bill in Equity regarding the distribution of Thomas's estate. Newton County Superior Court Minutes 1858–1863, March 1860, GDAH, 213, 291, 367; see also the Petition of Eliza G. Burge to the Court of Ordinary, Newton County Minutes Records 1863–1864, GDAH, 6.

10. Perhaps G. W. W. Stone, forty-one in 1860, a professor at Emory College. U.S. Census Records, State of Georgia, 1860, Population Schedules, Newton County, NAMP, 434.

11. Sandtown was the name for the area of Newton County later incorporated as Newborn. There were areas of the town that had a clear, fairly white sand.

12. The town of Monticello is about twenty miles southeast of Burge Plantation.

13. Young John Allen (1836–1907) attended Emory College and later transferred to Emory and Henry College. He was received on trial into the Georgia Conference of the Methodist Episcopal Church, South, and then appointed missionary to China. In December 1859, he, his wife, and their infant daughter sailed to Shanghai and served there for nearly five years without reimbursements for his board. In 1864, he was appointed to teach English at a government school. Later, he worked as a government translator and a newspaper editor and, in 1868, began his own paper. *DGB*, 19–20.

14. Amanda, who was ten at the time of the 1850 census, was the daughter of Manson and Minerva Glass. U.S. Census Records, State of Georgia, 1850, Population Schedules, Newton County, NAMP, 479.

15. S. W. Gresham lived in the house next to Dolly's during the 1860 federal census. He is listed as a thirty-three-year-old overseer with no real estate of his own and a personal estate worth $150. He lived with Frances, forty-two (perhaps his wife); Amy M., thirteen; and Josiah A., twelve. U.S. Census Records, State of Georgia, 1860, Population Schedules, Newton County, NAMP, 454.

16. Probably slaves: Martha, born in 1819; Middleton, Martha's son, born in 1846; and Sally (1830-1879), the eldest daughter of Elbert and Julia. In 1849, Sally married May Ansley and had at least three children: Mary (1852–1870), Mollie, and Mack. By 1880, May had remarried and lived next to Sally's father, Elbert. SBD; MDB.

17. Lizzie Dutton, usually referred to as Libby, and her sister Hattie were two unmarried sisters of Sara Ward Dutton Graves. Like Dolly, Sara had come to Covington from the North to teach and became the second wife of Iverson Lea Graves (1799–1864). Libby and Hatty came South to visit and never returned North. Dolly recorded Libby's wedding on January 1, 1867. HNC, 706–7.

18. Born in August 1846, Rachel was the daughter of Franklin and Hannah. She was also a house slave and Sadai's nurse. In 1867, she married Dock Davis and had two children, Marion and Thomas. SBD; MDB.

19. John M. Bonnell was president of Wesleyan Female College from 1859 to 1871.

20. Dolly frequently mentions Miss Johnson, probably a teacher, during the 1860s. She most likely taught at one of the several academies in Newton County. HNC, 103–17.

21. Probably slaves: Lewis, born in 1832, and John, born on August 19, 1838, the son of Lewis and Martha. SBD.

22. Probably Thomas S. Glass, twenty-four, the son of Manson and Minerva Glass, nearby neighbors of Dolly's. U.S. Census Records, State of Georgia, 1860, Population Schedules, Newton County, NAMP, 454.

23. Ransom Harwell (b. 1805) was the son of Jackson and Marthay (Patsy) Fretwell Harwell. Since Patsy was the sister of Thomas Burge's mother, Nancy Fretwell, Ransom was Thomas's first cousin. HNC, 725–26.

24. Thomas's uncle and his mother Nancy's brother.

25. Thomas Burge's mother was named Nancy Fretwell. This could be one of her nieces.

26. Again, Dolly wanted to record work accomplished a few days earlier.

27. Dolly mentions Mr. Thompson and Carrie Thompson several times. There were several Thompsons in Newton County, but I could find no "Carrie." U.S. Census Records, State of Georgia, 1850 and 1860, Population Schedules, Newton County, NAMP.

28. Probably the Thomas Burge Sr.'s nephew, who would have been about twenty-five at this time. U.S. Census Records, State of Georgia, 1850, Population Schedules, Newton County, NAMP, 478.

29. Probably William H. Evans (1814–1870), a Methodist minister active in the conference from 1842 to 1872. Harold Lawrence, ed. and comp., *Methodist Preachers in Georgia, 1783–1900* (Tignall, Ga.: Boyd Publishing Co., Ltd., 1984), 176–77.

30. The youngest daughter of Jackson Harwell by his third wife Rhoda, Amanda was twenty-three in 1861. *HNC,* 725–26.

31. Dolly mentions George Yarbrow, with alternate spellings, several times. Perhaps she is referring to J. W. Yarborough, a Methodist minister in the area at the time. At the 1860 census, he was forty-six years old and lived in Oxford with his wife Amanda, forty-two, and several children and students. U.S. Census Records, State of Georgia, 1860, Population Schedules, Newton County, NAMP, 440; Pierce, *History of Methodism,* 101.

32. Dolly is referring to the site of the first house the Burge family built on the property. Most likely, it was built by Thomas Burge's father, Wiley Burge, near the family graveyard.

33. At this point, Lou was sixteen years old and a student at Macon Female College.

34. David Henry Ansley (1828–1896) of Augusta. He married Sarah ("Sallie") Ann Neal Burge (1837–1896), the daughter of Hamilton Burge, Thomas's brother. David Henry was a major in the Fifth Infantry Regiment, CSA, during the Civil War and was wounded at Missionary Ridge in 1863. After the war, he farmed and served as ordinary of Newton County between 1887 and 1890. *HNC,* 559.

35. This is the Confederate assault on Fort Sumter on April 12.

36. Probably Laura Anne Heard Perry, wife of Josiah Patterson Perry. *HNC,* 866–67.

37. Probably Sarah N. Parks (b. 1840), Dolly's future step-daughter and the twenty-one-year-old daughter of William J. and Emily Parks. U.S. Census Records, State of Georgia, 1860, Population Schedules, Newton County, NAMP, 434; William J. Parks's Bible, IFP.

38. Probably Zelemma Glass, the nineteen-year-old daughter of neighbors Manson and Minerva Glass. U.S. Census Records, State of Georgia, 1850, Population Schedules, Newton County, NAMP, 479; ibid., 1860, Population Schedules, Newton County, NAMP, 454.

39. In the slave list at the back of Dolly's diary, it reads, "Charles formely belonging to My father i bought to day Dec 14 of Mr. Zachry Dec 1857. aged about 68." In other words, Charles had belonged to Thomas Burge's father, Wiley Burge, and was sold to a Mr. Zachry. Thomas purchased Charles from Zachry in 1857, when Charles was about sixty-eight years old. SBD; MDB.

40. Perhaps Frank and Hannah, both slaves born in 1819, went with their children to see the marriage of their third living child, Jane in the Burge diary, who was born in 1842 and sold to Mr. Pace in January 1856. SBD.

41. A beverage of wine or liquor and sweetened milk or cream which is beaten to a froth.

42. Cora Graves is Cornelia Lansing Graves, born in 1849 to Sara Ward Dutton (b. 1814) and Iverson Lea Graves (1799–1864). *HNC*, 706–7.

43. In February 1862, General Ulysses S. Grant captured Fort Henry on the Tennessee River and then Fort Donelson on the Cumberland River.

44. After forcing Confederate forces to withdraw from Kentucky and middle Tennessee, Grant moved south with forty thousand men. On April 6, the Confederates under General Albert Johnston surprised Grant's army just north of the Tennessee-Mississippi border and forced them back to the Tennessee River. The next day, Grant regained the territory, at an enormous cost of more than twenty-three thousand casualties. New Orleans fell in late April 1862.

45. Possibly Robert (b. 1844), the son of Franklin and Hannah. SBD.

46. The Confederate Congress passed the first draft in American history in April 1862, shortly after the defeat at Shiloh.

47. Newton Factory, south of the Burge Plantation in Newton County, was a thriving cotton mill and community along the Alcovy River. *HNC*, 218.

48. Chalybeate Springs (pronounced *ka-lib-e-at*) is in Meriwether County, one mile east of Manchester and approximately seventy miles southwest of the Burge Plantation. There was a popular resort there, named for the springs, where Louisiana and others sought healing. Kenneth Krakow, *Georgia Place-Names* (Macon: Winship Press, 1975), 39.

49. Barnesville is about fifty miles south of Atlanta. *HNC*, 39.

50. Perhaps John, the slave son of Lewis and Martha. SBD.

51. There were more casualties at the Battle of Antietam on September 17,

1862, than on any other day in American military history. Lincoln claimed victory, but Lee's troops were allowed to retreat into Virginia.

52. Rebecca was Thomas Burge's eldest daughter, who by this time had married her second husband, Augustus Lee. U.S. Census Records, State of Georgia, 1870, Population Schedules, Newton County, NAMP, 46.

53. Probably J. M. Codey, who in 1860 was a thirty-seven-year-old physician in Newton County. U.S. Census Records, State of Georgia, 1860, Population Schedules, Newton County, NAMP, 410.

54. There were many Robinsons in Newton County at the time, many descendants of Rev. Luke Robinson, who was born in Dublin, Ireland, in 1786. *HNC*, 891.

55. Probably Libby Dutton.

56. Dolly refers to the distribution of slaves that Thomas stipulated in his will but that some family members opposed because they believed it unfairly favored Dolly. Nevertheless, the court divided the slaves according to his will into two lots. The first lot went to Wiley, Eliza, and Louisiana Burge, and included Lewis, Martha, Winnie, Hester, Jane, Kit (perhaps Christopher), Corene (or Connie), Ann, Sally, Mary, Newton, Ned, John, and Oliver. The second lot went to Dolly and Sadai Burge and included Elbert, Julia, Willie, Uesley (or Ueole), Mid, Sam, Rachel, Lydia, Bob, James, Henry, Jackson, Frank, Hannah, Floyd, Millie, and Margarett. Both groups were valued at $34,900. Will of Thomas Burge, Newton County Will Records, Vol. 2, 1851–1871, GDAH, 117–18; Dolly S. Burge v. Mathew A. Mitchell and Wiley Burge, Court of Ordinary, Newton County Minutes Records 1852–1863, GDAH, 241–42. Newton County Estate Records, Inventories and Appraisements, Annual Returns 1862–1864, 607–8.

57. This is probably the daughter of President Longstreet of Emory (1839–1848) and wife of Lucius Q. C. Lamar, an 1845 graduate of Emory College. Lucius was elected to Congress from Mississippi in 1857, urged that state to secede before the war, returned to Congress in 1857, and urged conciliation between North and South. He was elected to the Senate in 1877 and later served as secretary of the interior under President Cleveland. In 1888, he was appointed associate justice of the United States Supreme Court, where he served until his death in 1893. Bullock, *History of Emory*, 82.

CHAPTER FOUR. In Sherman's Path

1. In 1860, within a few households of Dolly's, Jesse F. Mixon, a teacher and attorney, lived with ten (mostly young) people in his household. One of them was

Nelson Mixon, a twenty-nine-year-old teacher. U.S. Census Records, State of Georgia, 1860, Population Schedules, Newton County, NAMP, 458.

2. Hannah, wife of Frank, was born in 1819 and died "Sunday Morning Feb 20 1864*" according to the slave list at the back of Dolly's diary. SBD.

3. Clinton Lee was probably a son of Augustus Lee.

4. Eatonton was the seat of Putnam County, about twenty-five miles southeast of the Burge Plantation in Newton County.

5. During late May and throughout June, Sherman's forces were penetrating deeper into Georgia. On June 27, Sherman dispatched General George Stoneman and a force of five thousand men to move around Atlanta to the east, destroy the Macon railroad at Lovejoy's Station, and continue to Macon and Andersonville, where they would liberate imprisoned federal soldiers. Stoneman's troops went through Newton County on their way to Monticello and the east side of the Ocmulgee River opposite Macon. There they found that the bridge they had planned to cross had been washed away. Recognizing that the Confederate cavalry was pursuing them, Stoneman and his men retreated but were captured by General Alfred Iverson's cavalry on July 29. T. Conn Bryan, *Confederate Georgia* (Athens: University of Georgia Press, 1953), 158–61.

6. Probably James W. Hinton, approximately sixty-four years old and a Methodist minister in the area. A less likely candidate is John L. Hinton, who in 1860 was a twenty-six-year-old mechanic in the Newton Factory area. Pierce, *History of Methodism*, 232; U.S. Census Records, State of Georgia, 1850, Population Schedules, Newton County, NAMP, 477; ibid., 1860 Population Schedules, Newton County, NAMP, 470.

7. General Garrard led the Union cavalry through Georgia.

8. Perhaps Mary was a sister of Major David Henry Ansley. David Henry was a nephew of the prominent Newton County Thomas Ansley, and the husband of Sally Burge Ansley, Thomas Burge's niece who was raised by the Graves. *HNC*, 559.

9. Major General Joseph Wheeler, a native Georgian, commanded the cavalry under Johnston. Later in the war, Wheeler was censured for allowing his men to steal horses and destroy private property in Georgia. Bryan, *Confederate Georgia*, 171.

10. Born in 1842, Moses was the son of Elbert and Julia. Sanford was born in 1848 to Lewis and Martha. SBD.

11. The Federals' forty-day siege on Atlanta began in late July and ended with the evacuation and occupation of Atlanta on September 1 and 3, respectively. The diary's initial editor, Robertson, suggests that Dolly may have heard the Battle of

Jonesboro which occurred on September 1 and precipitated the final fall of Atlanta. Bryan, *Confederate Georgia*, 162–63; *Diary*, ed. Robertson, 95.

12. Mr. G is Iverson Lea Graves (1799–1864). Sally is probably Thomas Burge's niece, Sallie Burge Ansley (1837–1886), whom Iverson raised with his second wife, Sara Ward Dutton. Dut is probably Iverson's and Sara's second child, Iverson Dutton (1845–1907). *HNC*, 706–7.

13. Probably Rev. Albert Gray (1826–1884), a Methodist minister in Newton County at the time. Lawrence, *Methodist Preachers in Georgia*, 212.

14. There were a number of Browns in Newton County. *HNC*, 590.

15. There were several Iveys and Ivys in the area. Two served in the war: William Henry Ivy (1824–1894) and J. W. Ivey. The original editor, Robertson, indicated that this was Robert Ivey, who is listed as a sixty-three-year-old farmer in the 1860 census. *HNC*, 758, 275; *Diary*, ed. Robertson, 98; U.S. Census Records, State of Georgia, 1860, Population Schedules, Newton County, NAMP, 480.

16. Francis A. Usher was a thirty-nine-year-old widow in 1860. Four children, one elderly spinster, and the executor of her husband's estate lived with her. U.S. Census Records, State of Georgia, 1860, Population Schedules, Newton County, NAMP, 416.

17. On November 15th, Sherman began his infamous March to the Sea through the Georgia countryside. He divided his army into two equal divisions. The left wing moved southeast through Decatur, Oxford, Covington, Sandtown (the previous three towns were in Newton County), Madison, Eatonton, and Milledgeville on November 18–19. The right wing met the left at Sandersville and proceeded southeast. In addition, cavalry moved ahead of advancing troops and contributed to the devastation and plunder of the countryside and the Georgia home front. Bryan, *Confederate Georgia*, 166; *HNC*, 258 (map).

18. Newton (b. 1840), son of Lewis and Martha; Middleton (b. 1846), son of Lewis and Martha; and Jack (b. 1839), eldest son of Frank and Hannah. SBD.

19. James Arnold (b. 1838) was the son of Elbert. His mother probably was not Julia, but another slave. He married Miranda, circa 1867, and had at least six children: Amanda, Lucy, David, James, Willie, and "Baby." Henry (b. 1837) was the son of Lewis and Martha. Bob, or Robert (b. 1844), was the son of Franklin and Hannah. SBD; MDB.

20. Abe and Wiley Glass, two slaves on the neighboring Glass plantation, later explained that they were taken by the 22nd Indiana regiment and the 52nd Ohio regiment, respectively. They eventually made their way to Washington, D.C., before returning home after the war. Julian Street, *American Adventures*, 399–401.

McMillen, Sally. *Motherhood in the Old South: Pregnancy, Childbirth, and Infant Rearing*. Baton Rouge: Louisiana State University Press, 1990.

Moore, John Hammond, ed. *A Plantation Mistress on the Eve of the Civil War: The Diary of Keziah Goodwyn Hopkins Brevard, 1860–1861*. Columbia: University of South Carolina Press, 1993.

Newton County Historical Society. *History of Newton County, Georgia*. 1988.

Osterud, Nancy Grey. *Bonds of Community: The Lives of Farm Women in Nineteenth-Century New York*. Ithaca: Cornell University Press, 1991.

Pease, Jane H., and William H. Pease. *Ladies, Women, and Wenches: Choice and Constraint in Antebellum Charleston and Boston*. Chapel Hill: University of North Carolina Press, 1990.

Pessen, Edward. "How Different from Each Other Were the Antebellum North and South?" *American Historical Review* 85 (December 1980): 1119–49.

Pierce, Alfred M. *A History of Methodism in Georgia — February 5, 1736–June 24, 1955*. North Georgia Conference Historical Society, 1956.

Rable, George C. *Civil Wars: Women and the Crisis of Southern Nationalism*. Chicago: University of Illinois Press, 1989.

———. "'Missing in Action': Women of the Confederacy." In *Divided Houses: Gender and the Civil War*, edited by Catherine Clinton and Nina Silber. New York: Oxford University Press, 1992.

Robertson, James I., Jr. "The Diary of Dolly Lunt Burge." *Georgia Historical Quarterly* 44–46 (June 1960–March 1962).

———, ed. *The Diary of Dolly Lunt Burge*. Athens: University of Georgia Press, 1962.

Ryan, Mary P. *Cradle of the Middle Class: The Family in Oneida County, New York, 1790–1865*. New York: Cambridge University Press, 1981.

———. "The Power of Women's Networks: A Case Study of Female Moral Reform in Antebellum America." *Feminist Studies* 5 (spring 1979): 66–85.

Scott, Anne F. "The 'New Woman' in the New South." *South Atlantic Quarterly* 65 (autumn 1962): 473–83.

———. *The Southern Lady: From Pedestal to Politics, 1830–1930*. Chicago: University of Chicago Press, 1970.

———. "Women's Perspective on the Patriarchy in the 1850s." *Journal of American History* 61 (June 1974): 52–64.

Smith, Daniel Blake. *Inside the Great House: Planter Family Life in Eighteenth-Century Chesapeake Society*. Ithaca: Cornell University Press, 1980.

Stone, Lawrence. *The Family, Sex and Marriage in England, 1500–1800*. New York: Harper & Row, 1977.

Stowe, Steven M. *Intimacy and Power in the Old South: Ritual in the Lives of the Planters*. Baltimore: Johns Hopkins University Press, 1987.

———. "Seeing Themselves at Work: Physicians and the Case Narrative in the Mid-Nineteenth-Century American South." *American Historical Review* 101, no. 1 (February 1996): 41–79.

Street, Julian. *American Adventures: A Second Trip "Abroad at Home"*. New York: Century Co., 1917.

———, ed. *A Woman's War-Time Journal: An Account of Sherman's Devastation of a Southern Plantation*. By Dolly Sumner Lunt (Mrs. Thomas Burge). New York: Century Company, 1918; Macon, Ga.: 1927; Atlanta: Cherokee Publishing Company, 1994.

Wates, Wylma. "Precursor to the Victorian Age: The Concept of Marriage and Family as Revealed in the Correspondence of the Izard Family of South Carolina." In *In Joy and In Sorrow: Women, Family, and Marriage in the Victorian South, 1830–1900*, edited by Carol K. Bleser. New York: Oxford University Press, 1991.

Weiner, Jonathan M. "Female Planters and Planters' Wives in the Civil War and Reconstruction." *Alabama Review* 30 (April 1977): 135–49.

Welter, Barbara. "The Cult of True Womanhood, 1820–1860." *American Quarterly* 18 (summer 1966): 151–74.

———. "The Feminization of American Religion." In *In Dimity Convictions: The American Woman in the Nineteenth Century*, edited by Barbara Welter, 83–102. Athens: Ohio University Press, 1976.

Whites, Lee Ann. "The Civil War as a Crisis in Gender." In *Divided Houses: Gender and the Civil War*, edited by Catherine Clinton and Nina Silber. New York: Oxford University Press, 1992.

Williford, William Bailey. *The Glory of Covington*. Atlanta: Cherokee Publishing Company, 1973.

Wood, W. Kirk, ed. *A Northern Daughter and a Southern Wife: The Civil War Reminiscences and Letters of Katharine H. Cumming, 1860–1865*. Augusta: Richmond County Historical Society, 1976.

Wyatt-Brown, Bertram. *Southern Honor: Ethics and Behavior in the Old South*. New York: Oxford University Press, 1982.

21. Frank (b. 1819), husband of Hannah, took the surname Mitchell after the war. Rachel (b. 1846) was their daughter. SBD; MDB.

22. There were many Pitts families in Newton County. Perhaps this is John W. Pitts, who settled in the Newborn area and established himself as a colorful figure, lawyer, educator, and writer. Alternatively, this could be N. M. or Olin, both of whom served in the Civil War. *HNC*, 397, 871–73, 277.

23. Pro-Secessionist or pro-Confederate.

CHAPTER FIVE. A New Union

1. Dolly was still troubled by the distribution of Thomas's slaves, particularly those allotted to Louisiana who had willed hers to Dolly and Sadai. Major Lee and others disputed the distribution. Kit (also Christopher or Thomas, b. 1852) was the son of Elbert and Julia. SBD.

2. See also Newton County Inferior Court Minutes 1859–1874, March 23, 1865, GDAH, 44.

3. Perhaps James Madison, Gant, or Joe Mitcham, three of the original five brothers who fought in the war. Two did not survive. *HNC*, 819.

4. A kind of cap.

5. Frank (b. 1819) had been Thomas's slave and Dolly's coachman. Lydia was his second spouse, and he hers. Julia, Hannah, and Martha Burge were Lydia's sisters, but Lydia belonged to Richard Harwell in 1833 and later to Manson Glass. Her first husband was William, possibly a slave of Manson Glass. Her children (none by Frank) were Wyley (1838–1928) who married Jane circa 1861, and had eighteen children: Blanche, Oscar, Wyley, Julia, Lucy, Zach, Sidney, Abraham, Susan, Jim, Mack, Indiana, Mary J., Ella, Tracey, Catherine, Ada, and Thomas; Abraham (1853–after 1920) who married Ursula Mattocks in 1869 and Catherine Strong in 1887, and had nine children: Caesar, Fanny, Louisiana, Selema, Josephine, Joseph, Lassie, John W., and Willie F.; Fannie (b. 1858) who was living with her mother Lydia in 1870; Alexander; Wilson; Catharine Elvira; and Sidney Ann (1854–after 1920) who married Reverend George Gunn in 1875 and helped manage the Burge farm until their deaths; Julia (c. 1840–after 1880) who married Newton Burge (d. c. 1879) circa 1866 and Cary Wood circa 1879, and had Sanford, Mattie, Fanny, and Indiana; and Mack (1853–c. 1894) who married Tempe Webbon (d. 1879) in 1877 and Lulu Neal in 1883, and had Wyley, Cornelius, Connie, Sidney, Robert, Hattie, Claude, and Mack. SBD; MDB.

6. A destructive tornado swept through the Newborn section of the county the

evening of January 24. Mr. James C. Bailey and his wife of three months, the daughter of Colonel J. W. Pitts, were killed. *HNC*, 399.

7. Ol was probably Oliver (1842–after 1870), the child of Lewis and Martha. He married Antonette Montgomery (b. c. 1853) in 1869 and had ten children: Lulu, Peter, Martha, Selena, Cora, Newton, Della, George, Floid, and Thomas.

Prior to emancipation, Maz belonged to an Ansley. In December 1849, he married Sally, the slave daughter of Elbert and Julia (Burge) who was born June 1, 1830. Maz and Sally's daughter Marg was born Tuesday, April 29, 1852. SBD; MDB.

8. The Gays were a large family in the Newborn-Sandtown area, and it seems likely they had some connection to the two schools there and possibly a store as well.

9. Probably the twenty-year-old daughter of Manson and Minerva Glass. U.S. Census Records, State of Georgia, 1850, Population Schedules, Newton County, NAMP, 479.

10. At this point, Sadai was ten years old.

11. Parks's youngest child, Sarah N. (b. 1840), married Dr. Irby Harrison in 1865. William J. Parks's Bible, IFP.

12. M. E. Dutton and C. D. Pace were married by W. R. Branham. Newton County Marriage Records, Volume C., 1850–1867, GDAH, 309.

13. At this point, Eliza was twenty years old.

14. William J. Parks's home was the President's House in Oxford. It is now where the dean of Oxford College resides.

15. Probably *The Augusta Daily Chronicle and Sentinel*, a continuation of the *Augusta Chronicle and Gazette of the State*, founded in 1785.

16. Probably Elizabeth Parks, born in August 1783. William J. Parks's Bible, IFP.

17. Isaac Stiles Hopkins (1841–1914) graduated from Emory College in 1859 and two years later joined the Georgia Conference of the Methodist Episcopal Church, South, and pastored several rural churches. In 1869, he returned to Oxford as a pastor of a Methodist church and professor of natural science at Emory College. Hopkins later helped Emory College introduce an industrial education program, which eventually led to the establishment of the Georgia Institute of Technology. Hopkins served as ninth president of Emory College from 1884 to 1888, and as the first president of the Georgia Institute of Technology. *DGB*, 476–78.

18. Sarah N. Parks (b. 1840), William J.'s youngest child, married Dr. Irby Harrison in 1865. Mary E. Parks's (b. 1835) second husband was Rev. John Harris. William J. Parks's Bible, IFP.

19. James Parton (1822–1891) was a widely read biographer and contributor to literary magazines. In addition to *The Life and Times of Aaron Burr* (1857), he wrote well-respected biographies of Andrew Jackson, Benjamin Franklin, Thomas Jefferson, and Voltaire. *DAB*, 279–80.

20. The son of William J. Parks, Harwell H. Parks (1825–1895) married Sarah Ann Sillivan in 1845 and served as a Methodist minister in the Georgia Conference. William J. Parks's Bible, IFP; Pierce, *History of Methodism*, 159.

21. Jacob Abbott (1803–1879) was a Congregational clergyman, educator, and prolific author of religious, educational, literary, historical, and children's books. *DAB*, 21–22.

22. The original diary's editor identified him as one of the most widely traveled ministers in the conference. At the time of his visit to Parks, J. P. Duncan (1809–1881) had been blind for over twenty-five years. *Diary*, ed. Robertson, 131.

23. A pharmaceutical preparation of opium and ipecacuanha. (The latter is a root with emetic, diaphoretic, and purgative properties.)

24. Atticus Greene Haygood (1839–1896), who moved into Dolly and William J. Parks's Oxford home, graduated from Emory College in 1859 and returned to receive a divinity degree in 1870. He entered the ministry after college, served as an army chaplain during the Civil War, and pastored in Rome, Georgia, after the war. He was elected bishop in 1882, which he declined until a second election in 1890. He was president of Emory College from 1876 to 1884 and edited the church periodical, the *Wesleyan Christian Advocate*, from 1878 to 1882. After 1880, he was known as a spokesman for progressive New South doctrines, northern business ideals, commercial efforts, and liberal attitudes toward southern African Americans. *DGB*, 424–26.

25. Two of Sarah Lunt Comings's daughters.

26. Sadai married Rev. John Davis Gray (1852–1887) on December 16, 1875.

27. William Markham, a prominent Atlanta builder, built the Markham House in 1875. It remained an important Atlanta landmark until it burned in a major fire in 1896. Franklin M. Garrett, *Atlanta and Environs* (New York: Lewis Historical Publishers, 1954), 1:921–22, 2:336.

28. This tenant probably is David (1848–1879), son of Elbert and Julia. In 1868, he married Laura Rakestraw and had one child, Julia (1866–by 1880). SBD; MDB.

29. Probably the twenty-three-year-old daughter of Manson and Minerva Glass. U.S. Census Records, State of Georgia, 1880, Population Schedules, Newton County, 39.

Epilogue

1. Orrington Lunt to Henry L. Graves, December 10, 1892; William Lunt to J. D. Graves, April 14, 1897, IFP. Family members indicate that the children went initially to live with Stephen Purrington Lunt. The 1897 letter from William indicates that he was the children's guardian and reported on their progress.

2. MDB; Street, *American Adventures*, 399–401.

3. *The Diary of Louisiana Burge*, May 31, 1861, American Women's Diaries (Southern Women) (New Canaan, Conn.: Readex Film Products, 1988). The original is in the BGC.

4. Ibid., February 24, 1864; Richard B. Harwell, "Louisiana Burge: The Diary of a Confederate College Girl," *Georgia Historical Quarterly* 36 (1952): 144–63. Louisiana's northern cousin, Cornelia Gray Lunt, confirmed Lou's personal strength, passion, and determination, particularly in support of the South. See Cornelia Gray Lunt, *Sketches*, 45–49.

5. *The Diary of Sadai C. Burge*, August 16, 1874, American Women's Diaries (Southern Women) (New Canaan, Conn.: Readex Film Products, 1988). Bolton, *Little Sadai*.

SELECTED BIBLIOGRAPHY

Manuscript and Microfilm Sources

Burge, Dolly Sumner Lunt. The Diary of Dolly Lunt Burge. Original in Burge-Gray Collection, Special Collections Department, Robert W. Woodruff Library, Emory University. Microfilmed copy in American Women's Diaries (Southern Women) (New Canaan, Conn.: Readex Film Product, 1988).

Burge, Louisiana. The Diary of Louisiana Burge. Original in Burge-Gray Collection, Special Collections Department, Robert W. Woodruff Library, Emory University. Microfilmed copy in American Women's Diaries (Southern Women) (New Canaan, Conn.: Readex Film Product, 1988).

Burge, Sadai C. The Diary of Sadai C. Burge. Original in Burge-Gray Collection, Special Collections Department, Robert W. Woodruff Library, Emory University. Microfilmed copy in American Women's Diaries (Southern Women) (New Canaan, Conn.: Readex Film Product, 1988).

Burge-Gray Collection, Special Collections Department, Robert W. Woodruff Library, Emory University.

Family papers in the family's possession. Includes Bibles, obituaries, wedding announcements, and memorabilia.

Lunt, Cornelia Gray. Cornelia Gray Lunt papers, Northwestern University Archives, Evanston, Illinois.

Public Resources

Crawley's 1837 Survey in Madison. Map in the Morgan County Courthouse, Madison, Georgia.

Davis, Theodore, comp. *The Complete 1850 Federal Census of Newton County, Georgia.* Oxford, Ga.: Oxford Shrine Society, 1978.

————, comp. *The United States 1870 Census: Freedmen in Newton County, Georgia.* Oxford, Ga.: By the author, 1988.

Ingmire, Frances T. *Morgan County, Georgia Marriage Records, 1808–1865.* Madison, Ga.: privately printed, 1985. Morgan County Courthouse, Madison, Georgia.

Morgan County Marriage Records. Morgan County Courthouse, Madison, Georgia.

Morgan County Tax Digests. Morgan County Courthouse, Madison, Georgia.

Newton County Inferior and Superior Court Records, Georgia Department of Archives and History, Atlanta, Georgia.

Seventh Census of the United States, 1850. Vol. 1. Georgia Department of Archives and History, Atlanta, Georgia.

United States Census Records, State of Georgia, 1850, 1860, 1870, Population, Slave, and Agricultural Schedules, National Archives Microfilm Publications.

Morgan County; Newton County; Watson County Records.

Secondary Sources

Akers, Samuel Luttrell. *The First Hundred Years of Wesleyan College, 1836–1936.* Macon, Ga.: Beehive Press, 1976.

Bartlett, Irving H., and C. Glenn Cambor. "The History and Psychodynamics of Southern Womanhood." *Women's Studies: An Interdisciplinary Journal* 11 (1974): 9–24.

Bleser, Carol K. "Southern Planter Wives and Slavery." In *The Meaning of South Carolina History: Essays in Honor of George C. Rogers, Jr.,* edited by David R. Chesnutt and Clyde N. Wilson. Columbia: University of South Carolina Press, 1991.

Bleser, Carol K., and Frederick Heath. "The Clays of Alabama: The Impact of the

Civil War on a Southern Marriage." In *In Joy and In Sorrow: Women, Family, and Marriage in the Victorian South, 1830–1900,* edited by Carol K. Bleser. New York: Oxford University Press, 1991.

Bode, Frederick. "The Formation of Evangelical Communities in Middle Georgia: Twiggs County, 1820–1861." *Journal of Southern History* 60, no. 4 (November 1994): 711–48.

Boles, John B. "The Discovery of Southern Religious History." In *Interpreting Southern History: Historiographical Essays in Honor of Sanford W. Higginbotham,* edited by John B. Boles and Evelyn Thomas Nolen, 510–48. Baton Rouge: Louisiana State University Press, 1987.

Bolton, Dorothy G., editor. *Little Sadai: Journal of Miss Sadai C. Burge, 1874.* Atlanta: Keelin Press, 1952.

Bonomi, Patricia. *Under the Cope of Heaven: Religion, Society, and Politics in Colonial America.* New York: Oxford University Press, 1986.

Boylan, Anne M. "Evangelical Womanhood in the Nineteenth Century: The Role of Women in Sunday Schools." *Feminist Studies* 4, no. 3 (October 1978): 62–80.

Bryan, T. Conn. *Confederate Georgia.* Athens: University of Georgia Press, 1953.

Bullock, Henry Morton. *A History of Emory University.* Nashville: Parthenon Press, 1936.

Burr, Virginia. "A Woman Made to Suffer and Be Strong: Ella Gertrude Clanton Thomas, 1834–1907." In *In Joy and In Sorrow: Women, Family, and Marriage in the Victorian South, 1830–1900,* edited by Carol K. Bleser. New York: Oxford University Press, 1991.

Bynum, Victoria. *Unruly Women: The Politics of Social and Sexual Control in the Old South.* Chapel Hill: University of North Carolina Press, 1992.

Cashin, Joan. "Structure of Antebellum Southern Families: 'The Ties That Bound Us Was Strong.'" *Journal of Southern History* 56, no. 1 (February 1990): 55–70.

Cates, Gerald L. "Medical Schools in Ante-Bellum Georgia." Master's thesis, University of Georgia, 1968.

Censer, Jane Turner. *North Carolina Planters and Their Children, 1800–1860.* Baton Rouge: Louisiana State University Press, 1984.

Chambers-Schiller, Lee Virginia. *Liberty, A Better Husband: Single Women in America: The Generations of 1780–1849.* New Haven: Yale University Press, 1984.

A Checklist of Pennsylvania Newspapers. Harrisburg: Pennsylvania Historical Commission, 1944.

Clinton, Catherine. *The Plantation Mistress: Woman's World in the Old South.* New York: Pantheon Books, 1982.

Coleman, Kenneth, and Charles Stephen Gurr. *Dictionary of Georgia Biography*. Athens: University of Georgia Press, 1983.

Cott, Nancy F. *The Bonds of Womanhood: "Woman's Sphere" in New England, 1780–1835*. New Haven: Yale University Press, 1977.

Culpepper, Marilyn Mayer. *Trials and Triumphs: Women of the American Civil War*. East Lansing: Michigan State University Press, 1991.

Degler, Carl. *At Odds: Women and the Family in America from the Revolution to the Present*. New York: Oxford University Press, 1980.

Douglas, Ann. *The Feminization of American Culture*. New York: Anchor Press, 1988.

———. "Heaven Our Homes: Consolation Literature in the Northern United States, 1830–1880." *American Quarterly* 26, no. 5 (December 1974): 496–515.

Epstein, Barbara Leslie. *The Politics of Domesticity: Women, Evangelism, and Temperance in Nineteenth-Century America*. Middletown, Conn.: Wesleyan University Press, 1981.

Faragher, John Mack. "History from the Inside Out: Writing the History of Women in Rural America." *American Quarterly* 33, no. 5 (winter 1981): 537–57.

Farnham, Christie Anne. *The Education of the Southern Belle: Higher Education and Student Socialization in the Antebellum South*. New York: New York University Press, 1994.

Faust, Drew Gilpin. "Altars of Sacrifice: Confederate Women and the Narratives of War." *Journal of American History* 76 (March 1990): 1200–28.

———. "Confederate Women and Narratives of War." In *Divided Houses: Gender and the Civil War*, edited by Catherine Clinton and Nina Silber. New York: Oxford University Press, 1992.

———. *Mothers of Invention: Women of the Slaveholding South in the American Civil War*. Chapel Hill: University of North Carolina Press, 1996.

Fox-Genovese, Elizabeth. "Family and Female Identity in the Antebellum South: Sarah Gayle and Her Family." In *In Joy and In Sorrow: Women, Family, and Marriage in the Victorian South, 1830–1900*, edited by Carol K. Bleser. New York: Oxford University Press, 1991.

———. *Within the Plantation Household: Black and White Women of the Old South*. Chapel Hill: University of North Carolina Press, 1988.

Fraser, Walter J., and Wakelyn Saunders, eds. *The Web of Southern Social Relations: Women, Family, and Education*. Athens: University of Georgia Press, 1985.

Friedman, Jean E. *The Enclosed Garden: Women and Community in the Evangelical South, 1830–1900*. Chapel Hill: University of North Carolina Press, 1985.

INDEX

Few, James F., 226 (n. 64)

Finley, 97, 219 (n. 8)

Florence, 68, 200

Floyd, John Julius, 50, 57, 67, 98, 147, 180, 228 (n. 15)

Floyd, Mary, 228 (n. 15)

Floyd, Sarah, 5, 6, 17, 20, 32, 36, 88, 181, 220 (n. 8)

Foot, Willie, 203

Forsyth, Ga., xxiv, xxvi, 202, 211 (n. 7)

Fort Donelson defeat, 125, 235 (n. 43)

Fort Henry defeat, 125, 235 (n. 43)

Fort Sumter, 117, 172

Foster (attorney), 58

Foster (colonel), 30

Freedpeople from Burge plantation, 173, 174, 175, 176, 177, 184

Fretwell, Dick, 131

Fretwell, Leonard, 92, 110, 132, 170, 231 (n. 50)

Fretwell, Nancy, 111, 112, 125, 233 (n. 25)

Gay, 123, 179, 182

Gay's store, 179

Georgia Institute of Technology, 240–41 (n. 17)

Gilpin, John, 80

Glass (judge), 107, 109, 110, 116, 142, 164, 170, 191

Glass, Abe, 206, 217 (n. 37), 238 (n. 20)

Glass, Amanda, 105

Glass, Ben, 148

Glass, Floyd, 152, 155, 165

Glass, James, 227 (n. 4)

Glass, Manson, 100, 111, 112, 122, 131–33, 139, 184, 227 (n. 6), 233 (n. 22), 235 (n. 38), 239 (n. 5)

Glass, Mary, 227 (n. 6)

Glass, Minerva, 55, 56, 57, 58, 62, 64, 66, 67, 69, 74, 75, 78, 81, 87, 89, 91, 92, 136, 139, 156, 166, 179, 183, 189, 233 (n. 22), 235 (n. 38)

Glass, Minnie, 186, 240 (n. 9)

Glass, Pennie, 203, 242 (n. 29)

Glass, Shug, 150, 152, 173

Glass, Thomas S., 109, 233 (n. 22)

Glass, Wiley, 206, 217 (n. 37), 238 (n. 20)

Glass, Zacharia, 57, 140, 141, 151, 176, 181, 182, 183, 219 (n. 8), 227 (n. 6), 231 (n. 1)

Glass, Zelemma, 119, 123, 235 (n. 38)

Graham, William P., 86, 169, 230 (n. 42)

Grant, Ulysses S., 171, 235 (nn. 43, 44). *See also* Civil War

Graves (widow), 83

Graves, Cornelia Lansing, 122, 235 (n. 42)

Graves, Henry Lea, 40, 134, 135, 153, 154, 173, 190, 226 (n. 63)

Graves, Iverson Dutton, 152, 153, 154, 173, 190, 238 (n. 12)

Graves, Iverson Lea, 5, 37, 40, 98, 99, 117, 122, 125, 133, 140, 141, 146, 147, 148, 149, 152, 153, 154, 155, 182, 187, 226 (n. 60), 229 (n. 29), 233 (n. 17), 235 (n. 42), 238 (n. 12)

Graves, Oscar, 191

Graves, Sara Ward Dutton, 64, 82, 119, 123, 135, 136, 149, 154, 165, 166, 171, 172, 174, 176, 178, 185, 186, 188, 191, 194, 220 (n. 9), 229 (n. 29), 233 (n. 17), 235 (n. 42), 238 (n. 12)

Graves Academy, 66

Graves family, 205

Gray, Albert, 153, 156, 238 (n. 13)

Gray, Davis Burge, xli, 205

Potter, W. H., 148
Presbyterian Church, 14, 21, 23, 24, 28, 39, 224 (n. 45)
Purington, 181

Rakestraw, Louisa, 166, 227 (n. 8)
Rakestraw, Martha (elder), 227 (n. 8), 230 (n. 45)
Rakestraw, Martha (younger), 88, 112, 230 (n. 45)
Rakestraw, Mary, 88, 112, 166, 230 (n. 45)
Rakestraw, Robert (elder), 55, 63, 112, 125, 134, 149, 230 (n. 45)
Rakestraw, Robert M. (younger), 227 (n. 8)
Rees, M. J., 34
Reese (Hillsboro hostess), 105
Reese, Amarintha, 32, 33, 36, 41, 225 (n. 52)
Reese, Augustus, 225 (n. 52)
Reese, Elizabeth, 225 (n. 52)
Reid, Sarah E., 222 (n. 32)
Richmond battles, 128, 129, 171
Rivers (male acquaintance), 131
Rivers, Mary Homer Stearns, 10, 19, 20, 21, 22, 24, 25, 37, 221 (n. 21)
Roberts, 75, 77, 84
Robertson, James, xiv, 210 (n. 6), 215 (n. 29), 224 (nn. 46, 47), 227 (n. 6), 238 (nn. 11, 15), 241 (n. 22)
Robinson (female neighbor), 136, 182
Robinson, James, 140
Robinson, John T., 222 (n. 31)
Robinson, Nancy, 17, 32, 37, 40, 49, 222 (n. 31)
Robson, John, 30, 37, 222 (n. 31), 224 (n. 46)
Robson, Martha, 17, 22, 32, 40, 49, 222 (n. 31)

Roquemore, 87, 97, 102, 164, 230 (n. 43)
Round, George H., 22, 113, 220 (n. 13)
Round, Mrs. George, 6, 22, 220 (n. 13)
Russell, 10, 64, 65
Rutherford, Fanny Burge, 90

Saffold, Mary Thomas, 19, 20, 222 (n. 32)
Saffold, Thomas P., 19, 222 (n. 32)
Saffolds (neighbors), 5, 8, 22, 33, 49, 224 (n. 50), 225 (n. 57)
Sandtown, Ga., 60, 64, 69, 74, 77, 80, 81, 84, 101, 104, 109, 110, 111, 114, 118, 123, 132, 139, 143, 144, 148, 149, 156, 171, 172, 175, 177, 179, 181, 182, 183, 185, 188, 190
Sasanett, 82
Savannah, Ga., 154, 157, 166
Sectionalism. See Civil War
Seige of Atlanta, 152, 157
Shaw, Alfred, 32, 220 (n. 6)
Shaw, Horace T., 63, 70, 229 (n. 24)
Shaw, Mary Ann, 67, 80, 82, 229 (n. 24)
Shaw, Susan, 5, 6, 24, 32, 52, 68, 131, 155, 220 (n. 6)
Shepherd, Robert, 219 (n. 6)
Sherman's march to the sea, xi, xii, 157–73, 237 (n. 5), 238 (n. 17)
Shiloh battle, 126
Shoal Creek, Ga., 101, 167
Ski, Gus, 84
Slaves, xi, xxxiv, xli–xliii; emancipation of, xxxv, 173–74, 217 (n. 37); seen as causing trouble, 57, 85, 131; Christmas gifts for, 79, 166, 175; seperation of, 140, 215 (nn. 28, 29, 30), 216 (n. 24), 236 (n. 56), 239 (n. 1); and war, 147, 149, 150, 158,

Southern Voices from the Past

Women's Letters, Diaries, and Writings

CAROL BLESER, GENERAL EDITOR

The Diary of Dolly Lunt Burge, 1848–1879,
edited by Christine Jacobson Carter

A Heritage of Woe:
The Civil War Diary of Grace Brown Elmore, 1861–1868,
edited by Marli F. Weiner

Shadows on My Heart:
The Civil War Diary of Lucy Rebecca Buck of Virginia,
edited by Elizabeth R. Baer

Tokens of Affection:
The Letters of a Planter's Daughter in the Old South,
edited by Carol Bleser